D1446501

THE SHELLEY-BYRON CONVERSATION

THE
SHELLEY-BYRON
CONVERSATION

William D. Brewer

UNIVERSITY PRESS OF FLORIDA
Gainesville / Tallahassee / Tampa / Boca Raton
Pensacola / Orlando / Miami / Jacksonville

Library of Congress Cataloging-in-Publication Data
Brewer, William D. (William Dean).
The Shelley-Byron conversation / William D. Brewer.
p.   cm.
Includes bibliographical references (p.) and index.
ISBN 0-8130-1300-3
1. Shelley, Percy Bysshe, 1792–1822—Criticism and interpretation.   2. Byron,
George Gordon Byron, Baron, 1788–1824—Criticism and interpretation.   3. Byron,
George Gordon Byron, Baron, 1788–1824—Influence.   4. Shelley, Percy Bysshe,
1792–1822—Influence.   5. English poetry—19th century—History and criticism.
6. Authorship—Collaboration—History—19th century.
7. Influence (Literary, artistic, etc.)   I. Title.
PR5438.B735   1994
821'.7—dc20   94-11299

The University Press of Florida is the scholarly publishing agency for the State
University System of Florida, comprising Florida A & M University, Florida Atlantic
University, Florida International University, Florida State University, University of
Central Florida, University of Florida, University of North Florida, University of
South Florida, and University of West Florida.

University Press of Florida
15 Northwest 15th Street
Gainesville, FL 32611

FOR TRACY

Contents

Preface ix

Acknowledgments xi

A Note on Texts xiii

CHAPTER 1
Shelley, Byron, and Their Conversations 1

CHAPTER 2
In Switzerland: Wordsworth and Science 22

CHAPTER 3
The Conversational Style of Byron and Shelley 39

CHAPTER 4
The Cenci and Sad Reality 56

CHAPTER 5
Byron's *Sardanapalus:* The Shelleyan Hero Transformed 77

CHAPTER 6
The Diabolical Discourse of Shelley and Byron 92

CHAPTER 7
Byron, Goethe, and *The Triumph of Life* 109

CHAPTER 8
Byron Puffs the Snake 131

APPENDIX A

Byron and Shelley in Mary Shelley's *The Last Man* 151

APPENDIX B

Cash Rules: Money and the Byron-Shelley Relationship 157

Notes 161

Bibliography 177

Index 185

Preface

While critics traditionally have seen Shelley and Byron as two irreconcilable opposites, separated by both temperament and philosophy, this study of their relationship argues that they have much in common, and that their works, rather than simply presenting the contrasting outlooks of idealism and despair, go beyond these limited perspectives to deal with the human condition in a complex and often ambivalent way. In his pioneering work *Shelley and Byron: The Snake and Eagle Wreathed in Fight* (1976), Charles E. Robinson succeeds in showing the importance of the Shelley-Byron relationship, but his presentation of the poets' "philosophical antagonism" turns their relationship into a debate between Shelley's meliorism and Byron's pessimism. In contrast, my study argues that the Shelley-Byron association resembles a conversation rather than a debate, and that their personal and literary dialogues were often unstructured and exploratory in nature. It is thus appropriate, in my view, that Shelley subtitles *Julian and Maddalo*—a poem inspired by discussions that he and Byron had in Venice—"A Conversation." Through my analysis of the poets' interactions, the echoes and allusions found in their poems, their responses to other writers, and their poetic styles, I try to demonstrate that the relationship was more collaborative than contentious, and that the poets' similarities are more significant than their differences. This book on the conversations of Shelley and Byron is intended for all students of British Romanticism, including undergraduates, graduate students, and specialists in the field.

Acknowledgments

While this study owes many debts to the Shelley and Byron scholars who have preceded me, I would like to especially thank Professors Paul A. Cantor and Cecil Y. Lang of the University of Virginia, who responded encouragingly and thoughtfully to my early work on the Shelley-Byron relationship. I am also grateful to the two readers who evaluated this study for the University Press of Florida: their detailed comments and constructive advice helped refine and strengthen it. In addition, I would like to thank Dr. Walda Metcalf, editor-in-chief at the University Press of Florida, for her help and enthusiasm, and Dr. William Byrd, former dean of arts and sciences at Appalachian State University, for providing me with a summer stipend to work on this book. The staff of the Inter-Library Loan Department of Belk Library at Appalachian has also provided invaluable assistance. Versions of chapters 3 and 6 were published in the *Keats-Shelley Journal* and *Philological Quarterly*, respectively, and I am grateful to Professors Stuart Curran, E. B. Murray, and Stuart Sperry of the *Keats-Shelley Journal* and John E. Grant of the *Philological Quarterly* for their insightful responses to my work. Mary Hussmann, business manager of *Philological Quarterly*, and Stuart Curran of the *Keats-Shelley Journal* have generously given me permission to reprint (in revised form) the articles I published in their journals.

Finally, I would like to convey my deepest gratitude to my wife, Tracy, to my parents and hers, and to our children, who supported this project over many years.

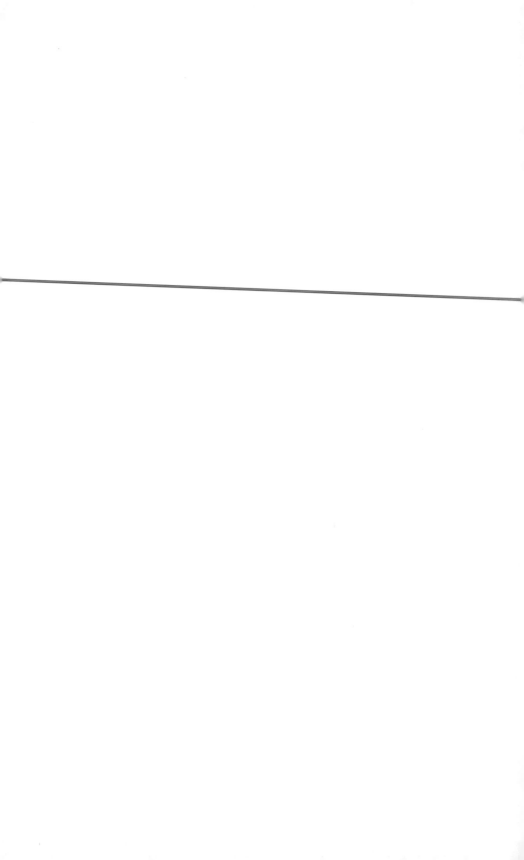

A Note on Texts

Unless otherwise indicated, all quotations from Byron's poetry and drama are taken from *Lord Byron: The Complete Poetical Works,* edited by Jerome J. McGann and Barry Weller, 6 volumes (Oxford: Oxford University Press, 1980–91). Quotations from *The Island* are taken from *The Works of Lord Byron: Poetry,* edited by Ernest Hartley Coleridge, 7 volumes (London: John Murray, 1898–1904). All references to Byron's letters are taken from *Byron's Letters and Journals,* edited by Leslie A. Marchand, 12 volumes (Cambridge, Massachusetts: Harvard University Press, 1973–82), abbreviated in the notes as BLJ.

Unless otherwise noted, all quotations from Shelley's works are taken from *Shelley's Poetry and Prose,* edited by Donald H. Reiman and Sharon B. Powers (New York: Norton, 1977). Quotations from Shelley's verse and prose not found in *Shelley's Poetry and Prose* are taken from *The Complete Works of Percy Bysshe Shelley,* edited by Roger Ingpen and Walter E. Peck, 10 volumes (London: Ernest Benn, 1926–30), *Shelley: Poetical Works,* edited by Thomas Hutchinson (Oxford: Clarendon, 1904; corrected by G. M. Matthews, 1970) (for *The Revolt of Islam*), and *The Poems of Shelley,* edited by Geoffrey Matthews and Kelvin Everest, 3 volumes planned (London: Longman, 1989), volume 1 (for Shelley's early poetry). Except where noted, all references to Shelley's letters are taken from *The Letters of Percy Bysshe Shelley,* edited by Frederick L. Jones, 2 volumes (Oxford: Clarendon, 1964), abbreviated in the notes as PBSL.

ONE

Shelley, Byron, and
Their Conversations

Like the famous relationship of Wordsworth and Coleridge, the Shelley-Byron friendship is difficult to characterize in simple terms. Because Shelley and Byron were contemporaries and lived near each other in Switzerland and Italy, our understanding of how they influenced one another depends almost as much on their personal relationship as it Does on the intertextual relationship of their poems. As in the case of Wordsworth and Coleridge, the friendship of Shelley and Byron had its positive side, particularly during the first months in Switzerland, and signs of tension and disharmony later on. It is significant, more-over, that Shelley wrote a poem to Byron which has some parallels to a poem Coleridge wrote to Wordsworth. Coleridge's "To William Wordsworth" bears witness to his awe of Wordsworth, ascending to join "the choir / Of ever-enduring men" (49–50), and his own feelings of inadequacy as a "corse" (74) being symbolically buried by Words-worth's greatness. And Shelley's "Sonnet to Byron," which Byron never saw, portrays a powerful genius whose "creations rise as fast and fair / As perfect worlds at the Creator's will" (7–8), a "God" (15) to whom a "worm beneath the sod" (14) (that is, Shelley) offers his unworthy homage.[1] As these emotionally charged poems suggest, any attempt to trace patterns of influence between poets who knew each other person-ally must consider both biographical and literary factors. The Shelley-Byron association, which had such a marked effect on the poetry and lives of both men, constitutes a good example of this kind of relationship and consequently deserves special scrutiny, both for what it teaches us about the poets' works and for the light it sheds on contemporary relationships in general.

Although there are several excellent biographical accounts of the six-year relationship of Shelley and Byron, there are relatively few studies of the ways in which the two poets influenced each other's poetry. The poems they composed during their association have interesting and often revealing intertextual relationships that are generally ignored in books which center on their personalities and on their meetings in Switzerland and Italy. Charles E. Robinson, in *Shelley and Byron: The Snake and Eagle Wreathed in Fight* (1976), has done much to rectify the critical silence on the ways in which Shelley and Byron influenced each other's poems. This present study is indebted to Robinson's meticulously researched work. In Robinson's view, the relationship of Shelley and Byron was characterized by "philosophical and aesthetic antagonism," and their works became, at least through 1821, part of a continuing debate in which Shelley argued for meliorism and Byron stood for the "skeptical denial of imaginative fulfillment."[2] Robinson argues that, from their first meeting in Geneva in 1816, Shelley and Byron had a profound effect on one another, and that their opposed "spirits" are figuratively "wreathed in fight" in nearly all of their major poems.[3] This view of the Shelley-Byron association has influenced many critics; in a recent study, *Shelley and His Audiences,* Stephen C. Behrendt goes beyond Robinson's thesis to argue that "Shelley wanted to answer Byron on his own turf, *in the press,* taking his case to the reading audience. If Byron's isolationist fatalism is 'poison,' then Shelley will offer his own works as antidote."[4] According to Behrendt, the poets' philosophical and aesthetic antagonism had a public as well as private dimension, although Shelley must have known that Byron's popularity and his own lack of it made such a public contest extremely unequal.

But while Robinson's analysis of Shelley's and Byron's influence on each other is often very helpful, he tends to simplify their literary relationship, to see each of their works primarily as either anti-Shelleyan or anti-Byronic in its philosophy or aesthetics. In Robinson's opinion, "Whatever else *Manfred* may be, it at least is an anti-Shelleyan tract (which Shelley, in turn, would answer in both *Julian and Maddalo* and *Prometheus Unbound*)."[5] Regarding Byron's *Cain,* Robinson claims that "Both Byron and Cain, according to Shelley, shared [the] 'vulgar' delusions [of Manichaeism] and consequently enslaved themselves in a world of their own making."[6] Even a seemingly minor work like the unfinished *The Deformed Transformed* becomes, for Robinson, another focal point for the rivalry and antagonistic disagreements between the two men: Shelley, he writes, "was personally humiliated by his rival's ingenious use of the devil as doppelgänger."[7] In other words, Byron writes *Manfred,* at least in part, to refute Shelley; and Shelley composes *Julian and Maddalo* and *Prometheus Unbound* as answers to Byron's pessimistic philosophy, pronounces that the ideas behind *Cain* are delusive, and is humiliated by *The Deformed Transformed.* Shelley's death, Robinson suggests, may have been a suicide, motivated by his unsuccessful rivalry with Byron, whose fame outshone Shelley's.[8]

While Robinson argues that Byron and Shelley responded to one another in the spirit of "philosophical antagonism" for most of their relationship, I believe that their interchanges were generally more collaborative than oppositional. In Robinson's opinion, *Julian and Maddalo* is a "debate"; I would describe it in the way Shelley himself subtitled the poem: as a "Conversation."[9] As with most conversations, it has points of agreement as well as disagreement, and is not bound, as debates generally are, by a logical structure or a clear argumentative progression. It becomes clear in the course of the poem, in fact, that Maddalo (who represents Byron) does not care to argue with Julian (Shelley), since he concedes that Julian could make his "system refutation-tight / As far as words go" (194–95). Toward the end of the conversation, moreover, a kind of consensus is reached; both men agree to try to resolve their argument by observing the Maniac, and afterward their disagreement is forgotten. As Maddalo says, parenthetically, to Julian: "(I think with you / In some respects you know)" (240–41). Through their conversation both men come to a deeper appreciation of human despair, an appreciation that seems to unite rather than divide them.

Shelley and Byron, of course, were very different in temperament, and they did have disagreements. Moreover, Byron was an aristocrat, whereas Shelley was a member of the rich landed gentry and, as such, Byron's social inferior. It is important, however, to see that as young poets, as post-Waterloo liberals, and as well-educated men of independent means they had much in common. *Julian and Maddalo,* their discussion of Shakespeare's *Hamlet,* and the many other conversations documented by their contemporaries, reveal the ease with which Shelley and Byron spoke to one another.[10] In writing *Julian and Maddalo* Shelley adopted "a certain familiar style of language to express the actual way in which people talk with each other whom education and a certain refinement of sentiment have placed above the use of vulgar idiom."[11] This conversational style is reflected in other works as well: in the speech of Byron's Sardanapalus, in the dialogue in *The Deformed Transformed,* and in the "fashionable" way Mephistopheles expresses himself in Shelley's translation of Goethe's *Faust.*[12] One of the reasons their relationship endured was that while they occasionally disagreed, they avoided open and acerbic confrontation, and learned from their disagreements. As John Buxton writes: "The friendship between them was of more significance than any other relationship of their lives, both for the development of their personal qualities and for the expression of these in their poetry. This was so because of their candour in recognizing, and their generosity in respecting, the contrast between them, so that each helped the other to be more completely himself."[13] Byron's and Shelley's six-year conversation clearly had high and low points, as well as occasional silences, but it was also stimulating, and it shaped and was shaped by their poetry.

In fact, as Shelley and Byron continued to converse, they often found themselves thinking along similar lines. Certainly, their liberal political aspirations were compatible, as was their dislike of moralistic cant. But even with respect to the arguments which critics use to show the essential differences between Shelley and Byron, they are often less opposed than is generally thought. For example, Shelley and Byron are usually seen as being unalterably opposed on the subject of Keats's merits: Shelley championing Keats, Byron denigrating him. But, as an article by P. M. S. Dawson has demonstrated, both poets came to believe that although many of Keats's productions were derivative—owing too much to the influence of Leigh Hunt—his *Hyperion* was a great poem.[14] *Hyperion,* wrote Shelley to Byron, showed Keats's "great . . . promise," and Byron agreed, calling *Hyperion,* in a letter to John Murray, "a fine monument."[15] And, although at first skeptical, Byron was eventually persuaded by Shelley that Keats's death was caused by a bad review. Another example of how Shelley and Byron are thought to be opposed involves their dramas. Robinson holds that the two poets had sharp differences over the merits of two of their tragedies, Byron's *Marino Faliero* and Shelley's *The Cenci*. According to Robinson, Shelley objected to *Marino Faliero* because it justified "an immoral revolutionary ethic."[16] Actually, the disagreement was strictly theoretical and literary in nature—Shelley believed in using Shakespeare as a model for his dramas, and Byron believed in preserving the Aristotelian unities. Whatever his reservations about Shelley's dramatic theory, Byron thought *The Cenci* was "perhaps the best tragedy modern times have produced" and assured Shelley that it "was a work of power, and poetry."[17] And Shelley's objections to *Marino Faliero* were directed against Byron's "system" of writing dramas, not against his misplaced revolutionary fervor.[18] In essence, both poets gave each other good literary advice: Shakespeare is a difficult dramatist to emulate, as Shelley discovered in composing "Charles the First," and most critics of Byron's plays agree that his use of the unities was unnecessarily restrictive. But Byron clearly respected *The Cenci* as a work of art, and Shelley, as far as I know, never condemned the political thinking behind *Marino Faliero*. In terms of their appreciation of Keats and each other's plays, Shelley and Byron were more attuned than many critics believe.

Perhaps the most wrongheaded conception of the Byron-Shelley relationship is that Byron invariably stood for pessimism, skepticism, and despair, while Shelley, an impractical dreamer, was unwaveringly optimistic and melioristic, a confident advocate of hope and reform. When one looks at the poets' works, one finds that they defy such simple formulations. As G. M. Matthews observes, "Shelley's fullest picture of the immediate future is in *The Revolt of Islam* (published 1818), where massacre, famine and disease reach their climax in the burning alive of the popular leaders. *The Mask of Anarchy* (written 1819) anticipated a far greater slaughter of unarmed civilians than at Peterloo. *Hellas* (written 1821) ended in the betrayal and massacre of the resurgent Greeks."[19] Byron, on the other hand, was not too pessimistic to be able to assert the possibility of an earthly utopia, such as Don Juan achieves for a time with Haidée, or as Sardanapalus maintains at the beginning of *Sardanapalus*. In fact, Byron's last long poem, *The Island,* describes a hero who achieves a terrestrial paradise on a South Sea island. Although

Byron, in many cases, is more pessimistic than Shelley, just as Shelley is often more optimistic than Byron, it would be inaccurate to identify these poets totally with either philosophical position.

If, however, Shelley and Byron were not philosophical opposites, how can their relationship be defined? A student of their association is faced with complexities and apparent contradictions. How can one, for example, square the harmony of their early relations in Switzerland with the apparent despair Shelley felt when he lived near Byron in Pisa? Certainly, if one stresses the months on Lake Geneva, a positive view of their relationship seems appropriate; if one concentrates on Shelley's complaints against Byron in Pisa, one is led to believe that the relationship had a negative effect on Shelley's creativity. In my opinion, neither view is completely accurate—their literary relationship was both helpful and inhibiting, and the conversation between Shelley and Byron, although for the most part positive, was sometimes marred by misunderstanding and contention. Two important points, however, need to be emphasized: as far as we know, the effect of Shelley on Byron was almost uniformly helpful and supportive, and, despite all the tensions in Pisa, an open break between the poets never occurred. But to get a clearer perspective of Shelley's and Byron's friendship, it is necessary to see how it evolved.

When Shelley and Byron first met in 1816, the primary impetus for their coming together was not literary but personal. Although Shelley had admired Byron and had sent him a copy of his *Queen Mab* as well as a brief 1814 note recently discovered by Robinson,[20] it was at the behest of Claire Clairmont, who was pregnant with Byron's child, that he agreed to meet Byron near Geneva. Claire Clairmont was Mary Shelley's stepsister and the Shelleys' traveling companion during their elopement. In many ways her association with the Shelleys was ambiguous—conjectures about her relationship with Shelley proliferated among their contemporaries. But about the nature of Claire's relations with Byron there can be no doubt. After a brief affair in England, and a short resumption of their intimate relationship in Switzerland, Byron rejected Claire with a dislike that grew into loathing. His cruelty toward Claire, which involved the enforced separation of Claire from their daughter, Allegra, threatened to poison Byron's relationship with Shelley. But the fact that Byron disliked and, to a certain extent, mistreated Shelley's wife's stepsister, who was also Shelley's own friend and companion of several years, never seriously threatened Shelley's association with Byron. This is a tribute to the strength of the Shelley-Byron friendship, particularly on Shelley's side. For Byron's part, he was content to accept Shelley as a friendly mediator between himself and Claire, and never let his dislike for her affect his regard for Shelley.

Shelley welcomed the opportunity to meet Byron, and Byron was glad to be in the company of the erudite and freethinking Shelley. Like Byron, Shelley had come to the continent after having endured a trying legal situation. Byron had just suffered through the separation from Lady Byron and the resulting scandal; Shelley had endured a chancery suit which made it impossible to get money from his estate, as well as the angry reproaches of Mary's father, William Godwin, who would not forgive her and Shelley for their elopement. The two poets seemed drawn together from the beginning and, according to Dr. Polidori, Byron's traveling companion, "talked, till the ladies' brains whizzed with giddiness, about idealism."[21] Another witness of these conversations, Mary Shelley, remembered Shelley's and Byron's talks after her husband's death: "I always saw them together, & when LB. speaks I wait for Shelley's voice in answer as a natural result."[22] It appears that from the beginning of their relationship Shelley and Byron inspired each other and those around them. From one of their early conversations, Mary got her idea for *Frankenstein:* "Many and long were the conversations between Lord Byron and Shelley, to which I was a devout but nearly silent listener. During one of these, various philosophical doctrines were discussed, and among others the nature of the principle of life."[23] At Byron's suggestion, each of the friends in Geneva attempted to write a ghost story: Byron wrote a sketch about a vampire, which later became Dr. Polidori's *The Vampyre,* Mary wrote her famous novel, and Shelley wrote a poetic fragment beginning "A shovel of his ashes took."[24] This is just one example of the many fruitful conversations that Shelley and Byron were to have; their later conversation in Venice inspired, of course, *Julian and Maddalo,* and also may have given Byron the impetus to write *Don Juan.* According to Shelley, Byron wrote *Don Juan* as a result of his encouragement: "at Venice, I urged Byron to come out of the dismal 'wood of error' into the sun, and to write something new and cheerful. 'Don Juan' is the result."[25]

The importance of the meeting in Switzerland is indisputable in Byron's case. Shelley's success in introducing Wordsworth to Byron left its mark on *Childe Harold's Pilgrimage,* canto 3, and, as Donald Reiman notes, Shelley's belief in the power of man to alter his condition is reflected in Byron's writings from the Geneva period: "in such poems as 'Sonnet on Chillon,' the third canto of *Childe Harold's Pilgrimage,* and *Manfred,* Byron asserts the autonomy of the human spirit as he does not do elsewhere in his mature poetry."[26] Newman Ivey White suggests that Byron's use of Ahrimanes in *Manfred* was inspired by a conversation with Shelley, who, along with his friend Thomas Love Peacock, was an enthusiastic student of Persian mythology.[27] Byron's effect on Shelley's poetry is less clear. Shelley's "Hymn to Intellectual Beauty" was the only major work actually written while Shelley was in Byron's company, but "Mont Blanc" was composed after Shelley separated from Byron and toured the Valley of Chamonix with Mary and Claire Clairmont. Besides these poems, two minor sonnets, "Upon the Wandering Winds" and "To Laughter," have come to light (in 1976) from this period in Shelley's career.[28] According to Geoffrey Matthews and Kelvin Everest, the first sonnet may have reflected Shelley's reading of the third canto of *Childe Harold:* after a passionate description of natural scenes, Shelley modestly mentions the "superior grace in others shown" (13), perhaps alluding to what he felt were Byron's "superior" descriptions of Switzerland.[29] Although it would be difficult to prove that Byron inspired these works, the fact remains that after a relatively unproductive period in England, Shelley came to Switzerland, met Byron, and achieved maturity as a poet. Shelley's long letter to Thomas Love Peacock of 12 July 1816 describes eloquently the poets' eight-day journey around Lake Geneva, an inspiring and joyful pilgrimage to Rousseau's old haunts which moved both men.[30] Whatever the reason, Shelley's and Byron's first encounter was clearly stimulating: Byron began a new phase in his poetic development, and Shelley moved back to England ready to embark on a major work, *Laon and Cythna,* which was later revised and published as *The Revolt of Islam.*

Although most of the conversations in Geneva were never recorded, conjectures about them can be made, based on the letters Shelley wrote to Byron from England. In his analysis of the 1817 letters from Shelley to Byron, Reiman notes that Shelley and Byron shared radical views on politics, and that Shelley sought to encourage Byron to reject common social mores in his poetry. According to Reiman, "Shelley was more insistent in communicating his radicalism to Byron than, say, to Peacock, Hogg, or Hunt. This was, presumably, a side of his character to which Byron responded favorably and an aspect of Byron's that Shelley desired to stimulate."[31] It is possible that neither man would have been quite so passionately interested in attacking the social injustices of their times had they not encouraged each other in this kind of thinking. Later, both of them became involved in Italian politics, and Shelley went even so far as to propose to Byron that they should organize an armed party to rescue a man about to be burnt for sacrilege.[32] Their conversations and letters confirm their shared political radicalism, but, paradoxically, did little to alter Shelley's deference to Byron's rank; he always addressed him as "My dear Lord Byron." This is true, despite the fact that Byron's other nonaristocratic friends, such as John Hobhouse and Thomas Moore, typically called him "Byron." Although the reason for this deferential treatment is unclear, Shelley's remark to Leigh Hunt in 1821 that "the canker of aristocracy wants to be cut out" of Byron suggests that Shelley referred to his friend as "Lord" because he felt that Byron was a bit of a snob.[33]

Another element in the relationship of Shelley and Byron involves their rejection of conventions, especially those having to do with the common morality of their day. After having suffered the vicissitudes of scandal and moral condemnation in England, Byron was probably relieved to discover Shelley, Mary, and Claire Clairmont, who professed to be essentially irreligious and freethinking in their views. Although Byron thought of himself as a Christian, he was extremely amused by Shelley's impieties. As Shelley writes in the preface to *Julian and Maddalo,* Maddalo-Byron "takes a wicked pleasure in drawing out [Julian's-Shelley's] taunts against religion." In an 1817 letter Shelley sought to reinforce Byron's rejection of the "common rules," a rejection which Shelley found present in Byron's productions during and after the summer in Geneva: the third canto of *Childe Harold, Manfred,* and *The Prisoner of Chillon.*[34] Shelley was, when he wrote the letter, working on *Laon and Cythna,* in which evil finally prevails, good goes unrewarded, and in which incest is presented sympathetically. Byron clearly agreed with Shelley's sentiments regarding incest: in *Cain,* he emphasizes the necessity and the basic healthiness of Cain's incestuous relationship with his sister Adah. Later, in 1822 Byron continued to praise Shelley as a man absolutely free from "humbug": "He, alone, in this age of humbug, dares stem the current, as he did to-day the flooded Arno in his skiff, although I could not observe that he made any progress. The attempt is better than being swept along as all the rest are, with the filthy garbage scoured from its banks."[35] Byron's and Shelley's determination to abandon conventional moral platitudes and religious cant, along with their shared political sympathies, were points of agreement which they discovered in Switzerland and to which they adhered for the remainder of their poetic careers.

While Shelley and Byron often questioned conventional morality, they differed in their attitudes toward sexuality. According to Nathaniel Brown, Shelley believed strongly in "sentimental love," whereas Byron believed that the sentiments were only a mask for sexual desire.[36] Despite his views on free love, Shelley was shocked when he visited Byron in Venice and found him debauching himself and "familiar with the lowest sort of these women, the people his gondolieri pick up in the streets. He allows fathers & mothers to bargain with him for their daughters."[37] Brown exaggerates, however, when he says that "the two great poets emerge from a dissection of the sexual mores of the age as complementary extremes."[38] Byron's attitudes toward sexuality were more complicated than cynical libertinism; Byron was capable, on occasion, of writing about love in a Shelleyan way. In fact, Shelley felt compelled to deny his influence on Byron's description of the nymph Egeria and "nympholepsy" in *Childe Harold's Pilgrimage,* canto 4.[39] Moreover, in describing Don Juan's tryst with Haidée and Torquil's relationship with Neuha in *The Island,* Byron proves himself capable of a sympathetic portrayal of "sentimental love." In 1821 Shelley wrote to John Gisborne that Byron was "quite cured of his gross habits," although "the perverse ideas on which they were founded [were] not yet eradicated."[40] Shelley and Byron had to agree to disagree on their attitudes toward sexuality, but there is little evidence that this was what, in Brown's words, "finally alienated Shelley from his friend."[41] An association which survived the vicissitudes of Byron's stormy relationship with Claire was not vulnerable to Byron's "perverse ideas," and it is simplistic to call Byron, who after all experienced a measure of domestic tranquillity with Teresa Guiccioli, a jeering libertine.

Of course, Shelley's complaint that Byron's Venetian debaucheries included his association "with wretches who seem almost to have lost the gait & physiognomy of men, & who do not scruple to avow practices which are not only not named but I believe seldom even conceived in England"[42] can be taken as an objection to Byron's homoeroticism, and it is likely that the poets had different attitudes toward homosexuality. But as Louis Crompton notes, Shelley's comments are difficult to decipher: "Were these men or transvestite street boys? Did Byron simply find them amusing company, or was he sexually involved?"[43] In the same vein, Doris Langley Moore remarks that "For all we know to the contrary, Byron, who had enjoyed the company of pugilists and jockeys in London and been delighted to have an escort of ex-robbers in Albania, entertained the 'wretches' with no more than his usual absorbing curiosity about every aspect of human character."[44] And in any case, Byron's homoerotic inclinations seem to have been dormant during the period in which he knew Shelley—according to Crompton, "After 1816 his homosexual side seems to vanish until his last days at Missolonghi."[45] Crompton also argues that Shelley's own attitudes toward homosexuality were enlightened for his time—in his "Discourse on the Manners of the Antient Greeks Relative to the Subject of Love," for example, Shelley makes "a conscientious effort to provide a candid, critical, and philosophical discussion of Greek pederasty" during an era in which translations of Plato's *Symposium* were bowdlerized to remove references to same-sex love.[46] Although we may never know whether or not the poets ever explicitly discussed the issue of homosexuality, it would certainly be inconsistent for Shelley to condemn it while at the same time sympathizing with "the aesthetic ideal of Greek pederasty."[47]

The most important conversation between the two poets took place on 23 August 1818 in Venice. Although they had corresponded during the two years after they parted in Switzerland, Shelley writing far more often than Byron, this encounter, like their first, came about because of Claire. Incensed by Byron's coldness and his refusal to let her see their daughter, Claire was using Shelley as a mediator between herself and Byron, an office that Shelley was to hold with increasing reluctance until Allegra's death in 1822. The meeting in Venice was followed by another period of intense creativity. Shelley's *Julian and Maddalo* was inspired by the meeting itself, and he returned to Este and began writing *Prometheus Unbound* during the following month. During that month, September 1818, Byron completed the first canto of *Don Juan,* and all of *Mazeppa.* Their famous conversation in Venice served to help them know themselves as well as each other, to find their poetic voices in their two masterworks. *Prometheus Unbound* is, in many ways, a dramatization of the discussion "Concerning God, free-will and destiny; / Of all the earth has been or yet may be" (42–43, *Julian and Maddalo*). And the composition of *Don Juan,* canto 1, marks a significant shift in Byron's poetry, toward an ironic and humorous view of the human condition. Shelley and Mary visited Venice together on 24 September 1818; their daughter Clara died upon their arrival, perhaps a victim of Shelley's excessive desire to visit his friend again. Soon after this tragedy, Shelley met with Byron, who read from canto 1 of *Don Juan* and who, in Shelley's opinion, had changed into the "liveliest, & happiest looking man [he had] ever met."[48] One of the results of this meeting was Shelley's "Lines written among the Euganean Hills" (October 1818), which idealizes Byron as "a tempest-cleaving Swan" (174). Shelley continued to encourage Byron's work on *Don Juan* during a period in which Byron's publishers and readers were scandalized by its supposed immorality.

After the visits to Venice, Shelley's next important encounter with Byron was in Ravenna, on 6 August 1821. This was at the beginning a very amicable visit, as Shelley wrote to Mary: "Lord Byron is very well, & was delighted to see me. He has in fact completely recovered his health, & lives a life totally the reverse of that which he led in Venice."[49] The poets talked late into the night, disagreeing on the correct way in which to write drama, but Byron cast a shadow over the visit by mentioning a malicious story related to him by their mutual acquaintances, the Hoppners. Mr. Hoppner believed, on the evidence of the Shelleys' maid, that Claire Clairmont had borne Shelley's child, and that the baby had been taken away from its mother and consigned to a foundling hospital.[50] Thus Claire continued to overshadow their relationship, giving it an uneasiness and ambiguity it may not have had otherwise. But, despite this disturbing scandal, Shelley stayed on in Ravenna until 16 or 17 August, persuading Byron to come to Pisa and take part in his dream of forming "a society of [their] own class, as much as possible, in intellect or in feelings."[51] The Ravenna talks also led Byron to begin a magazine, *The Liberal,* in partnership with Shelley's friend, Leigh Hunt. Most of all, Shelley came away from Ravenna with a renewed sense of Byron's greatness, which he found embodied in the early cantos of *Don Juan.*

It was at Ravenna that Shelley began to have doubts about his own poetic gift. He wrote to Mary: "I despair of rivalling Lord Byron, as well I may: and there is no other with whom it is worth contending."[52] Byron, for his own part, kept Shelley in Ravenna as long as he could, arguing that only Shelley and Teresa Guiccioli stood between him and the kind of libertinism and degradation he had succumbed to in Venice. In a letter to Mary, Shelley gives the following picture of his role as Byron's moral support: "I have the greatest trouble to get away & L. B. as a reason for my stay has urged that without either me or the Guiccioli he will certainly fall into his old habits.—I then talk, & he listens to reason."[53] Although Shelley's presence was beneficial to Byron, it evidently cost Shelley a great deal. Shelley wrote of his increasing inability to create in Ravenna: "I write nothing, and probably shall write no more."[54] Shelley, of course, did write more, but the demands of being an intermediary between Claire and Byron, and then between Leigh Hunt and Byron, began to wear him down. Unlike Byron, Shelley wrote best in seclusion. His sentiments about the poet's need for isolation are expressed in his works, most explicitly in *Epipsychidion,* and also in a Ravenna letter to Mary: "My greatest content would be utterly to desert all human society. I would retire with you & our child to a solitary island in the sea, would build a boat, & shut upon my retreat the floodgates of the world.—I would read no reviews & talk with no authors."[55] The scheme to gather a number of "authors" in Pisa, although seemingly beneficial to Byron, could only serve to exacerbate Shelley's growing feelings of poetic inadequacy, his inability to write in the proximity of other writers.

The conversations, however, continued. While the nature of the poets' Pisan discussions can never be completely known, according to Thomas Medwin the two men seldom had extended arguments, certainly not the debates that one would expect from two "antagonistic spirits." Medwin writes: "Byron was so sensible of his inability to cope with [Shelley, in argument], that he always avoided coming to a trial of their strength in controversy, which he generally cut off with a joke or pun; for Shelley was what Byron could not be, a close, logical, and subtle reasoner."[56] Of course, Medwin, Shelley's cousin and friend since childhood, was far from impartial in his appraisal of Shelley's superior intellectual prowess. The poets' debate on the merits of Shakespeare and *Hamlet* seems to reflect, however, Byron's desire to avoid any extended dispute; Shelley soon launches into a full-scale reading of the drama, to which Byron responds by falling asleep, like Charles XII does at the end of Byron's *Mazeppa*.[57]

Richard Holmes notes that Shelley and Byron observed certain formalities in their conversations: "Both men allowed each other a formal advantage: Shelley was absolutely rigid in his recognition of Byron's superior social status—'my dear Lord Byron'; Byron in turn always appeared to submit to Shelley's critical judgement on literary matters (it being understood that he regarded *Don Juan* and *Cain* as very great poems)."[58] Shelley gave Byron his due as a man of noble rank and as a great poet, while Byron regarded Shelley as a superior critic and intellect. In fact, Medwin wrote that "Shelley's disapprobation of a poem caused [Byron] to destroy it."[59] According to Edward Trelawny, Shelley's scathing criticism of *The Deformed Transformed* did lead Byron to throw half a sheet of his manuscript into the fire, a gesture which, since Byron later published the work as a fragment, may have been more symbolic than actually destructive.[60] Trelawny also noted Byron's quiet respect for Shelley's opinion: "I was then and afterwards pleased and surprised at Byron's passiveness and docility in listening to Shelley— . . . Byron knew him to be exempt from . . . the rivalry of authorship, and that he was the truest and most discriminating of his admirers."[61] Thus, even during the most tense periods of the poets' residence in Pisa, during a time when Shelley's marital and financial problems, his apparent loss of inspiration, and his irritation with Byron's seeming ascendancy over him conspired to drive him almost to distraction, there was no break between the poets, not even as far as we know a brief quarrel. Their conversation simply became more guarded, as each man deferred to the other's strengths and avoided controversy,

Byron using his humorous sallies to head off potentially acrimonious arguments.

Unfortunately, the Pisan period in Shelley's career was relatively unproductive. Soon after Byron arrived in Pisa Shelley wrote his haunting "Sonnet to Byron," in which heartfelt admiration for his friend is mixed with envy and self-denigration:

> If I esteemed you less, Envy would kill
> Pleasure, and leave to Wonder and Despair
> The ministration of the thoughts that fill
> The mind which, like a worm whose life may share
> A portion of the unapproachable,
> Marks your creations rise as fast and fair
> As perfect worlds at the Creator's will. (2–8)

As he continued to associate with Byron in Pisa, Shelley's dissatisfaction with his own failure to write grew, and he began to complain of Byron's influence over him. Shelley wrote to Leigh Hunt: "Certain it is, that Lord Byron has made me bitterly feel the inferiority which the world has presumed to place between us and which subsists nowhere in reality but in our own talents, which are not our own but Nature's—or in our rank, which is not our own but Fortune's."[62] In a letter to Horace Smith, Shelley complained that Byron's presence prevented him from writing: "I have lived too long near Lord Byron, & the sun has extinguished the glowworm."[63] After Shelley's failure to complete "Charles the First," he became hypersensitive to slights from his more prolific friend, and his feelings of animosity came to a kind of climax when Byron had "Don Juan" painted, in large letters, on the mainsail of Shelley's boat. It must have seemed to Shelley as if Byron meant to write the name of his masterpiece over everything that was Shelley's, thus aggressively outshining Shelley with the radiance of his own literary prowess.

Poetic competition was not, however, the only thing that Shelley came to find offensive in his relations with Byron. Indeed, Byron insisted in involving Shelley in a whole range of contests, including pistol shooting and billiards, and was willing to wager on almost anything. Even the weekly dinners with Byron became a strain, as Shelley complained to Horace Smith: "Lord Byron unites us at a weekly dinner where my nerves are generally shaken to pieces by sitting up, contemplating the rest making themselves vats of claret &c. till 3 o'clock in the morning."[64] And, of course, Claire Clairmont remained in the background, putting even more pressure on the poets' relationship. In an unsigned letter to Claire, Shelley suggested that he was prepared to challenge Byron to a duel: "for your immediate feelings I would suddenly and irrevocably leave this country which he inhabits, nor ever enter it but as an enemy to determine our differences *without words*" (Shelley's italics).[65] If one can judge from Shelley's correspondence, a complete break in his relations with Byron was imminent.

But a break never came. In fact, even as he wrote his dramatic letter to Claire, Shelley was successfully negotiating with Byron for a large loan to Leigh Hunt. Shelley seems to have been deeply divided, complaining bitterly about Byron in his letters but letting none of this show in his actual interchanges with his friend. Certainly, Byron valued Shelley's opinion; Trelawny wrote that Shelley was the only person in Pisa Byron took into his confidence: "During the time I knew Byron, he never talked seriously and confidently with any person but Shelley. Shelley was disconnected from all Byron's set, and from everyone that he knew, besides being a far superior scholar."[66] In fact, it is possible that critics, taking Shelley's sometimes histrionic letters at face value, have developed an overly negative view of the Pisan period of the poets' friendship. Byron was not the only source of Shelley's irritation, nor the only oppressive poetic influence with which Shelley had to contend. If one wants to point out a stifling influence, one might consider that Shelley was working on his translation of Goethe's *Faust* in the beginning of 1822, and that this poem became an obsession with him. It is also difficult to blame Shelley's failure to complete "Charles the First" fully on Byron's presence, particularly since the Shakespearean model would have been far more inhibiting to Shelley than would Byron's dramatic efforts. Shelley told Trelawny that he was trying for Shakespearean perfection in "Charles the First": " 'King Lear' is my model, for that is nearly perfect."[67] With such high expectations, he was virtually doomed to failure, whether living near Byron or not. Whatever his reservations regarding Byron's character, Shelley remained a sincere admirer of his poetry, and Byron's charm—what Mary Shelley was later to call "the delightful & buoyant tone of his conversation and manners"—was sufficiently disarming to prevent Shelley from actually quarreling with him.[68]

Of course, one must never forget that Shelley managed to compose during his last months a poem which many consider his masterwork, *The Triumph of Life*. The Shelleys had moved to San Terenzo, and Shelley was again able to write. In fact, there are indications that he projected an entire series of *Trionfi*, based on the Petrarchan model. The poem is, however, highly original and seems to point toward a shift in Shelley's work which he did not live to develop. The pattern begun in Switzerland and continued in Venice was then repeated in Pisa: in Byron's presence Shelley found it difficult to create but, immediately upon leaving Byron, he was exceptionally prolific. Again, it is important not to overemphasize the negative feelings Shelley had toward Byron during the Pisan period; they seem to have been temporary, and Robinson's assertion that "Byron's 'hateful' presence continued to torment [Shelley] into the last days of his life" is not entirely accurate.[69] Shelley's last days, "reading Spanish dramas & sailing & listening to the most enchanting music," were not those of a man devastated by "anxiety of influence," and *The Triumph of Life* is a powerful and eloquent manifestation of his poetic autonomy.[70]

The encounters between the two poets inspired their poetry, the difference between them being that Byron could write in Shelley's presence, but Shelley had to wait until he was away from Byron before he could be truly prolific. We still have the problem, however, of determining how their relationship affected individual poems. According to Robinson, many of the poems were assertions and rebuttals in Shelley's and Byron's debate between optimism and pessimism. As we have seen, however, Shelley and Byron were not consistently opposed to each other. In their poems they did indeed respond to one another, but with a view toward exploring their own apprehensions of reality rather than a desire to disprove or reject a rival vision. On occasion, Shelley contributed to their discussion his melioristic ideas, and Byron sometimes wrote pessimistically. But it is important to see this not as a *debate* between two poets who believe in only one perspective on life, but as a *conversation* in which Shelley and Byron try to clarify and develop complex and sometimes self-contradictory views on life and art. Shelley and Byron were not trying to simplify their perspectives by dogmatically insisting on opposing philosophical orientations: they used their discourse to develop and examine their attitudes and beliefs in relation to another poetic consciousness, striving for a sophisticated and well-rounded view of life.

The relationship between the poets' texts, like their personal relationship, is complex and difficult to characterize accurately. Harold Bloom's idea that intertextual relationships are dominated by "anxiety" about strong poetic "precursors" does not seem appropriate, since each poet was able to maintain his own poetic voice and neither poet clearly "preceded" the other.[71] And Robinson's description of the poets' "philosophical antagonism" covers only a part of their relationship, neglecting, I think, many of their similarities and points of agreement. In order to find a more appropriate description of their literary relations, I will turn to a concept found in both William Blake and Shelley, that of mental warfare, or, to quote from Shelley's *The Revolt of Islam,* the "war of earthly minds" (7.3134). Inasmuch as there is debate in *Julian and Maddalo,* it is a debate which seeks not to prove one view right and the other wrong, but which seeks to understand the human condition more completely, viewing it as a contradictory combination of man's idealistic aspirations and his bitter defeats. In the Eden of William Blake the sons of Eden fight "the great Wars of Eternity, in fury of Poetic Inspiration, / To build the Universe stupendous: Mental forms Creating" (*Milton,* plate 30.19–20)—Byron and Shelley also fought a mental "war" in order to inspire each other to create new poetic visions, "to build the universe stupendous" in their works.[72] True creativity, in Blake's prophetic poems, is collaborative, a mental struggle between poets which enlarges their perceptions, making new creation possible: "Our wars are wars of life, & wounds of love, / With intellectual spears, & long winged arrows of thought" (*Jerusalem,* plate 34.14–15). Although Shelley never read Blake, he too believed in the power of "the swift thought, / Winging itself with laughter" (*Julian and Maddalo,* 28–29), and the importance of intellectual struggle. As Cythna of Shelley's *The Revolt of Islam* improves her vision of reality by becoming familiar with "the shock and surprise / And war of earthly minds" (7.3133–34), Byron and Shelley used each other's visions to refine their own ideas on the human condition. While the Romantic concept of mental warfare implies aggressiveness, it is not a negative, antagonistic aggressiveness: it is a process of self-examination which seeks to illuminate rather than dominate.

In general, neither Shelley nor Byron has been given credit for their open-mindedness, their willingness to learn from each other or to change and develop their ideas. As Jerome McGann notes, Shelley and Byron were closely allied: "Both occupied the ideological vanguard of their period and both actively engaged in progressive social action at political and ideological levels. . . . In Shelley's contradictory futurism lies a fearful judgment upon what men were making of other men in Shelley's world. Byron's despair—both in its comic and its violent modes—must be seen in the same way."[73] By concentrating too much on the ways in which the poets respond to the same problem, critics tend to miss the fact that Shelley's and Byron's social-activist goals and their perceptions of man's benighted and tragic state have much in common. In fact, toward the end of their lives the poets made similar gestures, expressing their philhellenist aspirations in poetry (Shelley's *Hellas*) and action (Byron's work for the liberation of Greece).

It is in the works of Shelley and Byron that we see the "war of earthly minds" being waged. This study is, therefore, primarily an intertextual one, an analysis not only of the dialogue between Shelley and Byron but also of the dialogue between their texts. And, as an examination of the poets' letters and published conversations attests, Shelley and Byron read each other's works extensively. In his "Appendix A" to *Shelley and Byron: The Snake and Eagle Wreathed in Fight,* Robinson describes Shelley's pre-Geneva reading of Byron's works, a reading which included *English Bards and Scotch Reviewers,* Byron's 1808 edition of *Poems: Original and Translated,* and probably *Childe Harold,* cantos 1 and 2, as well as the tales (there is conclusive evidence that Shelley read *Lara*).[74] Shelley also sent a letter and a copy of *Queen Mab* to Byron between 1813 and 1816, but the letter, Thomas Moore later wrote, "miscarried."[75] Robinson has recently discovered another letter from Shelley to Byron, dated 2 June 1814, which "begs Lord Byrons acceptance of [an] inclosed poem," and speculates that this poem was Shelley's sonnet, "Feelings of a Republican on the Fall of Bonaparte."[76] The *Alastor* volume was sent to Byron in early 1816, and on 6 September 1819 Shelley asked his publisher Charles Ollier to send Byron copies of his books automatically upon publication.[77] This does not mean, however, that Byron saw all of Shelley's unpublished works; we cannot be entirely sure, for example, that Byron ever read *Julian and Maddalo,* although there is some evidence (which I discuss in chapter 3) that he may well have seen the poem in which he plays so important a part. But we can be certain that Byron read most of Shelley's works carefully, particularly, as I shall argue in this study, *Queen Mab, The Revolt of Islam, The Cenci,* and *Prometheus Unbound.* Shelley, on the other hand, read Byron even more extensively than Byron read Shelley: the useful Appendix 8 of Frederick Jones's edition of Shelley's letters indicates that Shelley was familiar with nearly all of Byron's important poems and dramas.[78] Of course, Shelley did not live long enough to read beyond canto 5 of *Don Juan* or to see any of *The Island,* but he was clearly an eager student of Byron's earlier writings.

According to the definition of intertextuality developed by Julia Kristeva, "Every text builds itself as a mosaic of quotations, every text is an absorption and transformation of another text."[79] Many of Shelley's and Byron's texts reflect their interest in reading, absorbing, and responding to one another's poems. For example, in the dedication preceding *The Cenci* (written in 1819), Shelley calls the drama "a sad reality," echoing a line from Byron's "Prometheus" (composed in 1816): "The sufferings of mortality, / Seen in their *sad reality,* / Were not as things that gods despise" (2–4, italics mine).[80] In this case, Byron's poem serves as a gloss for Shelley's use of this important phrase. Moreover, *The Cenci,* in its portrait of triumphant evil, has similarities, both in tone and perspective, to the vision in Byron's "Prometheus" of a world dominated by "the ruling principle of Hate, / Which for its pleasure doth create / The things it may annihilate" (20–22). Shelley does not simply reject Byron's text; he absorbs the ideas of "Prometheus" and transforms them in *The Cenci,* taking the concepts of "sad reality" and "the ruling principle of hate" and showing their human consequences in a way that Byron's much shorter work could not. Through an intertextual study of their poems, we can see how Shelley and Byron used each other's ideas and poetic visions to grapple with the problem of maintaining Promethean aspirations in a corrupt world.

In this study of the Byron-Shelley relationship, I have chosen to focus on works which are representative of the different ways in which

Shelley and Byron absorb and transform each other's poems, and works which explore themes which were of particular importance to both poets. For example, my discussion of *Julian and Maddalo* considers the conversational style which each poet came to employ; my analysis of *Cain* shows how it reflects Shelley's and Byron's interest in Prometheanism and their fascination with the devil; and my examination of *The Triumph of Life* includes an appraisal of the influence of Goethe's *Faust* on Shelley and Byron. Thus, while my primary focus is on a limited number of works, I seek to put them in the broader context of the relationship as a whole.

In his preface to *Prometheus Unbound* Shelley notes that it is impossible for any poet to "exclude from his contemplation the beautiful which exists in the writings of a great contemporary." And certainly Shelley and Byron contemplated one another's works with great interest. Thomas Moore wrote of the two men that they were drawn together because of their many differences: "The conversation of Mr. Shelley, . . . was of a nature strongly to arrest and interest the attention of Lord Byron. . . . As far as contrast, indeed, is an enlivening ingredient of such intercourse, it would be difficult to find two persons more formed to whet each other's faculties by discussion, as on few points of common interest between them did their opinions agree."[81] Of course, as Byron's biographer, Moore was interested in repairing his friend's reputation by separating him from the atheistical Shelley and making the two seem like polar opposites.[82] Trelawny also contrasted the poets, but in his account he denigrated Byron in order to elevate both Shelley and himself.[83] In this study, however, I will show that Byron and Shelley had points of agreement as well as disagreement, similarities as well as differences. Using the poetry of Shelley and Byron, I will examine the intertextual and personal sides of their six-year conversation, the "war of earthly minds" that helped shape some of the most important achievements of the Romantic era.

TWO

In Switzerland:
Wordsworth and Science

The Genevan period of the Shelley-Byron relationship began in May 1816 when Byron, Shelley, Mary Godwin, Claire Clairmont, and Byron's companion, Dr. Polidori, met and agreed to settle together on the southern side of Lake Geneva. The discussions that the poets had in the Villa Diodati were wide-ranging, and covered such topics as madness, Irish revolutionaries, idealism, "whether man was to be thought merely an instrument,"[1] Erasmus Darwin, the relative merits of Rousseau and Gibbon,[2] and ghost stories. They also discussed their great contemporary, William Wordsworth, at some length, and we can assume that in this instance Shelley did much of the talking. Wordsworth had been on Shelley's mind even before he met Byron: in a letter to Peacock dated 15 May 1816, Shelley associated his homesickness for England with the sentiments expressed in Wordsworth's "I Travelled Among Unknown Men." Until a man travels in foreign lands, Shelley declared, "like Wordsworth he will never know what love subsisted between himself and [the country of his birth], until absence shall have made its beauty heartfelt. Our Poets and our Philosophers our mountains & our lakes, the rural lanes and fields which are ours so especially, are ties which unless I become utterly senseless can never be broken asunder."[3] It is scarcely surprising, then, that Wordsworth became a common topic of conversation between the two expatriate poets—as Byron later told Medwin, "Shelley, when I was in Switzerland, used to dose me with Wordsworth physic even to nausea; and I do remember then reading some things of his with pleasure. He had once a feeling of Nature."⁴ Rather than analyzing each other's poetry, a practice which could have led to tensions between them, Shelley and Byron turned their critical intelligences to a third poet of an older generation and found themselves agreeing, at least at first, that Wordsworth was in some respects worthy of their admiration.

Of course, it may seem strange to assert that Byron held Words-worth in esteem—one thinks of his frequent references to the lake poet as "Turdsworth"⁵ and his less than respectful allusions to Wordsworth in *Don Juan*. But when Byron met Shelley, his opinion of Wordsworth was mixed. According to Lady Byron, her husband's one meeting with Wordsworth inspired a feeling of *"reverence"*⁶ in the younger poet, and from what Byron later told Medwin we might gather that Byron re-spected Wordsworth's "feeling of Nature," while at the same time ob-jecting to Wordsworth's politics. Speaking of Wordsworth's loss of revolutionary idealism, Byron remarked to Medwin that "It is satis-factory to reflect, that where a man becomes a hireling and loses his mental independence, he loses also the faculty of writing well. The lyrical ballads, jacobinical and puling with affectations of simplicity as they were, had undoubtedly a certain merit."⁷ Moreover, while Byron recognized Wordsworth's talent, he believed that Wordsworth had a tendency to misuse it. In an 1815 letter to Leigh Hunt he claimed that Wordsworth had declined as a poet: "his performances since 'Lyrical Ballads'—are miserably inadequate to the ability which lurks within him:—there is undoubtedly much natural talent spilt over 'the Excur-sion' but it is rain upon rocks where it stands & stagnates . . . —who can understand him?—let those who do make him intelligible."⁸

Shelley shared Byron's ambivalent view of Wordsworth to an extent. Kim Blank notes that "Shelley finds it painfully difficult to reconcile the older poet's political activity with his earlier poetical activity, the older man with the younger poet."⁹ While Shelley admired *Lyrical Bal-lads,* he objected strenuously to *The Excursion* (1814)¹⁰ and in 1816 he published a sonnet, "To Wordsworth," in which he mourned the older poet's lost idealism: "In honoured poverty thy voice did weave / Songs consecrate to truth and liberty,— / Deserting these, thou leavest me to grieve, / Thus having been, that thou shouldst cease to be" (11–14). In his "Verses Written on Receiving a Celandine in a Letter from England" (written in Switzerland), Shelley seems to be repudiating Wordsworth's "Ode 1815" (in which Wordsworth patriotically celebrates carnage): "the foul god of blood / With most inexpiable praise, / . . . / He has been bought to celebrate!" (45–48).[11] Moreover, Shelley was incensed when Peacock wrote to him in 1818 about Wordsworth's political allegiance to the Lowther family. In reply to Peacock's letter, Shelley wrote: "What a beastly and pitiful wretch that Wordsworth! That such a man should be such a poet! I can compare him with no one but Simonides, that flatterer of Sicilian tyrants, and at the same time the most natural and tender of lyric poets."[12] While Byron and Shelley agreed (Byron more grudgingly than Shelley) that Wordsworth was a great poet, they were also convinced that Wordsworth's reactionary politics had cast a shadow over his earlier poetic achievement.

But in Switzerland Shelley and Byron seem to have ignored Wordsworth's politics and wrote poems that reflected their shared interest in Wordsworth's "feeling of Nature, which he carried almost to a deification of it."[13] It is certainly true that echoes of Wordsworth's pantheism can be found in such poems as Byron's *Childe Harold's Pilgrimage,* canto 3, "[Epistle to Augusta]," and "The Dream," and Shelley's "Hymn to Intellectual Beauty" and "Mont Blanc," all of which were written in 1816.[14] It is also true, however, that in their presentations of nature Shelley and Byron often departed from the Wordsworthian model. For example, the focus of Byron's "The Dream" (1816)[15] is on the love of a youth for a maiden; for although the "living landscape" is carefully described, the young man only has eyes for his beloved:

> I saw two beings in the hues of youth
> Standing upon a hill, a gentle hill,
> Green and of mild declivity, the last
> As 'twere the cape of a long ridge of such,
> Save that there was no sea to lave its base,
> But a most living landscape, and the wave
> Of woods and cornfields, and the abodes of men
> Scattered at intervals, and wreathing smoke
> Arising from such rustic roofs;—the hill
> Was crown'd with a peculiar diadem
> Of trees, in circular array, so fix'd,
> Not by the sport of nature, but of man:

These two, a maiden and a youth, were there
Gazing—the one on all that was beneath
Fair as herself—but the boy gazed on her. (2.27–41)

Although the "wreathing smoke arising from . . . rustic roofs" seems to
recall the "wreaths of smoke" (17) observed in Wordsworth's "Lines
Written a Few Miles above Tintern Abbey," the youth does not see it,
and the maiden is looking for "her lover's steed" (2.73) rather than ap-
preciating nature's beauty. The irony of the scene is in the irrelevance of
the carefully described scenery to Byron's characters, whose attitudes
are not the least bit pantheistic. This section of "The Dream" is not so
much Wordsworthian as it is Wordsworth filtered through a Shelleyan
sensibility, and, as if to underscore this idea, Byron paraphrases two
lines from Shelley's *Alastor* three lines below the passage quoted above:
"the sweet moon on the horizon's verge" (2.44) echoes Shelley's "The
dim and horned moon hung low, and poured / A sea of lustre on the
horizon's verge" (*Alastor*, 602–3).[16] Nature in "The Dream" is seen as
secondary to the protagonist's (or Byron's) hopeless passion for his
beloved (Mary Chaworth), just as nature in *Alastor* is an "empty scene"
(201) compared to the "veiled maid" (151) of the poet's dream. While
both the lover of "The Dream" and the poet of *Alastor* are described as
"the wanderer" (see "The Dream," 6.145; and *Alastor*, 626), they are
quite different from the wanderer of Wordsworth's *The Excursion*, who
finds consolation in nature. Byron's character, like Shelley's, can never
find fulfillment without the object of his passion: neither Byron nor
Shelley present nature as a remedy for a lovesick soul.

As many critics have noted, *Childe Harold's Pilgrimage*, canto 3, contains many passages which recall Wordsworth, but in this canto, as in
"The Dream," one can find at least a trace of Shelley in the Wordsworthian "dose." The following stanza, for example, seems to combine
Wordsworth's enthusiasm for nature with a sense of social alienation
that is reminiscent of *Alastor:*

I live not in myself, but I become
Portion of that around me; and to me,
High mountains are a feeling, but the hum
Of human cities torture: I can see
Nothing to loathe in nature, save to be

A link reluctant in a fleshly chain,
Class'd among creatures, when the soul can flee,
And with the sky, the peak, the heaving plain
Of ocean, or the stars, mingle, and not in vain. (3.680–88)

Similarly, the poet of *Alastor* leaves "His cold fireside and alienated home" (76) to wander through nature and neglects his "fleshly" part to the point of self-destruction. And both *Childe Harold* (canto 3) and *Alastor* express a longing for death—the narrator of canto 3 looks forward to his body being "Reft of its carnal life" (700), and the poet of *Alastor* is impelled to "meet lone Death on the drear ocean's waste" (305). In canto 3 of *Childe Harold* Byron, still deeply depressed by his separation from Lady Byron and Ada, combined Wordsworthian pantheism with the asocial and suicidal sentiments of *Alastor; or, The Spirit of Solitude.* It is clear that Byron believed that canto 3 was more sophisticated than his earlier poetry—writing to Augusta Leigh, he said: "I am certain in my mind that this Canto is the *best* which I have ever written; there is depth of thought in it throughout and a strength of repressed passion which you must feel before you find; but it requires reading more than once, because it is in part *metaphysical,* and of a kind of metaphysics which every body will not understand."[17] The "metaphysics" Byron mentions in the letter are derived to a large extent from both Wordsworth and Shelley, who, along with Rousseau and "Monk" Lewis, were the major influences during his stay in Geneva. Although Byron may have felt dosed with Wordsworth "even to nausea," it seems clear that this dosage enabled Byron to compose poetry which was, in his own opinion, the best and most thoughtful that he had ever written.

Of course, while Shelley dosed Byron with Wordsworth in Switzerland, Byron reciprocated by impregnating Shelley's mind with Coleridge.[18] On 18 June Byron recited to Shelley some verses from Coleridge's *Christabel* (still in manuscript), and Shelley ran away shrieking when Geraldine's deformed bosom was described. Matthews and Everest argue that Shelley's "Mont Blanc. Lines written in the Vale of Chamouni" may have been a response to Coleridge's "Hymn: Before Sun-rise, in the Vale of Chamouny" (1802),[19] and in a 17 July 1816 letter to Peacock, Shelley expressed his growing interest in Coleridge: "Tell me of the political state of England—its literature, of which when I speak Coleridge is in my thoughts."[20] Later on in their careers, however, the poets began to write critically of Coleridge, although they never attacked him as they did the renegade Wordsworth: in "Letter to Maria Gisborne" (1820) Shelley describes Coleridge's "mind / Which, with its own internal lightning blind, / Flags wearily through darkness and despair" (204–6), and in the dedication to *Don Juan* (1819) Byron also takes Coleridge to task for a kind of mental blindness, "like a hawk encumber'd with his hood, / Explaining metaphysics to the nation— / I wish he would explain his Explanation" (Dedication, 14–16). But during their Genevan period Byron and Shelley acknowledged, at least for a time, the greatness of their Romantic precursors, and their discussions of Wordsworth and Coleridge during the summer of 1816 influenced their poetry for years to come.

* * *

Another important topic of conversation in Switzerland was contemporary science—in fact, in her famous preface to *Frankenstein* Mary Shelley describes a scientific conversation between Shelley and Byron that helped inspire her masterwork: "They talked of the experiments of Dr. [Erasmus] Darwin, . . . who preserved a piece of vermicelli in a glass case, till by some extraordinary means it began to move with voluntary motion. . . . Perhaps a corpse would be re-animated; galvinism had given token of such things; perhaps the component parts of a creature might be manufactured, brought together, and endued with vital warmth."[21] Shelley's interest in science was extensive and probably predated Byron's. In Shelley's early Gothic novella, *St. Irvyne; or, the Rosicrucian* (1811), he presents a character, Ginotti, whose intellectual progress seems to reflect Shelley's own mental development: "From my earliest youth, before it was quenched by complete satiation, *curiosity*, and a desire of unveiling the latent mysteries of nature, was the passion by which all the other emotions of my mind were intellectually organized. This desire first led me to cultivate, and with success, the various branches of learning which led to the gates of wisdom. . . . Natural philosophy at last became the peculiar science to which I directed my eager inquiries; thence was I led into a train of labyrinthic meditations."[22]

Thomas Jefferson Hogg noticed that Shelley's rooms in Oxford were filled with the paraphernalia of science, including "An electrical machine, an air-pump, the galvanic trough, a solar microscope, and large glass jars and receivers," and in 1811 Shelley read and began to translate some of the treatises of the great French naturalist, Georges Buffon.[23] As he reveals in a 23 November 1811 letter to Elizabeth Hitchener, he was also beginning to imagine lost civilizations:

> Imagination is resistlessly compelled to look back upon the myriad ages whose silent change placed [mountains] here, to look back when perhaps this retirement of peace and mountain simplicity, was the Pandemonium of druidical imposture, the scene of Roman Pollution, the resting place of the savage denizen of these solitudes with the wolf.—Still, still further!—strain thy reverted Fancy when no rocks, no lakes no cloud-soaring mountains were here, but a vast populous and licentious city stood in the midst of an immense plain, myriads flocked towards it; London itself scarcely exceeds it in the variety, the extensiveness of [or?] consummateness of its corruption![24]

Although Shelley does not speculate about how this imaginary metropolis was destroyed, he suggests that the present-day mountains were then "an immense plain" and that massive geological upheavals may have had something to do with the demise of this "licentious city."

Shelley returns to the theme of nature's power over civilizations in *Queen Mab* (composed between June 1812 and February 1813), in which climactic changes are related to the disappearances of cities:

> And from the burning plains
> Where Libyan monsters yell,
> From the most gloomy glens
> Of Greenland's sunless clime,
> To where the golden fields
> Of fertile England spread
> Their harvest to the day,
> Thou canst not find one spot
> Whereon no city stood. (2.216–24)[25]

Moreover, in one of the notes to *Queen Mab*, Shelley uses astronomical and geological theories to draw an analogy between "the progress of the perpendicularity of the poles [and] the progress of intellect."[26] If,

Shelley speculates, "Astronomy teaches us that the earth is now in its progress, and that the poles are every year becoming more and more perpendicular to the ecliptic," it is not unreasonable to assume that the earth's climates will grow more moderate, and that "the moral and physical improvement of the human species" will be achieved with the elimination of diseases caused by "the present state of the climates of the earth." To support this theory of the earth's progress, Shelley notes that "Bones of animals peculiar to the torrid zone have been found in the north of Siberia, . . . Britain, Germany and France were much colder than at present, and . . . their great rivers were annually frozen over." Thus Shelley considered global warming a real possibility and suspected that the moderation of the earth's climates would lead to humankind's moral and physical health. As Kenneth Neill Cameron notes, however, in this case Shelley is "running counter to the science of his time in order to support a theory which he finds aesthetically and politically attractive."[27] Pierre-Simon de Laplace, in *Exposition du système du monde* (1796), had already demonstrated that the earth's constant oscillation would prevent the perpendicularity that Shelley envisioned.

In Switzerland, however, the earth's climate seemed to be growing worse rather than better: the summer of 1816 was exceptionally cold and wet. In a recent article John Clubbe has described the weather conditions during that summer:

> 1816 stands out as having the coldest summer ever recorded in Europe. . . .
> The summer never came. The spring was unexceptional, and until mid-
> June the agricultural cycle proceeded normally. Then came the rains
> which, a few clear days excepted, lasted the summer. The sun on its
> few appearances was a pale disk. . . . In the spring, astronomers had
> sighted mysterious sunspots in their telescopes. During May and June
> these blemishes became large enough to be visible with the naked eye.
> . . . Superstitious folk, even some less so, concluded that the sun was
> dying; others thought a chunk of the sun would break off and destroy
> the world.[28]

Clubbe argues that this miserable summer had a profound influence on *Frankenstein,* and the abnormally cold weather may also have led Byron and Shelley to consider Buffon's idea of a progressively cooling world.[29] During a trip to Chamonix with Mary and Claire, Shelley viewed Mont Blanc and was strongly reminded of Buffon. Writing to Peacock on 22 July, Shelley declared: "The glaciers must augment, & will subsist at least until they have overflowed this vale.—I will not pursue Buffon[']s sublime but gloomy theory, that this earth which we inhabit will at some future period be changed to a mass of frost."[30] Mary was also greatly impressed by the cataracts and avalanches they saw and described the desolate scene in chapter 9 of *Frankenstein*. After their Chamonix trip Shelley and Mary returned to Byron and the Villa Diodati on 27 July, and, in their enthusiasm, conversed with Byron until midnight about their thrilling experiences.[31] Possibly as a result of this conversation, Byron composed "Darkness" (1816), which takes Buffon's theory to an apocalyptic conclusion: in the poem the world becomes "a lump, / Seasonless, herbless, treeless, manless, lifeless— / A lump of death" (70–72). The idea of a cooling world is also used in Byron's *Cain* (1821), in which the antediluvian Cain lives in a "clime which knows no winter" and is therefore bewildered when Lucifer mentions snow as a phenomenon which Cain's "remoter offspring must encounter" (2.2.317–18).

Shelley's more immediate response to Mont Blanc was expressed in the poem of that name, a poem in which the annihilating forces dominating the region are described in some detail:

> a flood of ruin
> Is there, that from the boundaries of the sky
> Rolls its perpetual stream; vast pines are strewing
> Its destined path, or in the mangled soil
> Branchless and shattered stand: the rocks, drawn down
> From yon remotest waste, have overthrown
> The limits of the dead and living world,
> Never to be reclaimed. The dwelling-place
> Of insects, beasts, and birds, becomes its spoil;
> Their food and their retreat is for ever gone,
> So much of life and joy is lost. The race
> Of man, flies far in dread; his work and dwelling
> Vanish, like smoke before the tempest's stream,
> And their place is not known. ("Mont Blanc," 107–20)

Although Shelley was aware of Horace Saussure's theory that glaciers "have their periods of increase & decay,"[32] in "Mont Blanc" glaciers inexorably advance and permanently destroy all life in their path.[33] Moreover, in "Mont Blanc" Shelley refers to Buffon's hypothesis, as set forth in "Epoques de la nature!" that the earth had slowly cooled from "a sea / Of fire" ("Mont Blanc," 73–74) into its present state.[34] What Shelley saw in Chamonix probably also reminded him of the theory of catastrophism, which argues that life on earth has been repeatedly annihilated by sudden and drastic geological events. Since Shelley and Byron shared an interest in catastrophism—besides Buffon's *Histoire naturelle,* Shelley had read James Parkinson's *Organic Remains,* and Byron was familiar with the writings of Georges Cuvier—it is likely that this theory of natural history was a common topic of conversation in Switzerland.

The theory of catastrophism may have been particularly attractive to Shelley and Byron because it had the virtue of making a phenomenon like the French Revolution seem almost like a natural occurrence. If geological catastrophes had destroyed the mastodons and, according to James Parkinson, past civilizations, a political cataclysm like the French Revolution should not be seen as anomalous: it has had, after all, many precedents in the history of the globe. As Martin Rudwick has noted, Georges Cuvier's use of the term "revolution" in his landmark work, *Recherches sur les ossements fossiles des quadrupèdes* (1812), had political implications: "Just as the institutions of the old regime had been suddenly swept away and replaced by new ones, so these fossil bones seemed 'to prove the existence of a world anterior to ours, destroyed by some kind of catastrophe.' "[35] Moreover, as Clubbe notes, the notion that climate affected human history had been widely accepted since the publication of Montesquieu's *De l'esprit des lois* in 1748, in which Montesquieu considers "climate as a determining factor in human history, in fact, *the* determining factor."[36] Thus, as Shelley and Byron discussed catastrophism during the summer of 1816, it is likely that they were particularly interested in its political ramifications.

Before writing *Queen Mab* Shelley had read James Parkinson's *Organic Remains of a Former World* (1804–11),[37] and Parkinson's discussion of the extinction of prehistoric civilizations and animal species had an influence on act 4 of *Prometheus Unbound,* written in 1819. In one section of act 4 Shelley even goes so far as to envision civilizations created by nonhuman beings. Shelley's Panthea mentions "The wrecks beside of many a city vast, / Whose population which the Earth grew over / Was mortal but not human" (4.296–98). Although Carl Grabo suggests that these lines indicate a belief in evolution,[38] they are also consistent with a nonevolutionary theory of extinction, such as the one developed by Cuvier. And as Cameron argues, Panthea's speech as a whole is "based on Cuvier's famed catastrophe theory, which posited neither a divine creation nor an evolutionary progression but a series of natural creations and destructions."[39] Thus Shelley invokes the theory that the earth was destroyed by floods when he has Panthea describe how "The jagged alligator" and the "earth-convulsing behemoth" fell victim to a "Deluge" (4.309–15). Panthea also suggests that this process may be repeated every time "some God / Whose throne was in a Comet, past, and cried— / 'Be not!'" (4.316–18).

Similarly, Byron uses the notion of prehistorical civilizations in *Cain,* his biblical closet drama. For example, in the note to his Preface to *Cain* Byron mentions the theory "that the pre-adamite world was also peopled by rational beings much more intelligent than man, and proportionably powerful to the mammoth."[40] The submerged beings described by Shelley's Panthea, while not necessarily as intelligent as the pre-Adamites discussed in *Cain,* seem equally mammoth-like: Panthea describes the "prodigious shapes" (4.300) of "Their monstrous works and uncouth skeletons, / Their statues, homes, and fanes" (299–300). There is no sense that these large and intelligent beings ever evolved (or degenerated) into present-day homo sapiens—rather, they went extinct as the result of a worldwide flood. And in both *Cain* and *Prometheus Unbound* there seems to be the suggestion that mankind, like the inhabitants of the dead civilizations described by Parkinson, could be annihilated by future geological revolutions. It is unclear what legacy these forgotten beings left, although Shelley's evil Cenci speculates that their sins may still need punishment: "I do not feel as if I were a man, / But like a fiend appointed to chastise / The offenses of some unremembered world" (*The Cenci,* 4.1.160–62).

In Shelley's works catastrophic change can be either positive or negative. In his note to *Queen Mab* he suggests that changes in the earth's climate could work for good; "Mont Blanc" describes the irreversible devastation wrought by glaciers. Shelley celebrates, however, the destructive force of change in his "Ode to the West Wind" (1819), in which the "wild West Wind" (1) is both "Destroyer and Preserver" (14), an "Uncontrollable" (47) and transformative power. According to Shelley, if the "Pestilence-stricken multitudes" (5) are blown away, new life, or "winged seeds" (7), will inevitably replace them. Thus catastrophic events should be welcomed, even if they cause widespread destruction; after all, "If Winter comes, can Spring be far behind?" (70). Similarly, the dynamic universe of Byron's *Cain,* which is modeled on Cuvier's theory of catastrophic change, opens up new possibilities and is, in a sense, intellectually liberating. At the end of their breathtaking tour through the abyss of space and Hades, Lucifer tells Cain to make up his own mind, to trust to reason rather than blind faith in the traditional cosmology:

> judge
> Not by words, though of spirits, but the fruits
> Of your existence . . .
> *One good* gift has the fatal apple given—
> Your *reason:*—let it not be over-sway'd
> By tyrannous threats to force you into faith
> 'Gainst all external sense and inward feeling. (2.2.456–62)

In a dynamic universe revolution is not only possible, it is likely, and visions of universal progress, or speculations about universal decay, can prove prophetic. Moreover, such catastrophic change can happen almost instantaneously—the drastic and extremely sudden change chronicled in act 4 of *Prometheus Unbound* is clearly consistent with the catastrophism of Parkinson and Cuvier.

The influence of catastrophism is perhaps most evident in Byron's "Darkness," *Cain,* and *Heaven and Earth,* in which Byron speculates about the degenerative effects of geological catastrophes. Thus in *Heaven and Earth* a "Spirit" predicts that after the great flood the new race of men will be inferior to the great antediluvians: "[Japhet's] new world and new race shall be of woe— / Less goodly in their aspect, in their years / Less than the glorious giants, who / Yet walk the world in pride" (1.3.129–32), and in *Cain* Lucifer claims that the races of intelligent beings who preceded mankind on earth were

> As much superior unto all [Cain's] sire,
> Adam, could e'er have been in Eden, as
> The sixty-thousandth generation shall be,
> In its dull damp degeneracy, to
> [Cain] and [his] son. (2.2.69–73)

In describing *Heaven and Earth* to Medwin, Byron says that the angels and their two mortal lovers "leave this globe to a fate which, according to Cuvier, it has often undergone, and will undergo again."[41] Thus these geological changes will continue to take place, resulting, presumably, in the establishment of new and increasingly inferior races of intelligent beings on earth. It is worth noting, however, that Byron does mention catastrophism in a positive context in *The Island* (1823), his treatment of the *Bounty* mutiny. The refuge of the poem's protagonist, Torquil, is a cave created by the earth's great upheavals, formed "When the Poles crashed, and water was the world; / Or hardened from some earth-absorbing fire" (4.150–51). In this passage Byron refers to the neptunist and vulcanist theories of catastrophic change and shows how the results of these events can save as well as destroy.

The poets' conversations about Cuvier in particular seem to have lasted until the last year of their friendship. In April 1822, soon before his death, Shelley sent for and received the first two volumes of Cuvier's *Recherches sur les ossements fossiles des quadrupèdes,* perhaps inspired to do so by Byron's use of Cuvier's theories in *Cain* (published December 1821). And in January of that year Byron was electrified by a letter from Bologna proposing that he help finance a steam-driven flying machine. He described to Medwin how science might enable man to resist future catastrophes:

> We are at present in the infancy of science. Do you imagine that, in former stages of this planet, wiser creatures than ourselves did not exist? All our boasted inventions are but the shadows of what has been,—the dim images of the past—the dream of other states of existence. Might not the fable of Prometheus, and his stealing the fire, and of Briareus and

his earth-born brothers, be but traditions of steam and its machinery? Who knows whether, when a comet shall approach this globe to destroy it, as it often has been and will be destroyed, men will not tear rocks from their foundations by means of steam, and hurl mountains, as the giants are said to have done, against the flaming mass?—and then we shall have the traditions of Titans again, and of wars with Heaven.[42]

In this speculation, science becomes man's ally in a war with heaven, as it perhaps was in the time of that early metaphysical rebel, Prometheus. And in *Don Juan,* canto 9 (published 1823), Byron shows himself capable of presenting the lighter of side of Cuvierian catastrophism:

> this world shall be *former,* underground,
> Thrown topsy-turvy, twisted, crisped, and curled,
> Baked, fried, or burnt, turned inside-out, or drowned,
>   Like all the worlds before, which have been hurled
> First out of and then back again to Chaos,
> The Superstratum which will overlay us.
>
> So Cuvier says;—and then shall come again
>   Unto the new Creation, rising out
> From our old crash, some mystic, ancient strain
>   Of things destroyed and left in airy doubt:
> Like to the notion *we* now entertain
>   Of Titans, Giants, fellows of about
> Some hundred feet in height, *not* to say *miles,*
> And Mammoths, and your winged Crocodiles. (9.291–304)

In this passage Cuvier's ideas are used to puncture modern man's sense of self-importance: humans are described as "maggots of some huge Earth's burial" (9.312), and Byron imagines future and much smaller "worldlings" (9.306) regarding the (relatively) huge bones of George IV with the curiosity of Lilliputian Cuviers, who "wonder where such animals could sup!" (9.307).

Both Byron and Shelley appear, then, to have been attracted to scientific theories which present the universe as dynamic and revolutionary rather than static and reactionary in nature. Thus once Shelley's Demogorgon goes into action, the fall of Jupiter, the unbinding of Prometheus, and the transfiguration of the universe seem to take place instantaneously, and the negative changes described in Byron's "Darkness" and *Heaven and Earth* are also swift and drastic. Byron suggests that the flood is not the last catastrophic episode in earth history, and even after the world has been remade in the joyous act 4 of Shelley's *Prometheus Unbound* Demogorgon warns that "with infirm hand . . . Eternity" (4.565) may still free "The serpent that would clasp her with its length" (4.567). Thus in a number of their works Shelley and Byron envision a universe that is ever-changing, punctuated by events that are as revolutionary as they are sudden. Part of their frustration as would-be revolutionaries was that after Napoléon's defeat European history became stagnant, not following the catastrophic model that so engaged their imaginations. In this respect, historical reality conformed neither to Cuvier's theories nor to the poets' political aspirations, and only Byron, as an organizer of the Greek revolution, found a practical outlet for his revolutionary ambitions. But, nevertheless, the scientific conversations in Switzerland were seminal, and had an important influence on the poets' later works.

*   *   *

The poets' summer on Lake Geneva is, of course, best known as a summer of ghost stories, including the germ of Mary Shelley's *Frankenstein.* But although Jerome McGann suggests that "Monk" Lewis "helped to shift the conversations with the Shelleys, Polidori, and B[yron] on to grim subjects,"[43] Lewis did not arrive in Geneva until 14 August, and the proposal that they should all write ghost stories may have been made as early as 16 or 17 June.[44] Without our discounting the influence of Lewis, there is evidence to support the idea that Byron was the main inspiration for the ghostly and Gothic atmosphere of that summer: it was he, Mary notes in her 1831 preface to *Frankenstein,* who proposed that they all write a ghost story, and Holmes argues that Byron was the purchaser of the French translation of a collection of German ghost stories, *Fantasmagoriana,* that turned the group's attention to horror fiction.[45] It is likely, moreover, that Shelley would have associated Byron with Gothic horror, since in Shelley's second Gothic novella, *St. Irvyne; or, The Rosicrucian* (1811), he plagiarized from Byron's early lyrics, "Lachin y Gair," and "I Would I Were a Careless Child,"[46] and also because several of Byron's longer works, such as *Lara* (1814), contain Gothic elements. In fact, a fragment in Shelley's Swiss notebook suggests that Shelley may have begun a contribution to the ghost-story contest:

> A shovel of his ashes took
> From the hearth's obscurest nook;
> With a body bowed and bent
>   She tottered forth to the paved courtyard,
> Muttering mysteries as she went.—
> Helen and Henry knew that Granny
> Was as much afraid of ghosts as any,
>   And so they followed hard—
> But Helen clung to her brother's arm
> And her own shadow made her shake.[47]

If we can judge, however, from this piece of doggerel, Shelley did not take the ghost-story writing very seriously. I will discuss the Gothic connections between the two poets further in chapter 4, but at this point, I would simply like to suggest that Byron, not Lewis, was the main inspirer of the grim themes that so fascinated the circle at Diodati.

A nonliterary interest the poets shared in Geneva should also be mentioned: as Mary Shelley repeatedly notes in her journal, Byron and Shelley went sailing virtually every day, and the passion for sailing was to continue until the end of their relationship, when Shelley died in a sailing accident. Jonathan Wordsworth speculates that these boating expeditions (from which Mary was excluded) may have done much to cement the poets' friendship: "Seated together for days on end at the tiller of their boat, with two boatmen aboard to work the sails; experiencing together the calm beauty of the lake and mountains (and on one occasion the danger of being wrecked in a sudden storm); visiting together the literary sites that called forth their different responses, and led inevitably to discussion of that difference; the two men built up at once companionship and respect."[48]

Perhaps the playful side of the Shelley-Byron relationship has not been sufficiently emphasized in accounts of their association: in Pisa, for example, the poets became obsessed with shooting, and even invented Italianate words to describe the action, such as "firing, *tiring;* hitting, *colping;* missing, *mancating;* riding, *cavalling.*"[49] Their friendship was, in fact, based on more than literary interests—Shelley and Byron genuinely enjoyed each other's company and often preferred sailing or shooting to intellectual discussions. When, in Pisa, Shelley sailed with Edward Williams rather than with Byron, it was a sign that their relationship had changed. But whatever else one might say about the poets' association, it is clear that it began extremely well.

THREE

The Conversational Style of Byron and Shelley

The odd poetic universe of *Julian and Maddalo,* with its manic-depressive fluctuations between extreme optimism and despairing pessimism, is perhaps the most intriguing product of the Shelley-Byron relationship. In the poem Shelley introduces three characters: Julian, who represents Shelley himself, Maddalo, who is a version of Byron, and the Maniac, a character who has never been definitively explained but who seems to represent a kind of tragic everyman, whose agony, the preface of the poem suggests, "will perhaps be found a sufficient comment for the text of every heart." Whereas Julian argues for hope, Maddalo insists on a pessimistic view of man's existence. The argument of these two friends is, however, never resolved, and the Maniac seems to confuse rather than illuminate the issues they have raised. *Julian and Maddalo* is a poem which refuses to interpret reality according to a single, unified perspective, a poem, moreover, partially written in a conversational style influenced by Byron, a style which is not by nature conducive to singleness of vision. The Shelleyan Julian does indeed try to deal with the Byronic Maddalo's influence, but he neither embraces nor completely disproves his friend's worldview. Maddalo's effect on Julian's idealism is, instead, to make Julian waver in his own beliefs and doubt the possibility of either understanding or overcoming human suffering. What results from Julian's troubled response to Maddalo and the madhouse world Maddalo presents is a narrative marked by uncertainty and ambiguity which has no real conclusion—as Julian says, "the cold world shall not know" (617) the final message of the Maniac's life story.

Shelley was at some pains to create a new style for *Julian and Maddalo*, a "familiar style of language" which he described in a letter to Leigh Hunt: "I have employed a certain familiar style of language to express the actual way in which people talk with each other whom education and a certain refinement of sentiment have placed above the use of vulgar idioms. I use the word *vulgar* in its most extensive sense; the vulgarity of rank and fashion is as gross in its way as that of Poverty, and its cant terms equally unfit for Poetry."[1] Through this style, which approximates the Horatian middle style in which he and Byron were trained at Eton and Harrow (respectively), Shelley tried to represent the conversations he had with Byron in Venice, conversations marked by the easy familiarity of two well-educated and literary men of the upper classes, unmarked by elevated poetic diction or "vulgar idioms." Although composition of Byron's *Beppo* predates the poets' meeting in Venice by almost one year, I do not believe that the conversational style of that poem was an important influence on *Julian and Maddalo*. In creating the "familiar" style of *Julian and Maddalo*, Shelley was responding to Byron's actual conversation, a mode of discourse which he describes in the preface (ostensibly referring, of course, to Maddalo): "He is cheerful, frank, and witty. His more serious conversation is a sort of intoxication; men are held by it as by a spell. He has travelled much; and there is an inexpressible charm in his relation of his adventures in different countries." Like Byron himself, Shelley was quick to see the potential of an informal style. Julian's facetious comparison between the friends' conversation and the epic debate of Milton's devils (41–42) and his humorous irony concerning the madmen's "stern maker" (113) are both instances of the wittiness that Shelley evidently considered an integral part of this Byronic mode of self-expression. Shelley's intention in creating a conversational style is not quite that of Wordsworth, who sought, in *Lyrical Ballads*, "to imitate, and, as far as is possible, to adopt the very language of men."[2] Rather, Shelley tried to imitate the language of a particular class of men, the relatively small group of refined and educated men capable of the kind of philosophical discourse found in *Julian and Maddalo*. As Earl R. Wasserman notes, *Julian and Maddalo* has "something of Byron's own Horatian manner of urbane poetic talk,"[3] and one can find a similar conversational tone in Byron's letters. Harold Bloom essentially agrees with this assessment, writing that "Byron is the dominant element in Shelley's . . . conversational *Julian and Maddalo*" and that "the earlier part of the poem, and its closing lines, introduce another Shelley, a master of the urbane, middle style."[4] Shelley also uses this conversational style in his *Letter to Maria Gisborne,* which, like the first part of *Julian and Maddalo* (1–299), is informal, literary, and concrete rather than abstract. While Julian observes the Venetian landscapes and Maddalo's young daughter, Shelley, in the *Letter,* describes the prosaic objects in his friend's study. And both poems reflect the way in which people of "education and a certain refinement of sentiment" express themselves in ordinary situations.

A good example of the conversational style can be found in the quick interchange which precedes Maddalo's pessimistic apostrophe to the madhouse:

> "What we behold
> Shall be the madhouse and its belfry tower,"
> Said Maddalo, "and ever at this hour
> Those who may cross the water, hear that bell
> Which calls the maniacs each one from his cell
> To vespers."—"As much skill as need to pray
> In thanks or hope for their dark lot have they
> To their stern maker," I replied. "O ho!
> You talk as in years past," said Maddalo.
> " 'Tis strange men change not. You were ever still
> Among Christ's flock a perilous infidel,
> A wolf for the meek lambs—if you can't swim
> Beware of Providence." (106–18)

In Maddalo's opinion, Julian is both a wolf among Christ's flock and a nonswimmer flouting Providence; the very manner in which Maddalo is free to mix his metaphors demonstrates the almost careless flow of the conversation, with its sudden shifts in tone and imagery. The passage moves smoothly from the simple description of the madhouse, to Julian's playful irony, to Maddalo's "O ho!" and amused rejoinder, and to the somber evocation of human despair that follows Maddalo's strange image of Julian as a wolf in danger of drowning.[5] What keeps the conversation unified is not an abstract idea or theme: it is the physical presence of the madhouse, the objective correlative that Maddalo returns to after his digressive response to Julian's witticism. This effectively hampers Julian's tendency to idealize, to escape from the stubborn material evidence of man's tragic limitations. And, of course, the politeness required of a gentleman in conversation prevents Julian from becoming too aggressively argumentative. Donald Davie describes the civilized intercourse of *Julian and Maddalo:* "It is in keeping that Julian should know little of Maddalo and not approve of all that he knows, but should be prepared to take him, with personal reservations, on his own terms. It is the habit of gentlemen; and the poet inculcates it in the reader, simply by taking it for granted in his manner of address."[6] This is the same restrained politeness that characterizes the conversation of the Archangel Michael and Satan in Byron's *The Vision of Judgment:* "between [Satan's] Darkness and [Michael's] Brightness / There passed a mutual glance of great politeness" (279–80). It is significant that Julian's and Maddalo's conversation cannot continue after the Maniac's unrestrained outburst. Although the Maniac is, according to the preface, "a very cultivated and amiable person when in his right senses," the maddened bitterness of his monologue violates the conventions of polite intercourse, as does the eavesdropping of Julian and Maddalo, who hover like fascinated tourists viewing Bedlam. The urbanity of the poem never fully recovers from the "unconnected exclamations" (preface) of the Maniac, in which the rules of punctuation and syntax, as well as those of the "familiar style," are disregarded.

Another characteristic of the conversational style, as it is employed in *Julian and Maddalo,* is that it leads to a kind of paralysis: the conversationalists are passive, eavesdroppers and voyeurs, not actors pursuing definite goals. As Julian and Maddalo perceive the Lido, the madhouse, Maddalo's daughter, and the Maniac, their conversation changes, and appears to be controlled by the transitory sense-impressions each man experiences rather than by any thematic unity. Julian's faith in the mind's power to transform reality is thus continually called into question by his own tendency to be either profoundly depressed or uplifted by what he sees and hears, and his own apparent aimlessness. The conversational style is, then, a relatively loose form, strongly grounded in material reality, and given to quick shifts in tone. Although *Julian and Maddalo* is quite different from Byron's *Beppo* and *Don Juan,* it has in common with these poems the tendency to incorporate within itself natural description, philosophical disquisitions, witticisms, and even poetry in a different style, like the Maniac's long monologue.

Despite its relative versatility, the conversational style is not an effective mode for a didactic poet or a polemicist. Its informal structure gives as much weight to clever rejoinder as to thoughtful argument; Maddalo easily undercuts Julian's theorizings with a cogent phrase: "You talk Utopia" (179). And since, in *Julian and Maddalo,* the environment of the conversationalists often intrudes upon their discourse, idealistic notions must continually be qualified in terms of material realities. Julian's response to the Lido is far from certain: "I love all waste / And solitary places; where we taste / The pleasure of *believing* what we see / Is boundless, as we *wish* our souls to be" (14–17, italics mine). The conversational style lends itself to uncertainty—it does not favor logical progressions and a structured format and, as a result, the certitude of a more unified and ordered poem. It poses questions well but never answers them, and it presents characters and scenes eloquently but never adequately explains them. It is a style particularly suited to Byron, who enjoyed urbane literary talk and was easily put off by philosophical disquisition, but Shelley employed it less often. The dialogue of Byron and Shelley regarding the character of Shakespeare's Hamlet, anonymously recorded, illustrates a crucial difference between the two poets: Byron contributes some of his opinions, and a few witticisms, but falls asleep as soon as Shelley begins to look at *Hamlet* in a methodical, analytical way.[7] Byron prefers the expression of opinion to the justification of it, and rejects the analysis of poetry as being "like making out one's expenses for a journey," while Shelley favors rational analysis and theorizing.[8] The conversational style was, then, an ideal mode for Byron, but Shelley tended to favor a more formal and ordered medium, with fewer digressions and shiftings in tone.

* * *

Julian, according to the preface of *Julian and Maddalo,* is "passionately attached to those philosophical notions which assert the power of man over his own mind, and the immense improvements of which by the extinction of certain moral superstitions, human society may yet be susceptible." His faith in these "philosophical notions" is, however, sorely tried in *Julian and Maddalo,* in which the pessimistic attitudes of Maddalo and the Maniac embody the "moral superstitions" that Julian wants to extinguish. The poem repeatedly moves from images of union, innocence, and joy to images of division, experience, and despair in a continual manic-depressive oscillation. In a sense, *Julian and Maddalo* presents a world that is a kind of ambiguous inkblot which anyone can interpret as he or she likes. Whether in a barren waste or a child's eyes, the aspiring Julian seeks a " 'soul of goodness' in things ill" (204). Maddalo looks, however, at madhouses and maniacs when he wants to find emblems for the human condition. Julian is simply a lone voice for meliorism, opposed to an even more adamant voice advocating fatalism and pessimism; Maddalo tells Julian that his "judgment will not bend / To [Julian's] opinion" (192–93). Moreover, as Kelvin Everest argues, the narrative voice of Julian contains "a note of wry self-distance [which is] worldly, and not in fact very far from Maddalo's frank disillusion-ment."[9] While Julian is clearly moved by what he sees of the maniacs' sufferings, he is also capable, as we have seen, of some humorous irony at their expense (111–13). And although Julian professes a desire to help the Maniac, he leaves Venice without so much as a nod of farewell to him. Thus Julian seems as changeable as the poem he narrates, which shifts suddenly from the "aerial merriment" (27) of two friends on the Lido to a sadder conversation similar to the one that "the devils held within the dales of Hell" (41).

As he seeks to defend his meliorism, Julian is, moreover, hampered by the inadequacy of language as a means of communication. Although Maddalo admits that Julian could probably prove his theories "As far as words go" (195), he says that he would not believe in them anyway. To him words prove nothing. This sense of language's limitations is not peculiar to *Julian and Maddalo*—even in Shelley's idealistic *Prometheus Unbound* words are often seen as useless. Saying that "words are quick and vain" (1.303), Prometheus rescinds his curse. Later he exclaims to Mercury, Jupiter's messenger: "How vain is talk!" (1.431). Accord-ing to William Keach, Shelley's linguistic skepticism is an important facet of *A Defence of Poetry:* "the more specific [Shelley] becomes in ex-amining [language's] unique resources, the more likely he is to reveal an underlying linguistic skepticism that runs throughout *[A Defence of Poetry]* like a counterplot."[10] Although in *Julian and Maddalo* Shelley attributes linguistic skepticism to Byron's surrogate, Maddalo, it would seem that Shelley's attitude toward language is actually more skeptical than Byron's. While Shelley often sees words as "vain," Byron, in *Don Juan,* canto 3, professes to believe that "words are things, and a small drop of ink, / Falling like dew, upon a thought, produces / That which makes thousands, perhaps millions, think" (3.793–95). The idea that "words are things," borrowed from Comte de Mirabeau, is also mentioned twice in Byron's letters [11] and in *Childe Harold's Pilgrimage:* "I do believe, / Though I have found them not, that there may be / Words which are things" (3.1059–61). Although this last pronouncement is qualified, Byron's belief in the power of words clearly contrasts with the skepticism Shelley exhibits in *Julian and Maddalo* and other works and indicates that Byron may not have shared Shelley's strongly ambivalent attitude toward language.

In *Julian and Maddalo* communication between individuals is at best momentary. Julian and Maddalo communicate harmoniously with each other only at the beginning of the poem (28–30) and, in a sadder vein, when they agree about the particulars of the Maniac's situation, having forgotten their argument. As they ride home from the Lido, however, Julian makes it clear that their discussions are futile; they "descant" on "All that vain men imagine or believe" (44). Much of the rest of the poem involves their argument, which is ultimately "vain" inasmuch as it is forgotten (520). The Maniac, who does not "dare / To give a human voice" (304–5) to his despair, is no help to them. As far as he is concerned, the page that depicts his sorrow is "this unfeeling leaf which burns the brain" (479) and the words he writes are "charactered in vain" (478). "How vain / Are words!" (472–73) he exclaims, calling into question the usefulness of giving vent to his soliloquy and of self-expression in general. The very incoherence of his disconnected ravings is an example of the limitations of language as a medium in which to express emotion. There is some irony in the fact that in order to resolve their argument the two men turn to an avowed madman who admits: "I know not what I say" (393).

The Maniac is, moreover, a man who presents a false front to the outside world. After listening to his soliloquy, the two friends conclude that because of the Lady's rejection of him the Maniac "had fixed a blot / Of fals[e]hood on his mind which flourished not / But in the light of all-beholding truth" (529–31). The Maniac himself indicates that he habitually hides his true nature; he says that he must

> wear this mask of fals[e]hood even to those
> Who are most dear—not for [his] own repose—
> Alas, no scorn or pain or hate could be
> So heavy as that fals[e]hood is to [him]—
> But that [he] cannot bear more altered faces
> Than needs must be, more changed and cold embraces,
> More misery, disappointment and mistrust
> To own [him] for their father . . . (308–15)

When language becomes a medium for deception, it leads to madness. Shelley describes, in *The Revolt of Islam,* some rabble-rousing priests who exemplify this, "some counterfeiting / The rage they did inspire, some mad indeed / With their own lies" (10.4189–91). To a certain degree the Maniac is mad with his own lies. The Lady's rejection of him has led him to hide his true emotions and thoughts—the Maniac must "smile on" (306) and play his pleasing melodies, not daring to communicate to anyone else his true grief. He is even more cut off from mankind than the solipsistic Maddalo, who can at least speak with Julian. The blot of falsehood that festers in his mind makes his words increasingly unreliable. In rejecting "the light of all-beholding truth" he is flirting with schizophrenia, the complete rejection of reality and all of the linguistic constructs that sane people use. He also demonstrates a high level of paranoia, which, as Timothy Clark argues, recalls the Rousseau of Byron's *Childe Harold,* canto 3:

> His life was one long war with self-sought foes,
> Of friends by him self-banish'd; for his mind
> Had grown Suspicion's sanctuary, and chose
> For its own cruel sacrifice, the kind,
> 'Gainst whom he raged with fury strange and blind.
> But he was phrenzied,—wherefore, who may know? (3.752–57)[12]

Like the Maniac, Rousseau is ultimately incomprehensible—his "fury strange and blind" is a result of a frenzy that has no reasonable explanation.

In composing the Maniac's dramatic monologue, Shelley probably benefited from Byron's earlier experiments in the form: *The Prisoner of*

Chillon (1816) and *The Lament of Tasso* (1817). *The Prisoner of Chillon* was, in fact, partially influenced by Shelley's reading of Dante, and a conversation the poets had after they had both visited Chillon Castle on 25 June 1816. In his notes to his edition of *The Prisoner,* McGann points out that Byron's poem owes a debt to the younger poet: "Not only does Shelley—in his *History of a Six Weeks' Tour*—name the castle as a monument of man's tyrannical inhumanity to man, it was he who showed B[yron] the Ugolino episode in Dante's *Inferno* (XXXIII)"[13] which became one of the inspirations for *The Prisoner of Chillon.* Later, Shelley mentioned *The Prisoner of Chillon* as one of the post-Geneva works which demonstrated that Byron had achieved "freedom from common rules."[14] Shelley probably also admired *The Prisoner* as a brilliantly conceived monologue in which the monologuist, Bonnivard, ultimately falls into a prison mentality.

The relationship between *The Prisoner of Chillon* and *Julian and Maddalo* has been discussed by Bernard Hirsch in an article on *Julian and Maddalo* as a dramatic monologue. According to Hirsch, "The potential of the dramatic monologue as a means of self-criticism may have suggested itself to Shelley through his reading of such Byron poems as *The Giaour* and *The Prisoner of Chillon.*"[15] Hirsch goes on to relate Julian's narration to Bonnivard's, although the similarities between the Maniac and Bonnivard appear more striking. In the dramatic monologues of both the Maniac and Bonnivard the emphasis is on self-exploration rather than self-criticism. And one finds in the Maniac's monologue some of the themes Byron develops in *The Prisoner:* the sense of isolation, the despair, and the mental imprisonment that neither Bonnivard nor the Maniac seem to be able to escape. While Byron's prisoner comes to accept his chains (391) and regains "freedom with a sigh" (394), the Maniac freely chooses to live in his madman's cell: "Till [he dies] the dungeon may demand its prey" (370). Of these two prisoners, Byron's seems more stoic, suffering with dignity and strength as his brothers die before him—the Maniac, disappointed in both love and politics, raves bitterly and, at times, almost self-indulgently. Thus in *Julian and Maddalo* Shelley presents a character who is even more bitter and despairing than Byron's prisoner of Chillon. It is almost as if in *The Prisoner of Chillon* Byron takes on Julian's point of view, that "much may be endured / Of what degrades and crushes us" (183–84), while

Shelley's Maniac embodies Maddalo's conviction of man's basic weakness (177). But in both *The Prisoner* and the Maniac's monologue, there is a sense that imprisonment, and the solipsism it leads to, has deeply affected Byron's and Shelley's prisoners, making it impossible for them to accept the very freedom they profess to love.

The connections between *The Lament of Tasso* and *Julian and Maddalo* have been explored thoroughly by critics, and by Carlos Baker in particular.[16] While Shelley admired *The Prisoner of Chillon,* his reaction to *The Lament of Tasso,* in which the imprisoned and heart-broken poet chronicles his woes, was more emotional: although Shelley did not think *The Lament* "so perfect and sustained a composition" as *Manfred,* he did find some passages "wonderfully impressive; and those lines in which [Byron] describe[s] the youthful feelings of Tasso . . . [made Shelley's] head wild with tears."[17] The Maniac, of course, changes like Byron's Tasso from a "love-devoted youth" (373) to an embittered inhabitant of a cell, and, as Tasso is stricken by his unrequited love for Leonora, the Maniac is tortured by his love for his Lady, whom he "loved even to [his] overthrow" (405). But unlike Shelley's Maniac, Byron's Tasso never completely despairs: "For I have battled with mine agony, / And made me wings wherewith to overfly / The narrow circus of my dungeon wall" (*Tasso,* 21–23). Again, Byron's protagonist asserts the power of the human mind to overcome what imprisons it, while Shelley's Maniac willfully chooses imprisonment. The Maniac has, in fact, much more in common with Shelley's Prince Athanase, another protagonist whose grief is somewhat mysterious in origin and completely debilitating, than with the characters of Byron's monologues: "like an eyeless nightmare grief did sit / Upon [Prince Athanase's] being; a snake which fold by fold / Pressed out the life of life" (*Prince Athanase,* 120–22). In essence, however, Maddalo presents Julian with a tragic figure who has counterparts in the works of both Shelley and Byron; a figure, moreover, to whom both Maddalo and Julian respond in similar ways.

While Shelley probably wrote the Maniac's lament with Byron's dramatic monologues in mind, he obviously made the Maniac more distraught, presenting his misery in "unconnected exclamations of . . . agony" (preface), not in the clearer, more controlled kind of verse found in *The Prisoner of Chillon* and *The Lament of Tasso.* The Maniac's lament is an experiment in this form, in which the monologuist presents his story in a confused, stream-of-consciousness manner, with the sections of the monologue demarcated by asterisks rather than the numbers that precede the stanzas of *The Prisoner* and *The Lament*. If Shelley was influenced in part by Byron's dramatic monologues in his composition of the Maniac's "unconnected exclamations," his treatment of this genre is innovative; he gives the Maniac's speech a hysterical, perhaps even insane quality which has an emotional immediacy not found in Byron's prison poems.

* * *

As I have shown, both the Maniac and Maddalo call into question language and its ability to represent reality. Moreover, Julian makes it impossible for the reader to interpret the Maniac's ramblings with any kind of objectivity, withholding information which Maddalo's daughter gave him, information which supposedly would explain how the Maniac arrived at his tortured mental state. Rather than giving us the means to interpret the Maniac's soliloquy, *Julian and Maddalo* depicts the impossibility of explaining the human condition with words. Until language is changed into "a perpetual Orphic song" (*Prometheus Unbound*, 4.415) which can truly interpret reality, arguments like Maddalo's and Julian's will be futile. As Shelley says in his essay *On Life*, "How vain is it to think that words can penetrate the mystery of our being."[18] Moreover, "the cold world shall not know" (617) is a statement uttered by a disillusioned poet who withholds information as a protest against an audience which will, presumably, misunderstand or perhaps mock the story Julian has heard. Like the Maniac himself, Julian will not "give a human voice to [his] despair" (305)—he chooses silence. Thus the conversational style of *Julian and Maddalo* breaks down and, in the end, the "conversation" between the poet's narrator and the reader is abruptly terminated. Julian ultimately seems to lose faith in his own poetic strategy.

Perhaps more than anything else, *Julian and Maddalo* is an experimental poem in which Shelley explores the conversational style, the limitations of language, and his own and Byron's ideas on the human condition. Insofar as it reflects, constructs, or interprets the manner in which Shelley and Byron conversed, it shows their commonality as well as their points of disagreement. Even the dualism with which the poem begins, in which there are two separate points of view—a Julian and a Maddalo—dissolves as they abandon their argument and unite in their compassion for the Maniac. The first person plural, referring to both Julian and Maddalo, is used frequently after the Maniac's soliloquy: "we wept," "we talked of him," "we agreed his was some dreadful ill," "we guessed not," and "we could not guess" (515–35). Julian seems far from comfortable with this close association with Maddalo, who is perceived as a threat to his metaphysics—at any rate, Julian leaves Venice abruptly, perhaps fleeing from Maddalo's "subtle talk" (560) which might "make [Julian] know [him]self" (561). As the poem progresses, the binary opposition between Julian and Maddalo, meliorism and skepticism, is shown to be an illusion. In the end Maddalo disappears and Julian remains, a changed Julian who maintains a vestige of his former idealism (calling his friend's daughter "a wonder of this earth" [590]) which is combined with Maddalo's pessimism ("there is little of transcendent worth" [591]). It becomes increasingly difficult to separate Julian from Maddalo, the idealist from his skeptical alter ego.

Maddalo is, of course, based on Byron in Venice and embodies the contradictory blend of positive and negative qualities that Shelley perceived in his fascinating and frustrating friend. In fact, Shelley echoes the "concentred recompense" (57) of Byron's "Prometheus" when he describes Maddalo as being "concentered" (preface to *Julian and Maddalo*). It is significant that when Shelley sought a model for the character of Mephistopheles in his translation of *Faust* Byron came to mind, the gentlemanly and conversational Byron who inspired both admiration and anxiety.[19] Although potentially heroic, Maddalo is also an ambiguous and slightly threatening figure. His philanthropy to the Maniac, for example, which seems benevolent, has the negative effect of making the madhouse seem attractive and of encouraging the Maniac's isolated residence there. His influence on Julian is also troubling—only in Maddalo's absence is Julian able to return to Venice. As Byron complained to Medwin, Shelley "does not make [him] cut a good figure" in *Julian and Maddalo*.[20] The very fact that the world is such a mixture of contradictory perceptions makes it possible for a man like Maddalo to present his gloomy views without being afraid that his ideas will be disproved. Since, moreover, Maddalo rejects rationality (193–95), Julian has no logical way to refute his theories. Julian has only words to work with, and words are shown to be inadequate, false to the reality they cannot either represent or transfigure. Betrayed by a style which promotes skepticism rather than a faith in man's ability to improve himself, Julian finally fails to prove the validity of his melioristic claims, and the exuberant feeling of the beginning of the poem is never completely regained.

In the preface Shelley uses irony to indicate that Julian, despite his "good qualities," is perhaps less than judicious in his passionate attachment "to . . . philosophical notions"; moreover, he is also "rather serious." Inasmuch as Julian is a surrogate for Shelley, he is a surrogate for Shelley as he questions himself and his ideals in the context of his relationship with Byron. The reflexive imagery offered at the beginning of the poem as a criticism of Maddalo, whose spirit has grown "blind / By gazing on its own exceeding light" (51–52), is echoed later in the poem with reference to both Julian and Maddalo, who are imagined sitting with the firelight reflected upon their faces (561–62).

Shelley's tendency toward self-deprecation and his dislike of enforcing didactic messages led him to be open-minded rather than antagonistic to influences such as Byron's. The conversation in *Julian and Maddalo* is, then, a conversation in which Julian seeks to both teach and learn from Maddalo. If he had stayed in Venice, Julian speculates, Maddalo's "wit / And subtle talk would [have made him] know [him]self" (559–61). The purpose of the conversation is not to divide the two men into philosophically antagonistic positions but allow them to better know themselves and the world in which they live. There is, in fact, reason to believe that Maddalo is not totally devoid of idealism—after all, he is attracted to idealists like Julian and the Maniac, who spoke like Julian when first visiting Venice. And the witty allusion to Byron's study of the Armenian language ("Maddalo was travelling far away / Among the mountains of Armenia" [586–87]) may also have reference to an idealistic impulse of Maddalo-Byron. In his letters Byron explained his study of Armenian in the following way: "my master the Padre Pasquale Aucher . . . assured me 'that the terrestrial Paradise had been certainly *Armenia*'—I went seeking it—God knows where—did I find it?—Umph!—Now & then—for a minute or two."[21] Byron was certainly capable of searching for the terrestrial paradise, and Shelley may have been indicating, through his sly reference to Maddalo's Armenian travels, that he recognized this aspect of Byron's temperament. In my view, the conversation in *Julian and Maddalo* provides a good portrait of the Shelley-Byron relationship because it shows their similarities as well as their differences, and because the conversation described in the poem was continued in many of the poets' other works. If Maddalo is flawed, so is Julian: neither character, given Julian's tendency to idealize and Maddalo's tendency toward pessimism, can hope to gain a comprehensive view of reality alone. Perhaps Julian's greatest mistake is not so much his desertion of the Maniac as his decision to interrupt his conversation with Maddalo, a conversation which has, in the course of the poem, already given him an important, if traumatizing, insight into the nature of human suffering.

* * *

While Shelley's *Julian and Maddalo* was profoundly influenced by Byron's Venetian conversations, two of Shelley's later works in the conversational style, *Peter Bell the Third* (completed 24 October 1819) and *The Witch of Atlas* (August 1820), owe much more to the first two cantos of *Don Juan* than to the Venetian period of the poets' friendship. Shelley was first exposed to *Don Juan* in October 1818,[22] less than two months after the visit that inspired *Julian and Maddalo*. During this second meeting in Venice, Byron read the first canto of *Don Juan* to Shelley and Shelley immediately responded to it as "a thing in the style of Beppo, but infinitely better."[23] The effect of the style of *Don Juan*, with its rapid movements from gravity to hilarity, can be seen throughout Shelley's *Peter Bell the Third*. As Richard Cronin notes,[24] the following lines from *Peter Bell the Third* are especially Byronic:

He had also dim recollections
    Of pedlars tramping on their rounds,
Milk pans and pails, and odd collections
Of saws, and proverbs, and reflexions
    Old parsons make in burying-grounds.

But Peter's verse was clear, and came
    Announcing from the frozen hearth
Of a cold age, that none might tame

The soul of that diviner flame
   It augered to the Earth[.] (428–37)

The abrupt shift from the concrete, everyday language of the first stanza to the much higher tone of the second is typical of Byron's *Don Juan* style. And in parts of *Peter Bell the Third* Shelley approaches the black humor of the shipwreck scene of *Don Juan,* canto 2: when Peter yells, the Parson drowns in Lake Windermere, where eels "kept / Gnawing his kidneys half a year" (34–35). Although Shelley had "dosed" Byron with Wordsworth in Switzerland, by 1819 both poets were ridiculing Wordsworth's later poetry; in a letter to Douglas Kinnaird, for example, Byron wrote that his *Marino Faliero* "is at least as good as Mr. Turdsworth's Peter Bell."[25] In *Peter Bell the Third* Shelley adapted Byron's *Don Juan* style and learned, as Cronin asserts, "the possibility of employing an uneven or mixed style, so that the reader is prevented from finding a point of reference in any one of the poem's styles and forced to consider the relation between styles as the poem's meaning."[26] In *The Witch of Atlas,* moreover, Shelley used this "mixed style" to create a poem at once conversational and visionary.

After writing *Letter to Maria Gisborne* in June 1820, Shelley continued his experimentations in the conversational style in August of the same year, when he wrote *The Witch of Atlas.* The use of the ottava rima stanza invites comparisons between *The Witch of Atlas* and the first two cantos of *Don Juan* (which Shelley had read before composing *The Witch*),[27] and the introductory stanzas in particular seem to owe something to the *Don Juan* style:

If you strip Peter [Bell], you will see a fellow
   Scorched by Hell's hyperequatorial climate
Into a kind of sulphureous yellow,
   A lean mark hardly fit to fling a rhyme at;
In shape a Scaramouch, in hue Othello.
   If you unveil my Witch, no Priest or Primate
Can shrive you of that sin, if sin there be
In love, when it becomes idolatry. (41–42)

In their lack of structure, both *The Witch of Atlas* and *Don Juan* resemble conversations—as Brian Nellist remarks, *The Witch* "has no internal design shaped by argument or action. In one sense the poem is endless, like *Don Juan* itself."[28] And *The Witch*, like Byron's masterwork, is given to quick shifts in tone and subject matter. For example, the pathos of the Witch's farewell to her nymphs (stanzas 23–25) shifts suddenly into a description of how "the sweet splendour of her smiles could dye" (254) her "pictured poesy" (252), and the Witch's pranks toward the end of the poem mix both humor and serious social commentary:

> The king would dress an ape up in his crown
>   And robes, and seat him on his glorious seat,
> And on the right hand of the sunlike throne
>   Would place a gaudy mock-bird to repeat
> The chatterings of the monkey.—Every one
>   Of the prone courtiers crawled to kiss the feet
> Of their great Emperor when the morning came,
> And kissed—alas, how many kiss the same! (633–40)

The comic presentation of the ape-king is suddenly interrupted by a dispirited recognition of the reality of this kind of self-abasement. Moreover, *The Witch of Atlas* has an ending as abrupt and arbitrary as Julian's "the cold world shall not know" or Byron's conclusion of *Beppo:* "My pen is at the bottom of a page, / Which being finished, here the story ends" (*Beppo*, 789–90). In *The Witch of Atlas* Shelley suddenly closes the poem with a jovial promise to continue it at another time:

>   what she did to sprites
> And gods, entangling them in her sweet ditties
>   To do her will, and shew their subtle slights,
> I will declare another time; for it is
>   A tale more fit for the weird winter nights
> Than for these garish summer days, when we
> Scarcely believe much more than we can see. (666–72)

The conversation in *The Witch of Atlas* is between Shelley, the storyteller of "these garish summer days," and the reader, a reader who is urbanely invited to share some of Shelley's views. At the beginning of the poem Shelley seems to be envisioning a reader who is, like him, a disillusioned visionary living in a world in which "Error and Truth . . . had hunted from the earth / All those bright natures which adorned its prime, / And left us nothing to believe in" (51–53). He also uses the first person plural in his description of the Witch's "Sounds of air" (154): they are "Such as we hear in youth, and think the feeling / Will never die—yet ere we are aware, / The feeling and sound are fled and gone, / And the regret they leave remains alone" (157–60). And later in the poem Shelley suggests that the reader shares with him a degree of helplessness: "We, the weak mariners of that wide lake / . . . Our course unpiloted and starless make / O'er its wild surface to an unknown goal—" (546–49). This conversation between Shelley and the reader continues at the whim of the poet, who seems more intent on poetic improvisation than the advancement of any argument or overall design. The poem was, of course, written in three days, in the swift, *improvvisatore* manner so admired by Byron (see *Beppo*, 257; and *Don Juan*, 15.160), and embodies Shelley's conversational style at its most playful.

Although Byron may never have seen the posthumously published *Witch*, his *Vision of Judgment* (1821) has some intriguing similarities to this poem, similarities which suggest that Byron's development of the conversational style in some ways paralleled Shelley's. As McGann has argued, "'The Witch of Atlas' and 'The Vision of Judgment' seize a visionary tradition far removed from the visionary emphasis of *The Prelude* and 'Kubla Khan,' and variant from 'Adonais' and *Childe Harold* III as well."[29] Both the "visionary rhyme" (8) of the Witch's story and the mock-visionary description of King George's trial before the gates of heaven have a light touch, a playful arbitrariness. And the visions in both poems tend to challenge the reader's preconceptions regarding the forces which rule the universe, forces which can be charming and somewhat heartless, like the Witch, or inflexible and occasionally befuddled, like God's angels and saints. Thus Shelley's *The Witch of Atlas* shares a great deal with Byron's brilliant satire, which is, like *The Witch*, an odd mixture of the visionary and the conversational.

FOUR

The Cenci and Sad Reality

In Charles Robinson's view, Shelley's tragedy *The Cenci* (1819) was at the center of a major dispute between Shelley and Byron. According to Robinson, the argument over the dramatic merits of Shelley's *The Cenci* and Byron's *Marino Faliero, Doge of Venice* "demonstrate[s] the two poets' continuing antagonism in 1819/20 and explain[s] Shelley's judgment in 1821 that he and Byron 'differed more than ever.' "[1] There is, indeed, some evidence that Shelley and Byron held to different sets of dramatic principles, and that this occasioned an argument. While Byron believed that dramas should be modeled after the tragedies of ancient Greece, with at least some adherence to the unities, Shelley looked to the Elizabethan and Jacobean playwrights as his models. A composer of tragedies would succeed, Byron claimed, "by writing naturally and *regularly*—& producing *regular* tragedies like the *Greeks*—but not in *imitation*—merely the outline of their conduct adapted to our own times and circumstances."[2] Shelley, on the other hand, held a different view: in his preface to *The Cenci* he asserted that "our great ancestors the antient English poets are the writers, a study of which might incite us to do that for our own age which they have done for theirs." But although Byron and Shelley clearly disagreed on this issue, their difference in opinion appears to have been limited to dramatic principles and does not in itself "demonstrate the two poets' continuing antagonism in 1819/20."

On 26 April 1821 Byron sent Shelley his response to *The Cenci*: "You . . . know my high opinion of your own poetry,—because it is of *no* school. I read Cenci—but, besides that I think the *subject* essentially *un*dramatic, I am not an admirer of our old dramatists *as models*. I deny that the English have hitherto had a drama at all. Your Cenci, however, was a work of power, and poetry. As to *my* drama, pray revenge yourself upon it, by being as free as I have been with yours."[3] Although this letter contains some praise as well as criticism, Shelley would have vehemently disagreed with the statement that his tragedy was "*un*dramatic"—he had originally hoped that the drama would be performed at Covent Garden, with the famous Eliza O'Neill in the role of Beatrice.[4] Since his hopes for a lucrative theatrical run had dimmed by 1821, Byron's assertion must have rankled. Moreover, as a staunch admirer of Shakespeare, Shelley also would have been somewhat irritated by Byron's odd claim that the English have not "had a drama at all," even though this pronouncement may well have been made facetiously. In 1815, as a member of the Drury Lane subcommittee of management, Byron had been intimately involved with the British stage, and had supported the production of such plays as Charles Maturin's *Bertram* and William Sotheby's *Ivan*. But while Shelley's respect for Byron's poetic talents and personal magnetism was immense, he generally seems to have felt that his own critical acumen was superior, and, as Donald Reiman has noted, Shelley continually sought to "establish himself as Byron's political and moral conscience as well as his tutor in philosophy, theology, and literary theory."[5] Byron's letter of 26 April 1821 suggests, however, that the pupil was developing literary theories of his own, and Shelley, the would-be tutor, was not at all pleased with this new development.

Moreover, Shelley's displeasure with Byron's reaction to *The Cenci* may well have colored his own response to Byron's *Marino Faliero*. While he visited Byron in Ravenna in August 1821, Shelley wrote a letter to Mary describing his opinion of Byron's tragedy: "We talked a great deal of poetry & such matters last night: & as usual differed & I think more than ever.—He affects to patronize a system of criticism fit only for the production of mediocrity, & although all his fine poems & passages have been produced in defiance of this system: yet I recognize the pernicious effects of it in the 'Doge of Venice,' & it will cramp & limit his future efforts however great they may be unless he gets rid of it. I have read only parts of it, or rather he himself read them to me &

gave me the plan of the whole."[6] Shelley seems to be responding with
some irritation to Byron's wrongheaded literary theorizings, although
he does not expand on what he means by Byron's "system of criticism."
In Robinson's view, however, Shelley not only rejects Byron's use of
the unities in *Marino Faliero,* he also opposes Byron's "enforcement of
dogmas" in his tragedy, which "might justify an immoral revolutionary
ethic."[7] In other words, Shelley is careful to show that Beatrice Cenci is
morally wrong in murdering her monstrous father, but Byron's Marino
Faliero seems *destined* to commit his acts of violence—this fatalism
seems to condone Faliero's actions. But while Robinson argues that
"Shelley feared that Byron portrayed Faliero too sympathetically and
that an audience might condone or at least willingly imitate his revenge,"[8] one might also contend, with some justification, that Beatrice
is presented sympathetically, and that readers might condone her vengeance as well.[9] Neither of the two poets were trying to present "dogmas" in their tragedies. Byron, as he later told Thomas Medwin, was
seeking "to record one of the most remarkable incidents in the annals
of the Venetian Republic"[10] when he wrote *Marino Faliero,* and he would
probably have agreed with Shelley's assertion, in his preface to *The
Cenci,* that "a drama is no fit place for the enforcement of [dogmas]." In
fact, in trying to liberate his city from tyranny, Faliero is attempting to
accomplish what Shelley suggests, in his preface to *Julian and Maddalo,*
Maddalo could (and should) achieve: "He is a person of the most con-
summate genius, and capable, if he would direct his energies to such
an end, of becoming the redeemer of his degraded country"—Venice.
Moreover, in his letter to Mary, Shelley never spells out what he means
by Byron's pernicious "system of criticism": it could be simply Byron's
use of the ancient Greek tragedies as models. A 26 August 1821 letter
to Leigh Hunt indicates that Shelley was more concerned with the *dramatic* form of the tragedies than with their moral effects: "Certainly, if
'Marino Faliero' is a drama, the 'Cenci' is not."[11]

   It should also be noted that Shelley's letter of 7 August 1821 (quoted
above) makes it clear that Shelley did not read *Marino Faliero* before
noting its "pernicious effects": Byron read parts of it to Shelley and
summarized the rest. While Shelley would certainly have been able to
respond to the dramatic qualities of *Marino Faliero,* it is unlikely that
he would have been able to get a full sense of its moral impact before

writing the letter to Mary. That he did impress his reservations about Byron's tragedies upon Mary cannot, however, be doubted. Ten years after her husband's death, Mary wrote to John Murray of Byron's pernicious "system of criticism" in language which seems to echo Shelley's: Byron's "school of criticism being of the narrow order, it confined his faculties in his tragedies & Lord Byron became sententious & dull—except where character still shone forth—or where his critical ideas did not intrude to Mar—."[12] Again, it is the deleterious effects of Byron's dramatic principles that Mary is decrying, not the drama's pernicious *moral* implications. Thus, while Shelley clearly had reservations about *Marino Faliero*, the grounds of his dislike were based on the form of Byron's tragedy and, perhaps, Byron's irritating response to *The Cenci*.

Moreover, Byron's sense that *The Cenci* was an *un*dramatic work did not take away from his admiration of the work's poetic quality: "Your Cenci," he wrote to Shelley, "was a work of power, and poetry." In a conversation with Medwin, Byron said: "The 'Cenci' is . . . horrible [in its subject matter], though perhaps the best tragedy modern times have produced."[13] And he ultimately came to consider his own *Marino Faliero* as essentially undramatic. When he discussed his two Venetian dramas with Medwin, he noted his "mistake": "There was one mistake I committed: I should have called 'Marino Faliero' and 'The Two Foscari' dramas, historic poems, or any thing, in short, but tragedies or plays. . . . I was ill-used in the extreme by the Doge being brought on the stage at all, after my Preface."[14] Thus he eventually decided that Shelley's *The Cenci* was "perhaps the best tragedy modern times have produced," while his own Venetian dramas were not tragedies or plays at all. Byron's initial assessment of *The Cenci* might have been even more positive had he not been engaged in his quixotic attempt to reform the English stage.

It also seems likely that Byron would have sympathized with the political ramifications of Shelley's tragedy. As an ardent supporter of Italian liberty, he would have noted, with some approbation, Shelley's depiction of the corrupt old regime as it is represented in *The Cenci* by the polymorphously perverse Cenci. *Marino Faliero* (written before Byron had read *The Cenci*) is also critical of Italian tyranny as it is personified in that drama by the ruling class of Venice, or "the foul aristocracy" (3.2.405). Byron's and Shelley's shared sympathy for the victims of tyranny was forcibly demonstrated in 1821 when they took up the cause of a man whom they erroneously thought was to be burned for sacrilege.[15] And Byron would have noticed a reference to one of his own works in the "Dedication" of *The Cenci* to Leigh Hunt. In this dedication Shelley refers to his tragedy as "a sad reality,"[16] quoting from Byron's lyric "Prometheus," in which "The sufferings of mortality" (2) are seen by the titan "in their *sad reality*" (3, italics mine). "Sad reality" does not, in the case of either Shelley or Byron, refer to the "realism" of their works—rather it refers to the fact that both "Prometheus" and *The Cenci* present visions of the human condition which mirror the sociopolitical situation of the poets' day, a situation which is symbolized in Byron's lyric by the bound titan and in Shelley's tragedy by the situation of Beatrice, the tortured victim of a system which is tyrannical and sadistic. *The Cenci,* like Byron's "Prometheus," is dominated by "The ruling principle of Hate" ("Prometheus," 20) in which the dominant figure, Cenci, likens himself to "a fiend appointed to chastise / The offences of some unremembered world" (4.1.161–62). It is significant that the composition of "Prometheus" was made possible by Shelley: as Byron later told Medwin, "Shelley, when I was in Switzerland, translated the 'Prometheus' to me before I wrote my ode."[17] Thus the poets' shared interest in Prometheus led to Byron's "Prometheus" and his idea of "sad reality," a conception which seems, in turn, to be behind Shelley's *The Cenci.*

There is also reason to believe that Byron used an idea given to him by Shelley in Switzerland to write his "Darkness," and that Shelley later used some of the imagery of "Darkness" in *The Cenci.* As I noted in chapter 2, several critics have speculated that Shelley suggested the idea of a world freezing into extinction to Byron in 1816, basing their belief on Shelley's 22 July 1816 letter to Peacock.[18] This "gloomy theory" was subsequently embodied in Byron's "Darkness." Images from "Darkness," in turn, can be found throughout *The Cenci,* written three years later. In *The Cenci* the count describes how he represents the forces of darkness: "I bear a darker deadlier gloom / Than the earth's shade, or interlunar air" (2.2.189–90). Cenci recognizes that Beatrice's "bright loveliness / Was kindled to illumine this dark world" (4.1.121–22) and thus seeks to snuff out this source of life and beauty. In *The Cenci,* as in "Darkness," "The bright sun [is] extinguished" ("Darkness," 2). And

when Beatrice, condemned to death, imagines that Cenci's darkness
has transformed the world, she echoes lines from "Darkness." Byron's
poem presents a vision of the sunless, desolated earth: "The world
was void, / The populous and the powerful—was a lump, / Seasonless, herbless, treeless, manless, lifeless— / A lump of death—a chaos
of hard clay" ("Darkness," 69–72). This description has some resemblances to Beatrice's description of a world in which Cenci's spirit has
triumphed: "If there should be / No God, no Heaven, no Earth in the
void world; / The wide, grey, lampless, deep, unpeopled world! / If all
things then should be . . . my father's spirit" (5.4.57–60).

The passage from "Darkness" is also recalled in *Prometheus Unbound*,
in which the bound Prometheus describes his surroundings as "Black,
wintry, dead, unmeasured; without herb, / Insect, or beast, or shape or
sound of life" (1.21–22). Like Beatrice, the agonized Prometheus recre-
ates the sunless world of "Darkness" in his own mind. Moreover, the
"lump of death" mentioned in "Darkness" is echoed in Cenci's promise
to transform Beatrice into a "monstrous lump of ruin" (4.1.95). Similarly, Beatrice's growing sensation of coldness (5.4.79–89) at the end
of *The Cenci* recalls the freezing world of "Darkness," in which the last
two survivors "shivering scraped with their cold skeleton hands" (61)
the ashes which will serve to reveal "their mutual hideousness" (67).
It is, then, likely that the conversation about Buffon's theory between
Shelley and Byron in Switzerland that helped inspire "Darkness" later
helped shape some of the imagery of *The Cenci* and act 1 of *Prometheus
Unbound*. In writing his drama of "sad reality," Shelley probably had
Byron's two 1816 lyrics in mind, as well as Byron's more ambitious
production from that period, *Manfred*.

The immediate inspiration for *The Cenci* was, of course, Shelley's
reading of the *Relation of the Death of the Family of the Cenci*,[19] but both *The
Cenci* and *Manfred* were influenced, in part, by ghostly and macabre conversations which took place in 1816, during the wet summer that Byron
and Shelley spent together in Switzerland. According to Dr. John Polidori, during that summer Byron recited part of Coleridge's *Christabel* to
Shelley, causing Shelley to fly out of the room:

It appears that one evening Lord B., Mr. P. B. Shelly [*sic*], two ladies
and [Polidori], after having perused a German work, entitled *Phantas-*

magoriana [*sic*], began relating ghost stories; when his lordship having recited the beginning of "Christabel," then unpublished, the whole took so strong a hold of Mr. Shelly's mind, that he suddenly started up and ran out of the room. The physician and Lord Byron followed, and discovered him leaning against a mantle-piece, with cold drops of perspiration trickling down his face. . . . [U]pon enquiring into the cause of his alarm, they found that his wild imagination having pictured to him the bosom of one of the ladies with eyes . . . he was obliged to leave the room in order to destroy the impression.[20]

As James Twitchell notes, Polidori takes "artistic license to link the July event with the earlier June meeting" at which the circle at Diodati pledged to write ghost stories,[21] but the description of Shelley's "wild" reaction to Coleridge's Gothic poem appears to be accurate. This response is significant, since many of the themes in *Christabel,* especially evil's power to infect good, are developed in *The Cenci.* Terry Otten develops some parallels between *Christabel* and *The Cenci:* "The meaning of both works is conveyed essentially by the delineation of the heroines and the demonic beings who destroy them. At one pole is the innocence of the heroine, a character living in a dark and ominous world but apparently free from guilt; at the other pole is the evil of her antagonist, more a symbol than a character, a demon bent on destruction. In the course of the conflict, the innocent and evil characters begin to mirror each other until we arrive at an enigmatic and insoluble mixture of seemingly antithetical forces."[22] The complex and strangely intimate relationship between good and evil is also found in *Manfred,* in which Manfred is described by the Abbot as "an awful chaos—light and darkness— / And mind and dust—and passions and pure thoughts, / Mix'd, and contending without end or order, / All dormant or destructive" (3.1.164–67). Both Shelley and Byron seem to have been influenced by Coleridge's presentation of human nature as an inextricably intertwined combination of good and evil, and both *The Cenci* and *Manfred* owe something to the Gothic tradition exemplified by Coleridge's fragment.

After the ghost-story conversation and the *Christabel* episode, Matthew "Monk" Lewis joined Shelley, Mary Godwin, Byron, Claire Clairmont, and Polidori in mid-August, and provided them with an oral translation of Goethe's *Faust.* As the famous author of *Ambrosio, or the Monk,* a Gothic classic, Lewis seems to have fascinated the circle at Diodati. The two poets were, of course, old hands at writing in the Gothic tradition: Shelley had written two Gothic novels, *Zastrozzi* and *St. Irvyne* in 1810, and one can find Gothic elements in many of Byron's oriental tales. But while the effect of Lewis's visit and translation of *Faust* on Byron's *Manfred* seems clear, Lewis's influence on Shelley is more difficult to discern. Three years later, when he began to write his own Gothic drama, *The Cenci,* Shelley may well have remembered the conversations with Lewis, but it is likely that the memory of the ghostly, Gothic atmosphere of that summer in Switzerland, Coleridge's *Christabel,* and Byron's *Manfred* were stronger influences. In fact, in his discussion of possible sites for hell in his essay *On the Devil, and Devils,* written soon after he completed *The Cenci,*[23] Shelley refers to *Manfred.* Some theorists, he notes, "have supposed Hell to be distributed among the comets, which constitute, according to this scheme, a number of floating prisons of intense and inextinguishable fire; a great modern poet adopts this idea when he calls a comet 'A wandering Hell in the eternal space.'"[24] Shelley is referring to Manfred's invocation of the spirits in act 1, scene 1, in which Manfred calls up "a tyrant-spell, / Which had its birth-place in a star condemn'd, / The burning wreck of a demolish'd world, / A wandering hell in the eternal space" (1.1.43–46). Of course, while Manfred refers to a star, Shelley, in his essay, mentions a comet, but it is clear that this Byronic image, "a wandering hell in the eternal space," made a strong impression on Shelley. Along with the "sad reality" of Byron's "Prometheus," and the nightmarish world of "Darkness," *Manfred* became associated, in Shelley's mind, with the despondent yet brilliantly conceived poetry that resulted from his meeting with Byron in Switzerland.

Another topic doubtlessly touched upon in Switzerland was vampirism, the subject of Byron's "Fragment of a Novel," which was written there, and a motif in both *Manfred* and *The Cenci.*[25] Earlier, in Byron's *Giaour* (published 1813), the vampire myth is alluded to in a passage which seems to foreshadow *The Cenci:*

> But first, on earth as Vampire sent,
> Thy corse shall from its tomb be rent;
> Then ghastly haunt thy native place,
> And suck the blood of all thy race,

There from thy daughter, sister, wife,
At midnight drain the stream of life;
Yet loathe the banquet which perforce
Must feed thy livid living corse;
Thy victims ere they yet expire
Shall know the daemon for their sire,
. . . But one that for thy crime must fall—
The youngest—most belov'd of all,
Shall bless thee with a *father's* name—
. . . Yet must thou end thy task, and mark
Her cheek's last tinge, her eye's last spark[.] (755–86)

The Giaour is never, of course, shown to be a vampire, but this description of a vampire turning against his family, especially a young daughter, has some resemblances to Cenci's treatment of his children. Cenci's "vampirism" is, however, a metaphor for a kind of moral bloodsucking. When Cenci drinks wine "As if [it] wert indeed [his] children's blood / Which [he thirsts] to drink" (1.3.176–77), his desire is not so much to kill them physically as to corrupt them morally and spiritually: "I rarely kill the body which preserves, / Like a strong prison, the soul within my power" (1.1.114–15). He is, in the words of Shelley's Spirit of the Hour, "a vampire among men, / Infecting all with his own hideous ill" (3.4.147–48, *Prometheus Unbound*). This nightmare vision of the vampire-father becomes deeply ingrained in the imaginations of both Lucretia and Beatrice; after Cenci's death Lucretia describes him as "a corpse in which some fiend / Were laid to sleep" (4.4.16–17). Beatrice invests Cenci with the vampire's power to rise from the grave and seek out victims: "the form which tortured" her seems to reappear in the last act (5.4.64). Although Cenci's vampirism may be more metaphorical than real, he assuredly gains strength from the dissolution of his children, staving off the effects of old age with the blood of youth.

Byron also uses the vampire motif in *Manfred* in a way that seems to prefigure Shelley's use of it in *The Cenci*. In *Manfred* the protagonist's "embrace [is] fatal" (1.1.88) and destroys his sister. And the blood-drinking in both works is presented as a kind of blasphemous transubstantiation: thinking of the dead Astarte, Manfred recoils from the cup of wine the Chamois Hunter offers him, exclaiming that "there's blood upon the brim!" (2.1.21). Similarly, Cenci wants to taste his children's blood "like a sacrament" (1.3.82). Manfred raves about his blood relation to Astarte to the puzzled Chamois Hunter:

MAN. I say 'tis blood—my blood! the pure warm stream
  Which ran in the veins of my fathers, and in ours
  When we were in our youth, and had one heart,
  And loved each other as we should not love,
  And this was shed: but still it rises up,
  Colouring the clouds, that shut me out from heaven,
  Where thou art not—and I shall never be. (2.1.24–30)

In both dramas vampirism takes the form of incest, an incest which ultimately destroys Astarte and Beatrice: Astarte dies and Beatrice is executed for parricide. As Manfred says to Astarte's phantom, their love was deadly: "it were / The deadliest sin to love as we have loved" (2.4.123–24). To the Witch of the Alps, Manfred describes Astarte's demise in terms of blood:

MAN. . . . I loved her, and destroy'd her!
WITCH.   With thy hand?
MAN. Not with my hand, but heart—which broke her heart—
  It gazed on mine, and withered. I have shed
  Blood, but not hers—and yet her blood was shed—
  I saw—and could not staunch it. (2.2.117–21)

Again, both vampirism and incest are suggested, but never mentioned explicitly—much as Cenci's rape of Beatrice is never described in words, although Beatrice staggers onstage, exclaiming that her "eyes are full of blood" (3.1.3).

But although there are some resemblances between the "crimes" committed in both *Manfred* and *The Cenci,* and a conscious use of the vampire motif in both dramas, there are important differences between Manfred's and Cenci's attitudes toward what happens to their victims. While Cenci wishes he could taste the "mingled blood" (1.3.81) of his dead sons, and then later imagines the wine he drinks is his children's blood (1.3.176–77), Manfred is stricken with remorse over his fatal relationship with Astarte. In his presentation of Cenci, in fact, it is almost as if Shelley is taking the idea of the Byronic hero to its final logical absurdity—to the point at which the moral confusion typical of many

Byronic heroes turns into a complete perversion of morality and an alliance with evil. Cenci has, in fact, at least a passing resemblance to the flawed hero of Byron's *Lara* (1814). While Lara seems "a stranger in this breathing world, / An erring spirit from another hurled; / A thing of dark imaginings" (315–17), Cenci also feels somehow extraterrestrial: "I do not feel as if I were a man, / But like a fiend appointed to chastise / The offences of some unremembered world" (4.1.160–62). If Cenci is, like Manfred, a Romantic overreacher, he is a demonic version, a sadistic villain who is utterly incapable of the remorse which paralyzes Manfred.

Byron's daring presentation of the incest motif in *Manfred* won Shelley's admiration—in a congratulatory letter, Shelley praised Byron for his "freedom from common rules"[26] in treating a taboo subject, incest. The entire circle at Lake Geneva was, in fact, condemned as a "League of Incest" by gossips back in England, who assumed that Claire Clairmont and Mary Godwin were sisters, and Byron later responded to this slander in an essay, unpublished in his lifetime, entitled "Some Observations upon an Article in *Blackwood's Edinburgh Magazine*" (1820).[27] Moreover, in defiance of "common rules," Shelley continued his exploration of the incest theme in *The Cenci*—the major reason that the play was never performed during Shelley's lifetime was the objection to this controversial topic—and he presents a villain who commits incest through rape. The two types of incest portrayed in *Manfred* and *The Cenci* are contrasted by Shelley in a famous letter to Maria Gisborne, dated 16 November 1819: "Incest is like many other *incorrect* things a very poetical circumstance. It may be the excess of love or of hate. It may be that defiance of every thing for the sake of another which clothes itself in the glory of the highest heroism, or it may be that cynical rage which confounding good & bad in existing opinions breaks through them for the purpose of rioting in selfishness & antipathy."[28] The brother-sister incest portrayed in Shelley's *Laon and Cythna* and Byron's *Manfred* is "the excess of love"; the father-daughter incestuous rape which is at the center of *The Cenci* is the "excess" of hate. Thus Cenci illustrates how a "very poetical circumstance" can become a vehicle for hatred rather than an expression of "the highest heroism." And *The Cenci* is by no means the poets' last word on the incest motif: in *Cain* (1821) Byron explores brother-sister incest as a natural institution in the post-Edenic world. In composing several works dealing with incest between 1816 and 1821, Shelley and Byron repeatedly demonstrated to each other their "freedom from common rules" and their willingness to defy public censure.

As overreachers, both Manfred and Cenci do the unthinkable—Manfred, through the intercession of Arimanes, calls up the spirit of the dead Astarte, and Cenci rapes Beatrice to damn her soul. The two figures consider the actions that they are about to undertake with a mixture of anticipation and dread:

> MAN. . . . Within a few hours I shall not call in vain—
> Yet in this hour I dread the thing I dare:
> Until this hour I never shrunk to gaze
> On spirit, good or evil—now I tremble,
> And feel a strange cold thaw upon my heart,
> But I can act even what I most abhor,
> And champion human fears.—The night approaches. (2.2.199–205)

> CENCI.   I said
> I would not drink this evening; but I must;
> For, strange to say, I feel my spirits fail
> With thinking what I have decreed to do.—
>
> *(Drinking the wine.)*
>
> Be thou the resolution of quick youth
> Within my veins, and manhood's purpose stern,
> And age's firm, cold, subtle villainy;
> . . . The charm works well;
> It must be done; it shall be done, I swear! (1.3.169–78)

They thus steel themselves to confront their victims, but this overreaching is ultimately self-destructive, since it leads to Manfred's death and Cenci's murder. Certainly, the kind of self-assertiveness which characterizes them is sterile and uncreative—far from the Promethean ideal admired by Byron and Shelley. In fact, both Byron and Shelley condemned overreachers of this sort, as their assessments of the fallen Napoléon demonstrate:

> But quiet to quick bosoms is a hell,
> And *there* hath been thy bane; there is a fire
> And motion of the soul which will not dwell

In its own narrow being, but aspire
Beyond the fitting medium of desire;
And, but once kindled, quenchless evermore,
Preys upon high adventure, nor can tire
Of aught but rest; a fever at the core,
Fatal to him who bears, to all who ever bore.
(*Childe Harold's Pilgrimage*, 3.370–78)

"Aye, alive and still bold," muttered Earth,
    "Napoleon's fierce spirit rolled,
    In terror, and blood, and gold,
A torrent of ruin to death from his birth.
Leave the millions who follow to mould
The metal before it be cold,
And weave into his shame, which like the dead
Shrouds me, the hopes that from his glory fled."
(Shelley's "Written on Hearing the News of the Death of Napoleon"
    [1821], 33–40)

The contemporary historical analogue to Manfred and Cenci is a man
who created unprecedented carnage across Europe—an object lesson
to Byron and Shelley of the dangers of hubris.

Moreover, like *The Cenci, Manfred* explores the dangers of excessive
self-examination. Manfred is a victim of a mental trait which is described in *The Cenci* as "self-anatomy." Orsino, the conspiring priest of
The Cenci, identifies the search for forbidden knowledge as a source of
evil for the Cenci family:

        'tis a trick of this same family
To analyse their own and other minds.
Such self-anatomy shall teach the will
Dangerous secrets: for it tempts our powers,
Knowing what must be thought, and may be done,
Into the depth of darkest purposes. (2.2.108–13)

Likewise, Manfred's thirst for knowledge leads to "Conclusions most
forbidden" (2.2.83)—like the Cenci family, he finds that "The Tree
of knowledge is not that of Life" (1.1.12). Ironically, self-knowledge
leads to evil rather than wisdom, as Manfred's self-analysis ends in his
own destruction and the obliteration of his Promethean powers to do

good for mankind, and the Cenci family's self-anatomy leads to perversion and parricide. The kind of knowledge Cenci seeks can only be
found through an examination of another's pain and sorrow. Indeed,
there is a ruthlessly scientific quality in Cenci's sadistic experiments, in
which he seeks to fix the limits of pain and perverted joy. In his essay
On the Devil, and Devils, Shelley compares the sadism of God and the
Devil to "naturalists anatomizing dogs alive,"[29] and it seems clear that
Cenci's attempt to spiritually dissect Beatrice is inspired by a feeling of
curiosity.

As early as 1811 Shelley warned Elizabeth Hitchener against the
"habitual analysis of [one's] own thoughts," a practice which leads inevitably to misery: "It is this habit, acquired by length of solitary labour,
never then to be shaken off[,] which induces gloom, which deprives the
being thus affected of any anticipation or retrospection of happiness."[30]
It is Manfred's and Beatrice's error to dwell on the acts of incest that
have so marred their lives in a solitary, self-conscious manner—they
simply increase their sufferings. Moreover, these characters deny themselves the therapeutic benefits that would come from self-expression.
They refer only obliquely and mysteriously to the incestuous encounters which have scarred them.[31] While Beatrice asserts that there are
no "words . . . to tell / [Her] misery" (3.1.111–14), Manfred dismisses
words more scornfully: "words are breath" (2.2.128). Their solipsistic
and wordless knowledge of evil leads both Manfred and Beatrice to violent and self-destructive acts, and sorrow unrelieved by an articulation
of their sufferings.

When Shelley composed Beatrice's nightmarish vision of her father
returning from the grave to drag her downward to her death, he may
have recalled Manfred's demise. Manfred, like Beatrice, is approached
by an infernal figure associated with darkness and hell. Describing the
apparition that comes to take Manfred, the Abbot says: "I see a dusk
and awful figure rise / Like an infernal god from out the earth; / His
face wrapt in a mantle, and his form / Robed as with angry clouds"
(3.4.62–65). Furthermore, after the spirit unveils his visage the Abbot
sees that "on his brow / The thunder-scars are graven; from his eye /
Glares forth the immortality of hell" (3.4.76–78). But no Demogorgon-
like figure can intimidate Manfred—he is satanically self-contained:

"The mind which is immortal makes itself / Requital for its good or evil thoughts" (3.4.129–30). And he welcomes death as a release from his painful consciousness of sin; after the demons disappear he passes away quietly, telling the Abbot " 'tis not so difficult to die" (3.4.151). Similarly, although Beatrice initially panics at the thought of death, she comes to welcome the prospect of escaping, through death, the misery she had experienced on earth: "Come, obscure Death, / And wind me in thine all-embracing arms! / Like a fond mother hide me in thy bosom, / And rock me to the sleep from which none awake!" (5.4.115–18). Like Manfred, Beatrice dies with quiet dignity, saying "Well, 'tis very well" (5.4.165). In both *The Cenci* and *Manfred* death is, to some extent, a welcome release from consciousness—from the knowledge which, in sad reality, inevitably leads to sorrow.

It seems clear that Byron's equation of sorrow with knowledge interested and troubled Shelley; later, in early 1821, he quoted from *Manfred* in a canceled preface to *Epipsychidion*. Speaking of the narrator of *Epipsychidion,* Shelley noted that "his fate is an additional proof that 'The tree of Knowledge is not that of Life.' "[32] In *The Cenci* Shelley also seems to be wrestling with the fact that knowledge can lead to error rather than enlightenment. Thus, through an analysis of Beatrice's mind, Cenci discovers a way to lead her, an exemplary being meant "to be admired" (preface to *The Cenci*), to commit parricide, and Manfred's will to "seek things beyond mortality" (2.3.159) ends in self-annihilation. The equation of knowledge with sorrow would haunt Shelley to the end of his career—at times he, like Byron, even doubted the usefulness of philosophy in solving the problems of mankind. In Manfred's words, "philosophy [is] / . . . of all our vanities the motliest, / The merest word that ever fool'd the ear" (3.1.9–11). As Rousseau, the disfigured philosopher of Shelley's *The Triumph of Life,* tells the poem's narrator, "If thirst of knowledge doth not . . . abate, / Follow it even to the night, but I / Am weary" (194–96). In both *Manfred* and *The Cenci* knowledge leads to tragedy and suffering rather than to wisdom.

*   *   *

After first meeting Byron in Switzerland, Shelley described his efforts to improve Byron's mind in a letter to Peacock recently published in its entirety:

Lord Byron is an exceedingly interesting person, & as such, is it not to be regretted that he is a slave to the vilest & most vulgar prejudices, & as mad as the winds? I do not mean to say that he is a Christian, or that his ordinary conduct is devoid of prudence. But in the course of an intimacy of two months, & an observation the most minute I see reason to regret the union of great genius, & things which make genius useless. For a short time I shall see no more of Lord Byron, a circumstance I cannot avoid regretting as he has shewn me great kindness, & as I had some hope that an intercourse with me would operate to weaken those superstitions of rank & wealth & revenge & servility to opinion with which he, in common with other men, is so poisonously imbued.[33]

After reading a number of Byron's 1816–17 works, however, Shelley congratulated his friend on freeing himself from "the common rules" which had been hampering his genius. Their intercourse had, Shelley thought, worked to weaken Byron's "superstitions." But by the time he wrote the preface to *The Cenci* Shelley had some reason to doubt Byron's freedom from some of the "things which make genius useless." Having observed Byron's assimilation into Italian society, a society marred, in Shelley's view, by error and superstition, Shelley seems to have felt that his friend was in some need of guidance. In a December 1818 letter to Peacock, Shelley deplores Byron's acceptance of Venetian mores: "for an Englishman to encourage such sickening vice is a melancholy thing. . . . He is not yet an Italian, & is heartily & deeply discontented with himself."[34] With this in mind, Shelley wrote his preface to *The Cenci,* a preface which is specifically directed to those from "Protestant countries" who may not understand the capability of an Italian Catholic like Cenci to be at once intensely religious and completely corrupt.

The religion of an Italian Catholic, Shelley writes in his preface, "is adoration, faith, submission, penitence, blind admiration; not a rule for moral conduct. It has no necessary connexion with any one virtue. The most atrocious villain may be rigidly devout, and without any shock to established faith, confess himself to be so. . . . Cenci himself built a chapel in the court of his Palace, and dedicated it to St. Thomas the Apostle, and established masses for the peace of his soul." Not only is this a startling generalization, it is also somewhat misleading with respect to Cenci's piety. As Shelley's primary source, *Relation of the Death of the Family of the Cenci,* notes, Cenci was actually an atheist and, "although he caused a small chapel, dedicated to the apostle St. Thomas, to be built in the court of his palace, his intention in so doing was to bury there all his children, whom he cruelly hated,"[35] not to try to save his soul. Cenci's adherence to the Catholic faith in the tragedy is, then, an invention of Shelley's that makes it possible to show how Catholicism can serve to inspire rather than discourage tyranny and criminal acts. Moreover, as Jerrold Hogle notes, Beatrice "remains caught within the circle of mirrors encouraged by Catholicism, which she allows to reflect her completely as though there were no other angles of interpretation on herself or other people."[36] As an instrument of tyranny, Catholicism can warp the imagination even of a potentially transcendent being like Beatrice.

When Shelley's attitude toward Italian Catholicism is compared to Byron's, one is struck by the great contrast. As early as 27 May 1817 Byron wrote to Augusta Leigh of his plans to place his illegitimate daughter Allegra "in a Venetian convent—to become a good Catholic—& (it may be) a *Nun*."[37] According to his valet, William Fletcher, Byron often made public demonstrations of his respect for the Catholic religion, although he denied that he was Catholic himself: "Even at the moment when my Lord was more gay than at any time after, in the year 1817, I have seen my Lord repeatedly, on meeting or passing any religious ceremonies which the Roman Catholics have in their frequent processions, . . . dismount his horse and fall on his knees, and remain in that posture till the procession had passed."[38] Among other things, the treatment of Catholicism in *The Cenci* may have been an attempt by Shelley to correct this tendency in his friend to sympathize with a religion which was, to Shelley, simply another instrument of tyranny and injustice. He did not, of course, succeed, and ultimately he and Mary Shelley agreed with Byron's decision to place Allegra in a convent, where she died at the age of five.[39] Even as late as April 1822 Shelley was still lamenting his inability "to eradicate from [Byron's] great mind the delusions of Christianity, which in spite of his reason, seem perpetually to recur, & lay in ambush for the hours of sickness & distress."[40]

Shelley also disapproved of Byron's dealings with the Italians in Venice, his willingness to indulge in practices which were "common enough in Italy" but which were not, in Shelley's mind, appropriate to an Englishman. While the Shelleys tended to socialize only with close friends and therefore knew few Italians intimately, Byron was almost immediately assimilated into Italian life. In *Beppo,* written in late 1817, Byron sang Italy's praises: "With all its sinful doings, I must say, / That Italy's a pleasant place to me" (321–22). Although Byron would not, of course, have condoned the criminal sexual practices described in the *Relation of the Death of the Family of the Cenci,* he was far from feeling, with Shelley, that Italian Catholicism was morally deficient as a religion, and he seemed, on the whole, to prefer Italian passion over English coldness and correctness. As Reiman has noted, Byron's "Italian acculturation"[41] contrasts sharply with Shelley's increasing sense of isolation: "Byron's letters and the letters to him support *Beppo* and his other poetry in portraying the successful human relationships and the sense of social solidarity that grew up in Italy around him, while Shelley's scattered letters and the few to him (so many of them involving unsuccessful financial arrangements of one kind or another) illustrate the increasingly negative aspect of his human involvements."[42] But while Shelley was appalled by the Italian practices and life-styles he observed when he visited Byron in Venice, not all Italian institutions disgusted him. In fact, when Byron eventually settled down as the *cavaliere servente* of Teresa Guiccioli, Shelley was overjoyed: "The connexion with la Guiccioli has been an inestimable benefit to him . . . he is becoming what he should be, a virtuous man."[43] Although he never seems to have felt fully comfortable in Italian society, Shelley came to accept and even applaud the beneficial effects of his friend's Italian acculturation.

* * *

Charles Robinson argues that in *Prometheus Unbound* "Shelley borrowed from the 'form' of *[Manfred]* but only insofar as he could use these 'borrowings' to assert his own 'spirit' and simultaneously denounce Byron's apostasy."[44] As Robinson points out, the parallels between Manfred and Prometheus are numerous: "Shelley created a Prometheus who, like Manfred, had the 'visions' and 'noble aspirations' to make his 'own the mind of other men, / The enlightener of nations' [3.1.104–7], and who also clouded his vision by an intellectual and moral error, destroyed his love, separated himself from his psychic complement, and caused his own pain and isolation."[45] In the first scenes of each dramatic poem the protagonists call on nature spirits, which are, in Prometheus's case, those of the mountains, springs, air, and whirlwinds (1.59–66), and, in Manfred's, the spirits of "Earth, ocean, air, night, mountains, winds, [and his] star" (1.1.132). Moreover, whereas Manfred asserts that "grief should be the instructor of the wise" (1.1.9), Prometheus, after "Three thousand years of sleep-unsheltered hours" (1.12), has learned to repudiate hate, for "misery [has] made [him] wise" (1.58). And while Manfred yearns for his antitype, Astarte, Prometheus longs for Asia—like Manfred, Prometheus seeks consolation from his female counterpart. The Manfred who defies the Spirits, declaring that his "Promethean spark" (1.154) is equal to their own, is clearly a precursor of Shelley's bound Prometheus, just as Byron's Arimanes, "Prince of Earth and Air!" (2.4.1), is the forerunner of Shelley's Jupiter.

But while Robinson's comparison of Byron's "Dramatic Poem" and Shelley's "Lyrical Drama" reveals some illuminating parallels between the two works, I disagree with Robinson's conclusion that in *Prometheus Unbound* and *Julian and Maddalo* Shelley "responded to Byron's misapprehension of life."[46] As I have demonstrated in this chapter, Shelley's *The Cenci* (written between the composition of acts 3 and 4 of *Prometheus Unbound*), echoes some of the ideas and themes found in *Manfred*— Shelley's sense of Byron's "apostasy" and "misapprehension of life" is certainly not evident in that other major drama of 1819. And as Robinson's own comparison of *Manfred* and *Prometheus Unbound* suggests, the two works have many more similarities than points of contrast, and their similarities go beyond mere form. Moreover, any discussion of their differences must take into account the situations of the two Promethean protagonists: while Manfred "is . . . a mortal / [who seeks] the things beyond mortality" (2.4.158–59) and Astarte is dead, Prometheus and Asia are immortal, and Prometheus only abandons his Manfred-like attitudes after 3,000 years of "torture and solitude, / Scorn and despair" (1.14–15). Whereas *Prometheus Unbound* is a work of nearly unadulterated idealism, presenting "the type of the highest perfection of moral and intellectual nature" (preface to *Prometheus Unbound*), Manfred's encounters with the Chamois Hunter and the Abbot locate him in a world which is not without its mundane elements. Thus it is reasonable to view *Prometheus Unbound* as a development rather than a refutation of *Manfred*—Shelley's lyrical drama takes Byron's theme of a Promethean hero confronted with sad reality and explores it in a work which is even more visionary and allegorical than its Byronic predecessor. And in any case, the fact that Shelley wrote a pessimistic companion drama to *Prometheus Unbound* suggests that Shelley responded to Byron's dramatic poem in a dialogical rather than a disputatious way, composing one work *(The Cenci)* which reaffirms the pessimism of *Manfred* and another work *(Prometheus Unbound)* which explores the earlier drama's themes and ideas from a more idealistic perspective.[47]

Thus, although it is probably true that by August 1821 Shelley and Byron were "differing more than ever" on dramatic principles, their common interests during the 1819–21 period of their relationship seem to have far outweighed their differences. For example, between 1819 and 1821 both poets independently experimented with Dante's terza rima, most notably in Shelley's "Ode to the West Wind" (1819) and Byron's *The Prophecy of Dante*. And they composed dramatic works, *The Cenci* and *Marino Faliero,* which have significant resemblances in their presentations of complex moral problems. While Beatrice must choose between parricide and being repeatedly raped by her demonic father, the Doge finds himself having to decide between violent rebellion and submission to tyrants who transform his people into "mere machines, / To serve the nobles' . . . pleasure" (1.2.302–3).

It is the dehumanization of tyranny that most appalled Byron and Shelley. After hearing of the Peterloo Massacre, Shelley wrote to Charles Ollier of "the torrent of [his] indignation." Quoting from *The Cenci,* he wrote that he, like the violated Beatrice, believed that " 'Something must be done . . . What yet I know not' " (see *The Cenci,* 3.1.86–87).[48] Both poets hoped for a free Italy, and *The Cenci* and *Marino Faliero* are, in part, portrayals of the tyranny and injustice that Shelley and Byron wanted to see ended. In February 1821 Shelley looked forward, in a letter to Peacock, to a battle between the Neapolitan and Austrian armies which he believed might "be the signal for insurrection throughout all Italy" and constitute "the birth of liberty."[49] Three days after Shelley wrote the letter to Peacock, Byron wrote about "free Italy" in his Ravenna Journal: "It is no great matter, supposing that Italy could be liberated, who or what is sacrificed. It is a great object— the very *poetry* of politics. Only think—a free Italy!!!"[50] Whatever their moral evaluations of Beatrice and Faliero, it is clear that Shelley and

Byron deeply sympathized with those who struggled against tyranny. And while Shelley's work of idealism, *Prometheus Unbound,* shows a titan freeing himself through pity and love for his antitype, *The Cenci* returns to the "sad reality" of Byron's Prometheus bound, to the tragic and essentially futile struggle against the power of the old regime that Shelley and Byron were observing in early nineteenth-century Italy. In this realm of sad reality even as admirable a woman as Beatrice Cenci can be "violently thwarted from her nature by the necessity of circumstance and opinion" (preface), and the movements of the Neapolitan army can come to nothing. Shelley's hopes for the future never blinded him to the tragic plight of a "violently thwarted" woman of the past, or to the reality of present tyranny. Thus, trapped in a historical situation over which she has no control, it is Beatrice's destiny to lead, like Byron's Prometheus, a "sad unallied existence" (52) in a world dominated by "The ruling principle of Hate / Which for its pleasure doth create / The things it may annihilate" ("Prometheus," 20–22).

FIVE

Byron's *Sardanapalus:*
The Shelleyan Hero Transformed

On 19 December 1821, John Murray published Byron's *Sardanapalus, The Two Foscari,* and *Cain* in the same volume. Of the three works, *Sardanapalus* seems to have been particularly difficult for Byron to write, at least at first; in his note at the end of the drama Byron outlined his progress: "I began this drama on the 13th of January 1821. and continued the two first acts very slowly and at long intervals.—The three last acts were written Since the 13th of May 1821. (this present Month.) that is to say in a fortnight."[1] *Sardanapalus* was completed on 27 May 1821. Soon after composing it, Byron wrote *The Two Foscari,* the weakest play of the volume, beginning work on it on 12 June and finishing it on 9 July 1821.[2] *Cain,* which was first envisioned along with *Sardanapalus* on 28 January 1821, was composed next, and Byron was occupied with the mystery play between 16 July and 9 September 1821.[3] The 1821 volume of dramas arguably contains Byron's most important work as a dramatist. In a recent book Martyn Corbett has argued that "*Sardanapalus* is unquestionably Byron's finest tragedy and a dramatic masterpiece by any standards,"[4] and *Cain* is generally considered Byron's most important metaphysical drama. This volume is also very important in the context of the Shelley-Byron relationship, since *Sardanapalus* and *Cain* both respond to themes developed in Shelley's works, particularly in *Queen Mab, The Revolt of Islam, Prometheus Unbound,* and *The Cenci.* Both *Sardanapalus* and *Cain* are works in which the protagonists are self-conscious idealists: Sardanapalus is a king who seeks to rule through peace and benevolence, and Cain murders, according to Byron, out of "rage and fury against the inadequacy of his state to his Conceptions."[5] Although Byron saw little of Shelley during the period he lived and worked in Ravenna, it is probable that Shelley had a significant influence on the two important dramas of 1821.

Robinson's insistence on the philosophical antagonism of Shelley and Byron notwithstanding, it is not difficult to establish Byron's respect for Shelley's "idealistic" works. Shelley himself reported Byron's admiration of *Prometheus Unbound* (published August 1820) in a 26 August 1821 letter to Leigh Hunt: "[Lord Byron] was loud in his praise of 'Prometheus.'"[6] And according to Medwin, *Queen Mab* was one of Byron's favorite sources: "Shelley's *Queen Mab* and Casti's *Novelle* were two of his favourite *cribbing* books."[7] In a 10 September 1820 letter to Richard Belgrave Hoppner, Byron defended the controversial *Revolt of Islam*, writing that "[Shelley's] Islam had much poetry,"[8] and two years later Byron welcomed the publication of Shelley's idealistic treatment of the Greek Revolution, *Hellas*; according to Mary Shelley, "Lord B. seem[ed] pleased with [*Hellas*]."[9] While *Sardanapalus* and *Cain* could not have been influenced by *Hellas*, they certainly could have been affected by *Prometheus Unbound, Queen Mab*, and *The Revolt of Islam*. Byron was not drawn to Shelley solely because Shelley occasionally wrote works dealing with "sad reality"; he was interested in Shelley primarily because Shelley, in Byron's words, was one of those poetic "visionaries out of [the world],"[10] a poet who was distinctive precisely because he was capable of sustained flights of idealism. Thus Byron admired *Prometheus Unbound* more than he admired *The Cenci*, and, far from feeling philosophically antagonistic toward it, praised it with enthusiasm. In the next chapter I will discuss Shelley's influence on *Cain*—in this chapter I will examine Shelley's influence on Byron's *Sardanapalus*, the portrait of a would-be pacifist king who, like Shelley's Prometheus, is punished for trying to become mankind's benefactor, for trying to "make [his] subjects feel / The weight of human misery less, and glide / Ungroaning to the tomb" (1.2.263–65).

In *Sardanapalus* Byron presents the legendary Assyrian monarch as a man who contains within his complex nature both comedy and tragedy, irony and pathos, lassitude and martial valor. Sardanapalus changes from a voluptuary almost too weak to lift a sword (2.1.194) to a warrior who in a supernatural fury "sweeps the air and deluges the earth"

(3.1.318). According to Richard Lansdown, Byron's portrait of Sardanapalus was partially influenced by the poet's own "revolutionary, or
near revolutionary, experience in Ravenna."[11] In 1820 and 1821, as a
member of an Italian nationalist organization, the Carbonari, Byron
faced the prospect of becoming involved in a war of liberation. Byron's
period of revolutionary activity in Ravenna was an abrupt departure
from his "Sardanapalian" life of debauchery in Venice and, in Lansdown's view, *Sardanapalus* represents Byron's fantasy of being swept
away by historical events beyond his control: Byron "could swap what
he felt to be a life of slothful self-indulgence for one of action, and forget his past altogether, as Sardanapalus forgets his."[12] Sardanapalus's
contradictions and mood swings can thus be seen as reflections of
Byron's own emotional turmoil as he waited for events to unfold in
Ravenna. Other critics have also viewed Sardanapalus as a Byronic self-
projection: while Bernard Blackstone conjectures that "Perhaps more
of Byron himself passes into [Sardanapalus] than into any of the earlier
heroes,"[13] Jerome McGann argues that the work as a whole is heavily
influenced by Byron's relationship with Teresa Guiccioli.[14]

That Sardanapalus is in many ways a reflection of Byron I do not
dispute; I would, however, argue that he also possesses some of the
attributes of Shelley's heroes, and that many of Sardanapalus's sentiments have more than a passing resemblance to Shelley's melioristic
ideas. Even Sardanapalus's manner of speaking is sometimes reminiscent of the Shelley-Byron dialogue. For example, Sardanapalus's
taunting reply to the suggestion that his forebears were gods calls to
mind Julian-Shelley's taunts against superstition in *Julian and Maddalo:*
"the worms are gods; / At least they banqueted upon your gods, /
And died for lack of farther nutriment" (1.2.269–71). Although Marilyn
Butler has condemned the language of the play as "stage blank verse,
here pompous, there threadbare, all the time insidiously moribund,"[15]
I would argue that Samuel Chew's assessment of the drama's style,
although dated, is closer to the mark: "Both Byron and Shelley were
very successful in reproducing the light small-talk of gentlemen, the
finest example of such work being *Julian and Maddalo.* Sardanapalus has
a good deal of this easy, well-bred conversation."[16] In fact, as Jerome
Christensen has shown, in at least one speech Sardanapalus's literary
knowledge and wittiness is that of a nineteenth-century Englishman

rather than an ancient Assyrian: he alludes to Herodotus, *Childe Harold*, canto 1, and *Biographia Literaria*, and plays on the similarity between the English words "king" and "kine" (see act 5, 480–87).[17] Although these anachronisms can be dismissed as incidental, they nevertheless suggest a link between the discourse of *Sardanapalus* and the familiar style shared by Shelley and Byron.

In fact, Byron's Sardanapalus seems in some ways much more Shelleyan than Byronic. He is, like Julian, a meliorist and optimist. His desire to create a secluded paradise with his beloved Myrrha resembles the goal of the speaker of *Epipsychidion*. And, like Shelley's Prometheus, he wants to be man's benefactor, to create a golden age for mankind. Moreover, in his idealism Sardanapalus resembles Shelley himself. After Shelley's death, Byron told Lady Blessington that his fellow poet had "a total want of worldly wisdom."[18] Sardanapalus, likewise, is impractical and, through the first two acts of the play, has a truly Shelleyan indifference to the mundane duties of everyday life. Sardanapalus does not, however, have an island retreat, like the poet of *Epipsychidion,* or a green isle like that in *Lines written among the Euganean Hills,* or a refuge like Prometheus's "Cave / All overgrown" (*Prometheus Unbound,* 3.3.10–11)—he cannot simply withdraw from his position as King of Assyria. Thus partly because he, unlike some of Shelley's characters, must operate within a specific (albeit largely imaginary) political-historical context, Sardanapalus changes in the course of the drama into a kind of Byronic hero and drenches his kingdom in blood. In the violent arena of Assyrian politics he finds it virtually impossible to maintain his Shelleyan ideals.

Byron had read *The Revolt of Islam* before writing *Sardanapalus,* and Byron may have created his protagonist with Shelley's Laon (the hero of *The Revolt of Islam*) in mind, especially since he chose to portray a king who suffers the same fate as the freedom-loving Laon—Sardanapalus dies by fire, with his mistress Myrrha, just as Laon is burned alive with his beloved Cythna. Although Laon and Sardanapalus are very different in their personality traits and backgrounds, they are both idealistic and must deal with an evil and threatening cosmos.[19] In the unjust world which they inhabit, their acts of forgiveness come back to haunt them. Laon persuades his followers not to murder the tyrant Othman (5.2008–25) and is executed by Othman's henchmen. Sarda-

napalus orders Salamenes to spare Beleses and Arbaces, but loses his
throne to the two men he pardoned. Because of their revolutionary
ideas, Sardanapalus earns the enmity of the fanatical priest Beleses and
Laon is hated and persecuted by priests who are described "Singing
their bloody hymns" (*The Revolt of Islam*, 12.4461), glorifying murder
and tyranny. In trying to free his subjects or make his people "monarchs in their mansions" (4.1.314), Sardanapalus becomes a threat to
the accepted order of things, just as Laon, "The friend and preserver of
the free" (5.1875), constitutes a menace to the status quo of Islam. Thus
both *Sardanapalus* and *The Revolt of Islam* are stern indictments which,
by implication, apply to the corrupt political systems of the poets' day.
The political radicalism of *The Revolt of Islam* finds an echo in Byron's
Sardanapalus.

But although they have some similarities, Laon keeps his ideals,
while Sardanapalus loses his. As Malcolm Kelsall notes, in a comparison
between *The Revolt of Islam* and Byron's Venetian plays, the "delightful
Laon and Cynthia [*sic*] belong to no age, no class, no race, but inspired
by a pure disinterested love of mankind founded on reading the sages
and poets of antiquity achieve social equality by the sheer force of their
oratory. Byron's characters, on the contrary, have to deal with recog-
nisable circumstances of time and place, social role, the corruption of
human nature."[20] Whereas in *The Revolt of Islam* Shelley is interested in
exploring an idealist's career in a somewhat visionary setting, in *Sardanapalus* Byron is more concerned with how this kind of idealist may act
in a world in which the "circumstances of time and place [and] social
role" must all be reckoned with. And while Shelley's heroic Laon is
shaped by a kindly hermit and an inspiring antitype, Cythna, Sardanapalus falls under the influence of Myrrha and Salemenes, who advise
him to be tyrannical and violent. At the end of *The Revolt of Islam* Laon
offers himself as a sacrificial victim to Othman and the fanatical priests
on the condition that Cythna be transported to the land of freedom
(America) (11.4437–39). Sardanapalus by contrast does not appear to
have altruistic goals in mind when he casts himself on his funeral pyre:
his self-immolation is an act of defiant self-assertion. While Laon's
death is a kind of martyrdom, Sardanapalus's death is a suicide: the
concept of martyrdom has no place in Sardanapalus's cynical world of
power politics.

Sardanapalus shares, however, with both Laon and Shelley's Prometheus a steadfast belief in the transcendent power of love. Charles J. Clancy notes that "Both Prometheus, in Shelley's *Prometheus Unbound*, and Sardanapalus are liberated by the power of love. . . . The Furies are unsuccessful because Prometheus understands their role as agents of evil, and pities them. He expresses his love for them and is set free. So too is Sardanapalus transformed by the insights of love, but he is led by these to death, and the hoped-for freedom which follows it."[21] Thus Sardanapalus, whose "life is love" (1.2.406), seeks to find fulfillment in his relationship with Myrrha rather than in military heroism, and Prometheus, asserting the vanity of "all hope but love" (1.808), uses his faith in Asia to resist the Furies' visions of suffering and despair. But, unlike Asia, Myrrha urges her lover to destroy rather than forgive his enemies (2.1.573–80). She is a masochist who claims that pain and pleasure are "*two* names for *one* feeling" (5.1.35). In fact, she seems to be close in temperament to the bloodthirsty Semiramis—at the end of Sardanapalus's nightmare the "ghastly beldame" fades away and is replaced by Myrrha (4.1.31–37), and, as a number of commentators have noted, the name "Se*mira*mis" has the name "Myrrha" enclosed within it.[22] Gordon Spence stresses another important difference between Byronic and Shelleyan heroes: "It is one of the contrasts between Byron and Shelley that, whereas Shelley endows his transfigured Prometheus with some feminine characteristics to express an androgynous ideal of harmony and completeness, Byron portrays a tragic hero with masculine and feminine tendencies in irreconcilable conflict."[23] Unlike Prometheus, Sardanapalus can never resolve the conflicts within himself or achieve harmony with his environment. And he can only become one with Myrrha in death: "commingling fire will mix [their] ashes" (5.1.471). In *Sardanapalus* love engenders death rather than life.

Myrrha is not, however, the only woman who attempts to influence Sardanapalus. Zarina, Sardanapalus's legitimate wife, presents to him the idea of a paradise in exile as an alternative to Myrrha's warlike vision of perpetual human conflict. The struggle between escapism and fatalism also takes place within Sardanapalus himself. He resembles the Promethean figures whom Byron's Dante (in *The Prophecy of Dante*) calls "poets but without the name":

For what is poesy but to create
From overfeeling good or ill; and aim
At an external life beyond our fate,
    And be the new Prometheus of new men,
    Bestowing fire from heaven, and then, too late,
Finding the pleasure given repaid with pain,
    And vultures to the heart of the bestower,
    Who, having lavish'd his high gift in vain,
Lies chain'd to his lone rock by the sea-shore? (4.10–19)

While Sardanapalus is a "new Prometheus," there are no "new men" to cherish his "high gift." Instead of oppressing his people, he has enjoyed "songs, and lutes, and feasts, and concubines" (1.2.234).[24] Rather than decimating his subjects, like Semiramis, he has founded cities and marked them with a "verse" which concludes " 'Eat, drink, and love; the rest's not worth a fillip' " (1.2.252). His ethic is constructive, while that of his forebears was destructive—he reveres pleasure, while they, like Shelley's Cenci, glutted their sadism with displays of violence. But Sardanapalus cannot pass on his poetic vision to his people, a race of warriors whose sensibilities are too crude to appreciate anything milder than mayhem. Like Dante's Promethean poet, Sardanapalus must inevitably find "the pleasure given repaid with pain." Or, in the language of Byron's "Prometheus," Sardanapalus's "Godlike crime was to be kind, / To render with [his] precepts less / The sum of human wretchedness" (35–37). The world is not ready for his hedonistic and pacifistic ideals and, in the final analysis, neither is he. He ultimately rejects the poetic life of creating pleasure and adopts, instead, the martial occupation of inflicting pain.

Sardanapalus's inability to accept the quiet, solipsistic life of a poet wholeheartedly resembles Byron's own ambivalent feelings toward his craft. In his Ravenna Journal, Byron asks: "As to defining what a poet *should* be, it is not worth while, for what are *they* worth? what have they done?"[25] As Lansdown says of Byron's Ravenna period, "His revolutionary enthusiasm, he felt, was in danger of being swamped by a powerful disinclination."[26] During the first two acts of the drama, Sardanapalus chooses inactivity, preferring instead to dream of a world in which all men are free to pursue lives of pleasure and in which war is an anachronism. When Beleses says that "Sloth is of all things the most fanciful" (2.1.120), he equates Sardanapalus's poetic fancifulness with sheer laziness. In the bellicose realm of Assyria the only acceptable professions are those of soldier and priest. But Sardanapalus is incapable of living the relatively passive, dreaming life of a poet indefinitely and finds himself forsaking the poet's garland of flowers for the helmet of war. And once he becomes embroiled in the struggles of sad reality, Sardanapalus ceases to be a poet and becomes, instead, what he most detests: a sanguinary, destructive ruler, like his grandmother Semiramis. While Shelley's Prometheus, through his imaginative will, is able to change the earth, Byron's Sardanapalus, hemmed in by both history and politics, is less effective and, rather than changing his environment, finds himself transformed by it. Like Byron's Cain, he has an imagination which aspires to recreate the world but is never quite able to transcend his tragic limitations. Perhaps it is this kind of poetic impotence that makes Byron prefer action to dreaming of another existence.

What Sardanapalus really longs for is a kind of terrestrial paradise. As the speaker of *Epipsychidion* seeks to take his loved one to his "pleasure-house" (491) to be the "lady of the solitude" (514), so Sardanapalus wishes he could throw away his crown "And share a cottage on the Caucasus" (1.2.452) alone with Myrrha, "and wear no crowns but those of flowers" (1.2.453). This urge to create a terrestrial paradise is, of course, a recurrent theme in both Shelley's and Byron's poetry, and is an urge which, in *Epipsychidion,* the Haidée episode of *Don Juan,* and *Sardanapalus,* seems like a form of escapism, a dream which must ultimately fade into the nightmare of sad reality. Certainly Myrrha, who is deeply concerned with the events of the violent outer world, cannot remain content with a lover "who ne'er looks / Beyond his palace walls" (1.2.109–10). And, when things go awry for Sardanapalus, all that is left to him is a death which is analogous to the climactic merger of the lovers in *Epipsychidion* (540–91). After Sardanapalus and Myrrha are cremated in the blaze of the funeral pyre, "the commingling fire will mix [their] ashes" into one last embrace. Harsh reality, armed and murderous, breaks into their "pleasure-house" and destroys it. Sardanapalus's desire to construct a personal paradise of type and antitype can never be fulfilled, simply because no island of peace and love can ever be inviolate in a hostile world. As even Shelley writes, in the fictional "Advertisement" of *Epipsychidion,* the ideals of the poet (who is said to have died) were not at all practical: "it was his hope to have realised a scheme of life, suited perhaps to that happier and better world of which he is now an inhabitant, but hardly practicable in this." Sardanapalus comes to realize that his desire to create a "pleasure-house" is not compatible with the realities of the human condition. Both Shelley and Byron shared a longing for a terrestrial paradise, but this longing was coupled with the recognition that such a situation was essentially untenable in the violent, corrupt world in which they lived.

A truly Shelleyan hero, like Prometheus or Laon, would probably abdicate a position of power rather than try to keep it by force and at the cost of human lives. Sardanapalus responds, however, to the rebels who threaten him by rejecting his life as a pacific, indulgent, and pleasure-seeking ruler and becoming another kind of monarch, a Byronic hero whose sanguinary exploits exceed those of the Corsair and the Giaour at their bloodiest. Byron hints at his repressed potential for violence in the first act, when Sardanapalus tells Salemenes that, although he loves peace, if roused he "will turn these realms / To one wide desert chase of brutes" (1.2.374–75). In Assyrian power politics there is no middle ground: if Sardanapalus's subjects will not accept him as a benevolent king of peace, he has no other alternative but to obliterate them. If he is not allowed to be a pacifistic Shelleyan hero, his only other choice is to become a violent Byronic hero. As the rebellion progresses Sardanapalus becomes virtually suicidal, refusing to flee with Zarina and then attacking the enemy prematurely, thus assuring his own defeat (4.1.573–75). The king who is at first so passive that he is willing to die languidly, to "fall like the pluck'd rose" (1.2.605), later becomes a Hercules (3.1.221–22) who longs for a warrior's death.

Sardanapalus's transition from the hedonistic narcissist of the first part of the play—whose aesthetic is based on the sensation of pleasure —to the virile narcissist of the last part of the play—whose aesthetic is based on masculine self-assertion and pain—comes to a psychological climax in his nightmarish vision of act 4. As the wounded king sleeps, Myrrha, his warlike lover, watches "the play of pain" (4.1.10) convulsing his features. Having undergone his baptism in blood, Sardanapalus dreams that his ancestors are welcoming him to a grisly banquet. Nimrod, the "Old hunter of the earliest brutes" (4.1.28) and Semiramis, the "ghastly beldame! / Dripping with dusky gore" (4.1.31–32) sit on his left and right. These beings, so dark and sinister, seem intent on initiating Sardanapalus into the violent fraternity of homicidal monarchs. Much to his disgust, Sardanapalus, the would-be "King of Peace," finds himself drawn to these monsters: "there was a horrid kind / Of sympathy between us, as if they / Had lost a part of death to come to me, / And I the half of life to sit by them" (4.1.124–27). Here Byron may be responding to the powerful image in *Prometheus Unbound* (which he may well have read before composing the fourth act) in which Prometheus gazes at the Furies and grows "like what [he] contemplate[s] / and laugh[s] and stare[s] in loathsome sympathy" (1.450–51).

Byron, like Shelley, recognized the power of evil, the way in which violent attitudes have the power to transform one's personality, to make even a would-be pacifist resemble a creature disfigured by hatred and corruption. While in both *The Cenci* and *Sardanapalus* tyranny is seen as violent and sadistic, in *The Cenci* the sadism is domestically centered and in *Sardanapalus* it operates at the core of public power. As Beatrice Cenci comes to realize the full extent of her father's effect on her in a nightmarish vision before her death (5.4.141–56), Sardanapalus is forced to gauge his decline from a peace-loving, benevolent king to a frenzied warrior in a nightmare which takes place shortly before his own death. In both cases the unconscious asserts what the conscious mind will not admit: that Beatrice and Sardanapalus have more in common with their monstrous forebears than they care to recognize. Even a virtuous daughter or a peace-loving king can become involved in an act of violence. Thus Beatrice feels as if her father were dragging her down, and Sardanapalus dreams that "all the predecessors of [his] line / Rose up . . . to drag [him] down to them" (4.1.175–76).

Like vampires rising from their graves, these ancestors return to torture their descendants, to twine their scions in grotesque embraces which pull them, morally and emotionally, downward. Acting like the "semi-glorious human monster" (1.2.181) she was in life, the phantasm of Semiramis attacks Sardanapalus. In fact, the king tells Myrrha that his grandam tried to rape him:

she flew upon me,
And burnt my lips up with her noisome kisses,
. . . while I shrunk from her, as if,
In lieu of her remote descendant, I
Had been the son who slew her for her incest. (4.1.149–58)

The dream, like Beatrice's vision, is incestuous and violent—Sardanapalus is tempted to emulate Semiramis's son and violently resist the monstrous spirit attacking him. He feels polluted by his forebears: awakening, he senses "a chaos of all loathsome things / Throng'd thick and shapeless" (4.1.159–60). Although he has devoted his life to love and peace and has allowed his subjects to live happily and unmolested, Sardanapalus cannot, any more than Beatrice, escape his heritage, the terrible weight of centuries of crimes and violence borne by every descendant of a corrupt aristocratic family. To Shelley and Byron the act of forcible incest symbolizes the sado-masochistic relationship between old age and youth. And, in the cases of Beatrice and Sardanapalus, the embraces of their unnatural forebears signify that these two protagonists recognize, if only in their unconscious minds, that they may never free themselves from the legacy of blood burdening them.

Thus Sardanapalus's aspirations to do good are foiled by a world which is evil and violent. Unlike Beatrice Cenci, however, Sardanapalus is the ruler of his world; rather than simply being an object of tyranny, he is driven to suicide because he will not be a tyrant. Whereas in *The Cenci* the cosmos is dominated by a god who supports acts of sadism, in *Sardanapalus* the problem comes not from above but beneath. The subjects who hate being ruled by a loving, benevolent king rise up against Sardanapalus because he will not oppress them. According to Byron, "*political* slavery . . . is men's own fault—if they *will* be slaves let them!"[27] As Sardanapalus says: "If then they hate me, 'tis because I hate not; / If they rebel, it is because I oppress not" (1.2.412–13). After the rebellion breaks out Sardanapalus realizes that he has been put in a situation over which he has little control: "Misplaced upon the throne—misplaced in life. / I know not what I could have been, but feel / I am not what I should be" (4.1.332–34). But he can no more accept a life in which would-be tyrants like Beleses and Arbaces rule than Beatrice is able to accept an existence in which she is vulnerable to her father's sadism.

Sardanapalus's transformation into a murderous warrior is not, however, due solely to Myrrha and the rebels, however much they serve to set the scene for his death. There are two facets of Sardanapalus's character which help propel him to his end: his innate aggressiveness, which he is never able to suppress, and his strong feelings of narcissism. These two personality traits combine to accelerate Sardanapalus's metamorphosis into a violent and suicidal Byronic hero. Without excusing violence, any more than Shelley excuses Beatrice's murder of Cenci, Byron seems to assert that every man inherits the curse of Cain, the will to murder. This idea is expressed most cogently by Byron's Marino Faliero; explaining why the rebels must strike soon, the Doge says:

> One stroke struck,
> And the mere instinct of the first-born Cain,
> Which ever lurks somewhere in human hearts
> Though circumstances may keep it in abeyance,
> Will urge the rest on like to wolves. (4.2.55–59)

Sardanapalus's sudden transformation from effeminate reveler to bloodthirsty warrior is not unique in Byron's canon; both Don Juan, whose face is "half-girlish" (*Don Juan,* 1.171), and the "she-king" Sardanapalus are equally adept at the soft life of the harem and the warrior's art of murder and mayhem.[28] Man does not only have the instinct to kill lurking, repressed, somewhere in his personality—he also has the physical potential to kill on a large scale, to wreak carnage at an amazing rate. Even Marino Faliero, a septuagenarian, is ready to go off to war at a moment's notice. Like Beatrice Cenci, an unlikely murderess, many of Byron's characters have a strong potential for violence. Although Sardanapalus may repress his homicidal instincts for a time, the blood of Nimrod runs through his veins and, in a martial world, aggressive tendencies must inevitably assert themselves. In *Sardanapalus* Byron presents these homicidal instincts in nightmarish fashion, in the form of a "ghastly beldame dripping with dusky gore," and his negative presentation of this propensity to murder seems to reflect Shelley's almost visceral loathing of violence.

*   *   *

Since Byron read *The Cenci* before he wrote *Sardanapalus,* it is possible that he may have noticed a similarity between Sardanapalus's method of suicide and Cenci's plans for self-destruction. After Lucretia tells Cenci that a voice from heaven has said that he must die, Cenci responds as follows:

> I will pile up my silver and my gold
> My costly robes, paintings and tapestries;
> My parchments and all my records of my wealth,
> And make a bonfire in my joy, and leave
> Of my possessions nothing but my name;
> Which shall be an inheritance to strip
> Its wearer as bare as infamy. (4.1.56–62)

This kind of suicide, which reaches out and destroys all of the victim's possessions, including, in Sardanapalus's case, a slave girl, is perhaps the most emphatically negative act that a man can commit. Such a self-destructive holocaust constitutes a small apocalypse, the incineration of not only the person committing suicide but also of all material evidence of that person's existence: it is a death meant not only to destroy oneself but to disinherit one's children or dispossess one's enemies. That Shelley attributed the desire for this kind of end to a deranged domestic tyrant, and Byron chooses to present, sympathetically, a king who planned the same method of suicide, suggests different attitudes toward suicide and defiant self-assertion. But even in Sardanapalus's case his suicide represents a sad falling off from his earlier dreams of a peaceful and joyous reign. It would be difficult, certainly, for Byron to argue that Cenci's preferred mode of self-destruction is a thing to be desired. While in 1816 Byron could argue that Prometheus makes "Death a Victory" ("Prometheus," 59), in 1821 he presents Sardanapalus's death as, in some ways, an admission of defeat, a warning to others to "avoid the life / Which led to such a consummation" (5.1.448–49). He had, I think, learned from Shelley the emptiness of violent self-immolation.

It is clear, however, that Sardanapalus has much more in common with Beatrice than he does with her psychopathic father. Although Sardanapalus seems superficially different from Beatrice simply because he is a king, whereas she is her father's dependent chattel, their situations are less far apart than one might think. Sardanapalus finds himself required to "make a prison of [his] palace" (1.2.636); "coop'd" and "captive," he cannot "even breathe / The breath of heaven" (1.2.573–75). Like Beatrice, who is virtually a prisoner in her father's palace and then in his castle, Sardanapalus finds himself surrounded by hostile forces, people who hate him—as Cenci hates Beatrice—for his virtues rather than his vices. Sardanapalus and Beatrice are young people struggling against the oppressive legacy of their ancestors; Cenci's incestuous attack and Semiramis's repulsive embrace symbolize, in graphic terms, the loathsome power that evil old age and the old regime still have over the Italian girl and the Assyrian king. As post-Waterloo liberals, both Byron and Shelley were disgusted at the restoration of the ancien régime, the renewed embrace of the old order, and to an extent *Sardanapalus* and *The Cenci* reflect this political frustration.[29] As the Fury of *Prometheus Unbound* says, "The good want power, but to weep barren tears. / The powerful goodness want: worse need for them" (1.625–26).

In order to achieve liberty, Sardanapalus and Beatrice feel compelled to commit acts of violence. For them, freedom can only be won at the cost of their lives: a beheading and a self-consuming inferno end their short but traumatic existences. Sardanapalus's tragedy is not simply that of a Romantic victim who dies in an unjust universe: it is also a tragedy of personal corruption, the transformation of a man from an idealist struggling against tyranny into a sanguinary warlord who forsakes nearly all of his earlier principles. Like Beatrice, Sardanapalus rejects a murderous forebear only to end up as murderous as his ancestor. He also resembles the Maniac of *Julian and Maddalo,* who first cherishes melioristic hopes and then comes to wish for death. Sardanapalus begins with an affirmation of peace, love, and happiness, and then turns from his orgy of pleasure to an orgy of pain, in which death, either for his enemies or himself, is his only goal. Although he is the titular ruler of a vast realm, he becomes the slave of a slave: Myrrha drives him to his fate, overmastering his idealism with her pragmatic notions of kingship. Sardanapalus's failure to transcend the evil cosmos he lives in limits his imagination and makes him a victim in Myrrha's dark arena of violent self-assertion. In the world of power politics even the best mind cannot "make / Good out of evil" (4.1.320–21), but good deeds always "Turn poison in bad minds" (4.1.320).

Byron and Shelley recognize in *Sardanapalus* and *The Cenci* the fact of human weakness, man's general inability to act positively and effectively against the evil of the old regime. Sardanapalus and Beatrice are not simply ordinary people; they are presented as extraordinary figures, capable of greatness. But they are no matches for the evil beings who haunt them like omnipresent nightmares, and thus "all best things are . . . confused to ill" (*Prometheus Unbound,* 1.628). This does not mean, however, that Shelley and Byron were fatalists. Shelley, when he wrote *The Cenci* and *Prometheus Unbound,* was not prepared to accept human weakness, and neither was Byron, who believed enough in political activism to join in the Greek revolution in 1823. In the end Sardanapalus and Beatrice fail, but they serve, nonetheless, as object lessons for others who might not fail. Thus Sardanapalus pledges to create "a light / To lesson ages" (5.1.440–41) with his funeral pyre, and Beatrice begs Bernardo not to err "in harsh despair, / But tears and patience" (5.4.144–45). They both point toward other Promethean figures who will be stronger than they, who will transform fallen reality rather than being transformed by it. While it is true that Byron and Shelley recognized the problem of human weakness in a corrupt and corrupting world, they also recognized the possibility of change, and the importance of remaining true to one's revolutionary principles.

SIX

The Diabolical Discourse
of Shelley and Byron

Shelley's praise of Byron's *Cain* was immediate and enthusiastic. In a
12 January 1822 letter to John Gisborne, he asked: "What think you of
Lord Byron now? Space wondered less at the swift and fair creations
of God, when he grew weary of vacancy, than I at the late works of
this spirit of an angel in the mortal paradise of a decaying body."[1] Elsewhere, Shelley used such terms as "apocalyptic" and "revelation" to
describe Byron's mystery play.[2] Part of Shelley's enthusiasm for *Cain*
could be explained by the fact that *Cain* treated themes he himself had
explored in *Queen Mab, Prometheus Unbound,* and *On the Devil, and Devils.*
And Byron's use of Lucifer in *Cain* would also have intrigued Shelley,
who, like Byron, enjoyed speculating about the nature and character of
the archfiend. It seems likely, moreover, that *Cain* was at least partly
inspired by the poets' discussions of metaphysical and religious questions during their meetings in Switzerland and Italy. What might be
called Byron's and Shelley's diabolical discourse began when Shelley
sent Byron a copy of his highly controversial *Queen Mab* (possibly in
1813)[3] and did not end until the last year of Shelley's life, when both
Byron (in *The Deformed Transformed*) and Shelley (in his translation
of scenes from *Faust*) found themselves responding imaginatively to
Goethe's Mephistopheles.

   Thomas Medwin was among the first to see the parallels between
Shelley's visionary *Queen Mab* and *Cain,* particularly in Shelley's and

Byron's descriptions of the vastness of space.[4] In *Queen Mab* Shelley writes:

> Earth's distant orb appeared
> The smallest light that twinkles in the heaven;
> Whilst round the chariot's way
> Innumerable systems rolled,
> And countless spheres diffused
> An ever-varying glory.
> It was a sight of wonder. (1.250–56)

Byron has Cain describe a similar view:

> CAIN.   As we move
> Like sunbeams onward, [the earth] grows small and smaller,
> And as it waxes little, and then less,
> Gathers a halo round it, like the light
> Which shone the roundest of the stars, when I
> Beheld them from the skirts of Paradise:
> Methinks they both, as we recede from them,
> Appear to join the innumerable stars
> Which are around us; and, as we move on,
> Increase their myriads. (2.1.34–43)

But while *Cain* and *Queen Mab* both deal with space travel, the results of the journeys in these works are radically different. Ianthe learns from her interstellar flight with Queen Mab that "when the power of imparting joy / Is equal to the will, the human soul / Requires no other Heaven" (3.11–12). In contrast, Lucifer teaches Cain that "the human sum / Of knowledge [should be] to know mortal nature's nothingness" (2.2.421–22) and leads Cain to despair. Behind both works is an interest in the discoveries of nineteenth-century science, particularly in astronomy, but while Shelley's perception of scientific knowledge and voyages through space is positive, Byron is more wary: rather than being uplifted, Cain is cast down by his vision of the cosmos. In Byron's words, by showing Cain "infinite things," Lucifer suggests Cain's comparative "abasement."[5] Knowledge, in *Cain,* is dangerous; what Cain learns in act 2 leads to the tragic violence of act 3.

It is clear, then, that Byron, while willing to borrow the idea of space travel from Shelley's *Queen Mab,* uses this device to draw different conclusions. Shelley's utopian belief that "A garden shall arise, in loveliness / Surpassing fabled Eden" (*Queen Mab,* 4.88–89) contrasts radically with Byron's vision in *Cain* of a universe in which everything progressively degenerates (2.2.67–74). But before too much emphasis is put on this difference in the poets' visions, it is important to remember that *Queen Mab* was published in 1813, *Cain* in 1821: the mature Byron, in effect, is arguing with a very young Shelley. It also should be noted that *Queen Mab* was both pirated and reissued in 1821, and that it was raising considerable interest in England at about the time Byron was composing *Cain.*[6]

In *Prometheus Unbound* Shelley refined the utopianism of *Queen Mab:* Prometheus, unlike Ianthe, pays a very high price for his wisdom. Moreover, *Prometheus Unbound* confronts the problems of man's self-defeating urge to hate and denounce the God of this world, the urge which leads Prometheus to enshrine and then curse Jupiter, and which inspires Cain to strike out in frustration and kill his brother. Byron's reservations about the meliorism presented in *Queen Mab* do not seem to extend to Shelley's *Prometheus Unbound,* published seven years later: as I noted in the previous chapter, Byron was reported to have been "loud in his praise of 'Prometheus.'" While *Cain* differs from *Prometheus Unbound* in many respects, a comparison of the two works is enlightening, and serves to show how Shelley and Byron continued the conversation begun in Venice on "God, freewill and destiny; / Of all that earth has been or yet may be / All that vain men imagine or believe, / Or hope can pain or suffering may atchieve" (*Julian and Maddalo,* 42–45).

As I noted in chapter 4, the determination of Byron and Shelley to write poems about Prometheus probably dated from the summer of 1816. Writing to John Murray on 12 October 1817, Byron claimed that Aeschylus's *Prometheus Bound* was an important influence on much of his poetry: "The Prometheus—if not exactly in my plan—has always been so much in my head—that I can easily conceive its influence over all or anything that I have written."[7] Byron composed his "Prometheus" in 1816, without the benefit of having read Shelley's *Prometheus Unbound* (1819), and he tended to think of Prometheus bound rather than unbound, defiant rather than pitying, a static "symbol" and "sign" ("Prometheus," 45) rather than a being capable of change. Byron's Prometheus has a certain moral authority, strong enough to make Jove's lightnings tremble (34), but it is not clear that his rebellion will ever accomplish anything. Similarly, Manfred's "Promethean spark" (*Manfred*, 1.1.154) is never used to threaten Arimanes' dark reign; Manfred's goal proves, in fact, to be self-destruction. In *The Prophecy of Dante* Byron writes that even when a poet seeks to become a "new Prometheus of new men, / Bestowing fire from heaven" (4.14–15), this gift will be repaid with pain, and there is no indication that any other outcome is possible. Cain is yet another potential Prometheus, an aspirer to better things for himself and mankind, a would-be rebel against divine authority, and a protester against death. But Byron presents him differently from his other Promethean figures: *Cain* is a portrait of a metaphysical rebel who becomes an ironic rather than heroic figure. Wolf Hirst describes the irony of Cain's act of violence succinctly: "The irony of Cain's surrender to fury, to irrationality, after vainly pleading with his brother for reason, is enhanced by the circumstance that Cain's murderous frame of mind was caused by Lucifer, the advocate of reason."[8] While Byron's other Promethean figures rely on their moral superiority to their tormentors to make them heroic, if bound, personages, Cain finds himself on the defensive, a criminal who can no longer judge his creator without seeming hypocritical. The simple conflict between the righteous rebel and the tyrannical and unjust God becomes in *Cain* a complex confrontation between a man who has condemned and then caused death and a Jehovah who is invisible and therefore inscrutable.

One looks in vain through Byron's works for the kind of positive apocalypse that is found in Shelley's *Prometheus Unbound*, in which the universe is revitalized and changed for the better. In fact, Byron's apocalyptic view, as presented in "Darkness" and in Lucifer's speeches to Cain, has to do with a constant loss of energy, a kind of entropy which makes each race of intelligent beings less vital and noble than the race before. The successive falls mount up: the superior race of pre-Adamites are annihilated and replaced by the less intelligent Adam and Eve, who fall from paradise; their son, Cain, is banished from Eden and, in Byron's *Heaven and Earth,* his offspring the Cainites are annihilated by the flood. This is not, as Byron suggests in his preface to *Cain,* simply a "poetical fiction" to help Lucifer make his case: the notion that the history of the universe is marked by a constant downward spiral is an integral part of the myth he presents in *Cain* and elsewhere. It is a situation that man can deplore but not reverse. While Adam's fatalism seems abject, Cain's rebellion is clearly counterproductive, and neither attitude will lead to paradise regained. In *Cain,* of course, Byron was to some extent bound by the text of Genesis. But it remains signifi-cant, I think, that Byron chose this biblical context for an exploration of Prometheanism or, in other words, that he chose a context in which Promethean aspirations cannot be realized without violating the integ-rity of the original text. Shelley's vision of Prometheus unchained and the world renewed seems to have no place in Byron's poetry.

It would be incorrect to say, however, that Byron's and Shelley's metaphysical outlooks have nothing in common. One should not forget that Shelley's apocalypse is not final, and that future falls are possible even after the apocalypse of *Prometheus Unbound.* Demogorgon's speech at the end of the lyrical drama is revealing:

> if, with infirm hand, Eternity
> Mother of many acts and hours, should free
>   The serpent that would clasp her with his length—
> These are the spells by which to reassume
> An empire o'er the disentangled doom. (4.565–69)

Shelley's "serpent" does not disappear after Prometheus's triumph, and there is a possibility that "Eternity" will become "infirm," that en-tropy will affect Shelley's cosmic myth as well as Byron's. Moreover, both poets show that violence is a misguided response to injustice and tyranny, whether divine or temporal. To Shelley, violence makes the rebel morally equivalent to the tyrant, and Prometheus's hatred must give way to pity before he can end Jupiter's evil reign. Byron, on the other hand, shows that violence, directed against a god like Jehovah, tends to miss its target (the creator-tyrant) and hit an innocent by-stander (Abel) instead. And in *Cain,* as in *Prometheus Unbound,* love is presented as a viable alternative to the barren and self-destructive man-versus-God scenario. Prometheus recognizes the importance of Asia's love—"Most vain all hope but love" (1.808)—and Asia becomes a vital part of his unchaining and the renewal of the universe. But while Prometheus realizes the necessity of love, Cain tends to view Adah as basically irrelevant to his goals and aspirations, and leaves her to be with the skeptical Lucifer, a being devoid of love. This is a crucial mistake: apart from Adah, Cain despairs and ultimately turns to violence. In these works love constitutes man's only hope for salvation. Separated from Asia, Prometheus remains bound and tortured; while away from Adah, Cain becomes bitter and potentially murderous. Although *Cain* does not explore the possibility of a redeeming apocalypse, it, like *Prometheus Unbound,* shows the error of a rebellion based on hatred and the necessity of love as a counterbalance to man's tendency toward despair when he is faced with human suffering and divine injustice.

Another resemblance between *Cain* and *Prometheus Unbound* has to do with the psychological nature of the metaphysical rebellions that Byron and Shelley are describing. Lucifer, Cain says, speaks to him "of things which long have swum / In visions through" (1.1.167–68) his own mind, and Adah is quick to warn Cain of demons who tempt man with his "own / Dissatisfied and curious thoughts" (1.1.402–3). Jehovah can be seen as a projection of Cain's pessimistic speculations, merely articulated by Lucifer, much as Jupiter can be interpreted as a vision of tyranny and injustice created by Prometheus. And if both Cain and Prometheus create out of their own minds the problems which beset them, then they, not simply some exterior beings such as Jehovah and Jupiter, are to blame for their sufferings. Cain's banishment to the land east of Eden and Prometheus's binding are caused by failures of the imagination: Cain's failure to understand the true nature of death, which he ends up causing, and Prometheus's foolish decision to enthrone Jupiter. The fallen nature of reality is not caused solely by "something out there" but by the erring minds of men.

Moreover, both Cain and Prometheus have antitypes, Adah and Asia, female reflections of themselves. Adah, of course, is Cain's twin sister and wife, and Asia is presented as a "golden chalice" into which part of Prometheus's "being overflowed" (1.809–10). As James Rieger notes, the reverse of incest (self-love) is fratricide (self-hatred): "The mirror connects incest with fratricide in the . . . sense that both are born out of self-love. Narcissus presses his lips to the looking-glass; Cain smashes it with a rock."[9] While Prometheus is able to disarm his negative mental imagery with the self-love personified by Asia, Cain allows his nihilistic vision to create in him the violent self-hatred symbolized by his murder of his brother. Shelley and Byron use their closet dramas to explore the psychological ramifications of the Prometheus and Cain myths. Cain's view of a Jehovah who creates only to destroy is never actually verified by anyone other than Lucifer, who can only be seen as an unreliable source, and may well tell us more about Cain's perspective on reality than about the universe or its creator. Perhaps Cain makes his own universe in a negative way, as Prometheus positively re-creates his world.

Like Shelley's Prometheus, Cain has some of the attributes of a poet, but he is clearly a fallen poet, his vision corrupted by his rage and despair.[10] Of course, Byron's vision of Cain as a poet predates his reading of *Prometheus Unbound*—in a letter to James Hogg written in 1814 Byron speculates on Cain's status as a poet: "Milton's Paradise Lost is, as a whole, a heavy concern; but the two first books of it are the very finest poetry that has ever been produced in this world—at least since the flood—for I make little doubt that Abel was a fine pastoral poet, and Cain a fine bloody poet, and so forth; . . . Poetry must always exist, like drink, where there is a demand for it. And Cain's may have been the brandy of the antediluvian, and Abel's the small [?] still."[11] The Old Testament notes that among Cain's descendants are Jubal, the first man to play the harp and organ, and Tubal-Cain, the first artificer in brass and iron (Genesis 4:21, 22).[12] In *Paradise Lost* Michael warns Adam of Cain's descendants, artisans and inventors who spurn God:

> Those Tents thou sawst so pleasant, were the Tents
> Of wickedness, wherein shall dwell his Race
> Who slew his Brother; studious they appear
> Of Arts that polish life, Inventors rare,
> Unmindful of their Maker, though his Spirit
> Taught them, but they his gifts acknowledg'd none. (3.607–12)

The aspiring, inquisitive Cain is the predecessor of those artists who seek to supplant the Creator by becoming creators in their own right. He is an exemplar of the self-destructive side of the poetic temperament, as represented by such figures as Manfred and the self-defeated Rousseau of *The Triumph of Life*. Every Promethean poet has the power to create or destroy, and the tragedy of *Cain* is that the protagonist tries to change the world in a positive way, but only succeeds in committing the first murder.[13] Like a rebel artist who rejects traditional religious beliefs in order to create his own worldview, Cain turns his back on his father's religious orthodoxy and tries to define the nature of the universe for himself. But Cain's perspective is affected by "the corrupting blight of tyranny"[14] that Shelley claimed made Tasso a lesser poet than Dante. In the universe in which he finds himself, Cain can only perceive Infernos. Cain is similar to the type of poet described in Grimm's *Correspondance,* quoted by Byron in his letters: "a poet, or . . . a man of genius in any department, . . . must have 'une ame qui se tourmente, un esprit violent'."[15] According to this description, continues Byron, he himself would be a poet "per excellenza," since he possesses a self-torturing soul and a violent spirit. Like many of the Romantic poets, Cain is more interested in the rebellious Lucifer, with his Satanic pride and resolute heroism, than in the tyrannical Jehovah, who inspires simple-minded devotion from Adam and Abel. He also has a powerful imagination capable of transcending everything Lucifer shows him in their tour through the universe. Cain tells Lucifer: "thou show'st me things beyond *my* power, / Beyond all power of my born faculties, / Although inferior still to my desires / And my conceptions" (2.1.80–83). Even before Lucifer describes his vision of the universe, Cain has imagined it (1.167–68). In fact, Cain's imagination is Napoléonic in its ambition; he is tortured by "Thoughts which arise within [him], as if they / Could master all things" (1.177–78). Despite the universal scope of his imaginative vision, Cain is capable of extemporizing a paean to Adah, in which he says that she is superior to "the bird's voice— / The vesper bird's, which seems to sing of love" (2.2.263–64). Cain is a fancier of "the lights above us, in the azure, / Which are so beautiful" (1.280–81) and looks to the stars for beauty as he aspires to greater things than a farmer's lot. Cain has the temperament of a poet who wants the world to match his imaginative conceptions—without that, he deems life not worth living.

As Byron noted in a letter to John Murray, Cain goes into a rage inspired by "the inadequacy of his state to his Conceptions," which expresses itself in violence directed against "the author of Life" rather than against the actual victim, Abel.[16] The injustice that most outrages Cain is that he cannot re-create the world to match his own "conceptions." Shelley's Prometheus, who is responsible for Jupiter's oppressive rule, succeeds in transforming his vision of reality, in eventually presiding over a creation which does, in fact, fulfill his aesthetic requirements. Cain cannot, however, overcome his vision of a Jehovah-dominated world, and therefore his poetic idealism becomes a chimera that haunts him, that reduces him to rage against the more prolific, if less imaginative, creative power of "the author of Life."

In his ultimate frustration, and violent reaction to what he perceives as an unjust universe, Cain has far more resemblance to Beatrice Cenci than he does to Shelley's Prometheus. We know that Byron had read *The Cenci* at least by 10 September 1820,[17] so it is possible that Shelley's tragic heroine influenced his conception of Cain. Alan Richardson has drawn some useful parallels between *The Cenci* and *Cain*. For example, Beatrice and Cain are at first "young, morally integral, idealistic, but critically lacking in self-awareness,"[18] but they are soon affected by older, sophisticated beings who tempt them to commit acts of violence. The result of the influence that Cenci and Lucifer have on the young protagonists is a loss of innocence and a growing self-consciousness: this self-consciousness, Richardson notes, "pays for its emergence with a loss of integrity,"[19] and both Beatrice and Cain commit crimes which violate the ideals they once held sacred. The journey to self-consciousness in *The Cenci* and *Cain* is symbolized by crossing an abyss.[20] In Beatrice's case the abyss is found at the spot where she plans to have Cenci ambushed:

> there is a mighty rock,
> Which has, from unimaginable years,
> Sustained itself with terror and with toil
> Over a gulph, and with the agony
> With which it clings seems slowly coming down;
> Even as a wretched soul hour after hour,
> Clings to the mass of life; yet clinging, leans;
> And leaning, makes more dark the dread abyss
> In which it fears to fall. (3.1.247–55)

The disorienting image of the abyss is also used in *Cain*, in which Lucifer conveys Cain across "The Abyss of Space,"[21] taking him on a voyage which is both liberating and completely alienating. In *The Cenci* and *Cain* Shelley and Byron explore the problems confronting Romantic idealists, the disillusionment, pain, and injustice that can lead beings like Beatrice and Cain to act exactly like those they most detest, as Beatrice reacts to Cenci's violence against his children by conspiring to assassinate him, and Cain protests against the Jehovah who dooms man to death by committing murder.

* * *

Byron's presentation of Lucifer, the other metaphysical rebel in *Cain,* may owe a great deal to Shelley's influence. Both poets had a half-whimsical interest in the devil and delighted in attributing demonic qualities to each other. In *Julian and Maddalo* Shelley compares the discourse between himself and Byron to the discussions that "The devils held within the dales of Hell" (41), and Byron, inspired by a quotation from Goethe's *Faust,* nicknamed Shelley "the Snake."[22] In his account of the Shelley circle in Pisa, Trelawny relates the story of Byron nicknaming Shelley "the Snake" and adds: "Byron was the real snake—a dangerous mischiefmaker."[23] Coincidentally, both Shelley and Byron were inspired as young men to imitate a satire written by Coleridge and Robert Southey entitled "The Devil's Thoughts" (1799).[24] Shelley composed "The Devil's Walk: A Ballad" in 1812, and Byron, in the same year, wrote "The Devil's Drive." Both poems use the idea of the devil visiting England as a vehicle for radical social and political satire. Byron's interest in portraying the devil went, of course, far beyond this relatively juvenile effort: the coldly intellectual Lucifer of *Cain,* the haughty, aristocratic Satan of *The Vision of Judgment,* and the Mephistophelian Stranger/Caesar of *The Deformed Transformed* all serve to illustrate his continuing fascination with the archfiend. Shelley presented diabolical beings in his Byronic *Peter Bell the Third,* in the fragmentary prologue to *Hellas* (heavily indebted to Goethe's prologue to *Faust*), and in his humorous essay *On the Devil, and Devils,* as well as in other works. In his translation of scenes from Goethe's *Faust,* Shelley depicted Mephistopheles brilliantly, and one can certainly see his Cenci as a type of Satan. Although often tongue in cheek, the poets' common interest in demonology is reflected in many of their works, and may well have helped shape Byron's Lucifer.

Both Shelley and Byron parted company with Milton in their refusal to identify the devil with the serpent who tempted Adam and Eve. As Shelley writes in his essay *On the Devil, and Devils,* the transformation of the serpent of Genesis into the devil of Christian mythology is a willful misreading of the Bible: "The Christians have turned this Serpent into their Devil, and accommodated the whole story to their new scheme of sin and propitiation."[25] Byron's Lucifer takes pains to disabuse Cain of any notion that he might be implicated in the serpent's crime: "I tell thee that the serpent was no more / Than a mere serpent / . . . Thy / Fond parents listen'd to a creeping thing, / And fell" (1.231–42). In removing the devil from the story of man's fall, Shelley and Byron remain consistent with the actual text of Genesis, and suggest that man himself, not a demon, is to blame for his expulsion from the Garden of Eden. The fact that Byron's Lucifer did not lead Adam and Eve into temptation allows him to approach Cain with a certain degree of self-righteousness; it also makes original sin a part of God's creation, not something imported into Eden by an evil demon, since the tempter is a serpent created by God, and Adam and Eve are God's creations as well. In *On the Devil, and Devils* Shelley challenges the reader to rethink the notion of a God who is both omnipotent and benevolent by questioning the idea that the devil can be blamed for all evil. Shelley writes that Christians "have tortured themselves ever to devise any flattering sophism, by which they might appease [God] . . . , endeavoring to reconcile omnipotence, and benevolence, and equity, in the Author of an Universe where evil and good are inextricably intangled and where the most admirable tendencies to happiness and preservation are for ever baffled by misery and decay. The Christians, therefore, invented or adopted the Devil to extricate them from this difficulty."[26] Similarly, Byron's Lucifer tells Cain not to use him as a scapegoat for the evil that God the creator has made:

> if he gives you good—so call him; if
> Evil springs from *him,* do not name it *mine,*
> Till ye know better its true fount; and judge
> Not by words, though of spirits, but the fruits
> Of your existence, such as it must be.
> *One good* gift has the fatal apple given—
> Your *reason:*—let it not be over-sway'd[.] (2.2.454–60)

But although Shelley's heterodox opinions probably influenced the speeches of Byron's Lucifer, it would be difficult to separate Shelley's heresies from Byron's. In Shelley's *Julian and Maddalo* both Julian and Maddalo delight in diabolical conversations, and one gathers that Shelley and Byron encouraged one another to make speculations which would be considered heretical by many of their contemporaries. And although they pursued these speculations with some interest, they did not take the concept of hell entirely seriously. For example, Byron professes to doubt the existence of eternal punishment in *The Vision of Judgment*, even though "one may be damn'd / For hoping no one else may e'er be so" (106–7), and, in a letter dated 10 April 1822, Shelley disputed the idea that "after sixty years of suffering . . . we [are] to be roasted alive for sixty million more in Hell."[27] Both poets seem, then, to have suspected that hell and the devil were superstitions, fictions which were created to make evil a place and an entity separate from heaven and God.

Besides Shelley's and Byron's conversations about the devil, the portrait of Ahasuerus in *Queen Mab* may also have had an influence on Byron's portrayal of Lucifer. Shelley's Ahasuerus, after being cursed by Christ, begins his wanderings in the spirit of defiance:

> But my soul,
> From sight and sense of the polluting woe
> Of tyranny, had long learned to prefer
> Hell's freedom to the servitude of heaven.
> Therefore I rose, and dauntlessly began
> My lonely and unending pilgrimage,
> Resolved to wage unweariable war
> With my almighty tyrant, and to hurl
> Defiance at his impotence to harm
> Beyond the curse I bore. (7.192–201)

Byron's Lucifer expresses similar sentiments when he describes his "unweariable war" with Jehovah:

> I have a victor—true; but no superior.
> Homage he has from all—but none from me:
> I battle it against him, as I battled
> In highest heaven. Through all eternity,

And the unfathomable gulfs of Hades,
And the interminable realms of space,
And the infinity of endless ages,
All, all, will I dispute! (2.2.429–36)

These immortal beings seem to exist solely to oppose the divine rulers of creation in a war that seems both endless and futile, and Shelley's and Byron's portraits of these two metaphysical rebels underline the uselessness as well as the admirable tenacity of Ahasuerus's and Lucifer's defiance of heaven.

Whatever sympathy we may have for the rebels' viewpoints, they do not present perspectives on reality that are helpful to either Ianthe or Cain. The Fairy waves her wand and Ahasuerus disappears as a "phantasmal portraiture / Of wandering human thought" (7.274–75), a desolate dream which is replaced by a vision of a much brighter future. Likewise, Lucifer's worldview is negative and counterproductive: it leads to Cain's frustration and his murder of Abel, a murder which makes Cain recognize that he has been influenced by "a dreary dream" (3.378). While Jehovah may be a tyrant, and while Christianity itself may have serious flaws, eternal hatred of the reigning divinities is not seen as a viable stance in either *Queen Mab* or *Cain*. Ianthe can escape Cain's bitterness because she, unlike Cain, can look toward the future with hope. While both Shelley and Byron are capable of presenting divine injustice and human suffering in a very pessimistic way, Shelley's futurism gives *Queen Mab* and *Prometheus Unbound* positive conclusions, whereas Byron's *Cain* ends in virtual despair. Although Lucifer may have many admirable qualities, his relentless skepticism leads Cain to an act which is as irrevocable as it is tragic.

As they developed their revisionist views of the devil, Shelley and Byron tried to determine the nature of his powers. New astronomical studies shaped their speculations, and, as a result, their devil became something of an astronaut. In *On the Devil, and Devils* Shelley considers the problem of a devil who has the job of doing evil in innumerable worlds: "It is discovered that the earth is a comparatively small globe, in a system consisting of a multitude of others, which roll round the Sun; and there is no reason to suppose but that all these are inhabited by organized and intelligent beings. . . . There is little reason to suppose that any considerable multitude of the planets were tenanted by beings better capable of resisting the temptations of the Devil than ours. But is the Devil, like God, omnipresent? If so he interpenetrates God, and they both exist together."[28] Similarly, Byron's Lucifer professes himself ready to struggle against Jehovah throughout the vast universe, over which they *both* reign (2.2.392). The earth becomes a tiny part of a war that stretches across infinity and eternity, and man, who imagines himself the center of the struggle between good and evil, begins to seem almost insignificant. Thus the devil attains God's power of omnipresence, becoming, in this respect, God's equal. Byron and Shelley suggest that the recent discoveries by astronomers further bring into question the orthodox views of the devil.

The speculation that God and the devil work in a sort of partnership, God creating man to be burned by the devil in hellfire, is explored in both Shelley's essay *On the Devil, and Devils* and Byron's *Vision of Judgment,* as well as in *Cain.* In Shelley's words, "These two considerable personages are supposed to have entered into a sort of partnership, in which the weaker has consented to bear all the odium of their common actions."[29] Satan and the archangel Michael are seen as friends with "political" differences in *The Vision of Judgment* (stanza 62), in which God's minions and the devil cooperate in trying to decide the fate of George III. In *Cain* the Manichean Lucifer makes his relationship with God mysterious and chastises Cain for wishing to know "the great double Mysteries . . . the *two Principles*" (2.2.404), but he does agree that they reign together (2.2.392). That there is, in fact, an understanding between Jehovah and Lucifer is indicated by what happens to Cain: Lucifer puts the would-be rebel in the state of mind that leads him to kill Abel, and Jehovah promptly sends down his angel to pronounce sentence on the first murderer. In order to further antagonize Cain, moreover, Jehovah spurns his sacrifice. The kind of partnership described in Shelley's *On the Devil, and Devils,* in which the devil leads man astray so God can condemn him, also seems present in *Cain.*

Thus Shelley's views of the devil and Byron's presentation of Lucifer reveal the poets' desire to subvert and even poke fun at the orthodox Christian belief in the archfiend. Both Shelley and Byron were inspired by Milton's Satan, but neither poet was blinded by Satan's heroic stature. As Shelley wrote, Satan has the "taints of ambition, envy, revenge, and a desire for personal aggrandisement" (preface to *Prometheus Un-bound*), and Byron's Lucifer, who professes himself unable to love, has similar flaws. According to Richardson, "Lucifer belongs to the tradition of demonic seducers exemplified by Satan, Iago, and the Witches of *Macbeth*."[30] But, nevertheless, in refusing to accept blame for man's fall and arguing against the idea of an omnipotent and benevolent Jehovah, Lucifer expresses many of the poets' irreverent notions. In an 11 April 1822 letter to Horace Smith, Shelley wrote that if he had any influence on Byron, he would certainly "employ it to eradicate from his great mind the delusions of Christianity, which in spite of his reason, seem perpetually to recur, & to lay in ambush for the hours of sickness & distress."[31] While he did not succeed in banishing all of Byron's Christian beliefs, he did seem to have an effect on Byron's conception of the devil. But whereas Shelley simply mocks popular notions of the devil in his *On the Devil, and Devils*, in *Cain* Lucifer is taken more seriously: his nihilism, his belief in man's nothingness, leads Cain to violence and misery.

In some ways *On the Devil, and Devils* has more in common with Byron's *The Vision of Judgment* than it does with *Cain*, although both *The Vision of Judgment* and *Cain* were written during the latter half of 1821. Like Shelley's *On the Devil, and Devils*, *The Vision of Judgment* is deflationary rather than tragic in its implications, seeking to question traditional Christian beliefs through irony and humor. On the other hand, Lucifer is one of the intellectual cherubs, not simply a common devil pandering to man's base appetites, or a restrained, gentlemanly personage like the urbane Satan of *The Vision of Judgment*. As such, he presents more of a threat to the poetic, aspiring Cain than would a demon who, in Byron's words, promised Cain "kingdoms, etc."[32] Although his discussions with Shelley probably influenced Byron's idea of the devil, in *Cain* he takes his conception of the archfiend one step further, presenting a demoniacal intelligence capable of perverting the Promethean aspirations of a would-be metaphysical rebel. In part, Lucifer leads Cain to despair by showing him the "high, / Intelligent, good, great, and glorious" (2.2.66–67) beings of the past, who were destroyed; Lucifer suggests that these noble victims demonstrate the destructive nature of Jehovah and the ultimate futility of man's aspirations. Significantly, in his "Prologue to *Hellas*" (written in October 1821) Shelley seems to realize the potency of this kind of argument, and puts it in the mouth of his Satan, who points to the ruin of Greece and uses the fact of Greece's fall from its golden age to argue against the possibility of its return to greatness. Christ responds to Satan by dismissing this vision, which "seest but the Past in the To-come" (Prologue to *Hellas*, 161).[33] In Shelley's view the future is not condemned to repeat the past, and later descendants of Adam and Eve may still succeed in re-creating their world. But, while Shelley's and Byron's outlooks for the future differed, they seemed to agree that the real threat to modern man comes not from a devil with horns and a forked tail but from the nihilistic despair a limited rationalism such as Lucifer's can inspire.

It is significant that in Shelley's last year both he and Byron wrote fragments which were influenced by Goethe's characterization of Mephistopheles in *Faust*: Shelley composed a relatively free translation of scenes from *Faust* in the spring of 1822, and the Stranger/ Caesar figure of Byron's *The Deformed Transformed* (written in early 1822) is clearly Mephistophelian.[34] In the next chapter I will discuss how Shelley's translation of *Faust* altered the original German to transform Mephistopheles into "a gentleman of fashion."[35] The Stranger of *The Deformed Transformed* also has a gentlemanly, even snobbish quality:

> ARNOLD.   I said not
>   You *were* the Demon, but that your approach
>   Was like one.
> STRANGER.   Unless you keep company
>   With him (and you seem scarce used to such high
>   Society) you can't tell how he approaches;
>   And for his aspect, look upon the fountain,
>   And then on me, and judge which of us twain
>   Look likest what the boors believe to be
>   Their cloven-footed terror. (1.1.94–102)

Thus the poets' interest in the figure of the devil, manifested in their 1812 imitations of Coleridge's and Southey's "The Devil's Thoughts," continued to the end of their relationship, when Shelley's and Byron's fascination with Goethe's Mephistopheles led to their writing two intriguing, if fragmentary, works. Unfortunately, their *Julian and Maddalo*–style conversation on "God, freewill and destiny" was interrupted by Shelley's death, which was soon followed by Byron's—we will never know how or if it would have continued. But there can be little doubt that Byron's and Shelley's diabolical discourse helped inspire some of their most important works.

SEVEN

Byron, Goethe, and
The Triumph of Life

The Triumph of Life is a fragment and, as such, presents special problems for critics. Although in its unfinished state the poem seems to present a pessimistic view of life, it is certainly possible that, had Shelley lived to complete the work, he would have given it an optimistic ending or have rewritten it entirely. As G. M. Matthews writes, "it might [also] be true that the unwritten conclusion of the poem would have followed Dante in balancing the *Inferno* with a *Paradiso,* or that several successive 'Triumphs' were planned, on the model of Petrarch's six *Trionfi,* in which Love or Ideal Beauty would have confirmed its dominion over all secular tyrannies."[1] Thus any judgment on how *The Triumph* should be interpreted must be qualified, simply because we can never know how Shelley planned to complete it. But while it is possible that Shelley would have altered the tone and meaning of his poem in the unwritten part of *The Triumph of Life,* it seems to me more probable that this missing conclusion would have reinforced the poem's pessimistic appraisal of quotidian life.[2]

Perhaps more than any of Shelley's other poems, *The Triumph of Life* shows him trying to come to terms with his contemporaries, with the "endowment of the age" in which he lived. Harold Bloom has outlined the ways in which Shelley's last major poem parodies Wordsworth and Coleridge and goes so far as to say that Rousseau, the fragment's central figure, "might just as well be named Wordsworth or Coleridge . . . , except that Shelley was too tactful and urbane to thus utilize those who were still, technically speaking, alive."³ In comparison with Words-worth, Byron has been underestimated as an influence on Shelley's fragment. Although Carlos Baker and Charles E. Robinson have noted some echoes of Byron's *The Prophecy of Dante* in *The Triumph of Life*, they never fully demonstrate the profound effect that Byron had on this poem, which constitutes Shelley's last pronouncement on the issues discussed in his *Julian and Maddalo*.⁴ In my view, after the collapse of his Promethean aspirations during the latter part of his career, Shelley found himself confronting the "darker side" (*Julian and Maddalo*, 49) of life. He turned increasingly to translation or transliteration rather than more original composition, and became obsessed with Goethe's *Faust*, which affected him in a personal as well as literary way. As early as October 1821 Shelley was quoting lines from *Faust* to express his feelings of poetic failure:

> I try to be what I might have been, but am not very successfull. I find that (I dare say I shall quote it wrong)
>
> "Den herrlichsten, den sich der Geist empängt
> Drängt immer fremd und fremder stoff sich an." [*sic*]
> [Whatever noblest things the mind received
> More and more foreign matter spoils the theme.
> —Walter Kaufmann translation]⁵

Although many sources, including Rousseau and Dante, helped shape Shelley's fragment, in the letters written around the time of the composition of *The Triumph of Life* Shelley was most concerned with the two preeminent literary figures of his era: Byron and Goethe. It is important, I think, to consider *The Triumph of Life* in the context of Shelley's relationship with Byron, whose presence in Pisa both stimulated and disturbed him, and also with regard to his and Byron's shared interest in *Faust*.

Before he composed *The Triumph of Life* Shelley began a translation of Goethe's *Faust*, part 1, a work which became a common topic of conversation for the poets in Pisa. Earlier, during a visit to Switzerland in 1816, "Monk" Lewis had given Byron an oral rendering of *Faust*. Because of this impromptu translation, Richard Holmes has argued, "Goethe's poem was clearly associated in Shelley's mind with Byron's presence,"⁶ an association which was probably strengthened by the profound influence Goethe's poem had on Byron's *Manfred*. Gratified by Goethe's generous praise of his works, Byron later dedicated the second edition of *Sardanapalus* and the first edition of *Werner* to him. Shelley's enthusiasm for *Faust* in Pisa increased Byron's admiration for Goethe, and he began to welcome rather than repudiate the comparisons readers were making between it and *Manfred*. In fact, he began to write a new drama based on the character of Goethe's Mephistopheles, *The Deformed Transformed*, a work which, if we can believe the sometimes dubious testimony of Medwin, Shelley disliked. According to Medwin, Shelley's criticism moved Byron to dramatic action:

> "Shelley, [Byron said,] I have been writing a *Faustish* kind of drama: tell me what you think of it."
> After reading it attentively, Shelley returned it.
> "Well," said Lord Byron, "how do you like it?"
> "Least," replied he, "of anything I ever saw of yours. It is a bad imitation of 'Faust;' and besides, there are two entire lines of Southey's in it."
> Lord Byron changed colour immediately, and asked hastily what lines? Shelley repeated,
> > 'And water shall see thee
> > And fear thee, and flee thee.'
> "They are in 'The Curse of Kehama.'"
> His Lordship, without making a single observation, instantly threw the poem into the fire.[7]

Byron evidently overcame Shelley's disapprobation, however, because *The Deformed Transformed* survived and was later published as a fragment, with the offending lines from Southey removed. *Faust* was also discussed by the poets in a less serious context. As Trelawny writes, *Faust* inspired Byron to nickname Shelley the "snake": "Goethe's Mephistopheles calls the serpent that tempted Eve, 'My Aunt—the renowned snake'; and as Shelley translated and repeated passages of 'Faust'—to impregnate, as he said, Byron's brain,—when he came to the passage, 'My Aunt, the renowned snake,' Byron said, 'Then you are her nephew,' and henceforth he often called Shelley the Snake; his bright eyes, slim figure, and noiseless movements strengthened, if they did not suggest, the comparison."[8]

Byron encouraged Shelley to put his oral translations of *Faust* into verse and asked him to explain Goethe's memoirs to him, and Shelley, although professing himself unequal to the task, translated the Prologue in Heaven and Walpurgis-Night scenes in the spring of 1822.[9] While Byron's "Faustish" drama, *The Deformed Transformed,* was clearly influenced by Shelley's effort to "impregnate" Byron's brain with *Faust,* Shelley's translation of Mephistopheles' lines owes a great deal to the style of some of Byron's verse, particularly in *The Vision of Judgment* and possibly in *The Deformed Transformed,* which Shelley probably read and criticized before embarking on his translation.[10] Richard Holmes suggests that Shelley's rendering of Mephistopheles' speeches derived from Byron's style of talk, which, in Pisa, was both aristocratic and chatty, "a dilution," Medwin writes, "of his letters."[11] Shelley clearly needed an informal style for Mephistopheles, who tells God in the Prologue in Heaven that the formal discourse of the Archangels is not for him: "You will excuse me if I do not talk / In the high style which they think fashionable" (Shelley's translation, 1.36–37),[12] and Byron, the undisputed master of the conversational style, was a natural model for Shelley's portrayal of Mephistopheles.

Writing to John Gisborne, Shelley professed dissatisfaction with his rendering of the scenes: "I feel how imperfect a representation, even with all the licence I assume to figure to myself how Göthe wd. have written in English, my words convey."[13] But, despite these reservations, Shelley translated Mephistopheles' lines with particular zest: he continued to share with Byron a lively and sometimes facetious interest in the devil. The excellence of the translation is all the more remarkable considering the fact that Shelley often abandoned Goethe's meter and even added lines. According to Timothy Webb, Shelley altered the original German to add a new quality to *Faust* which has "the effect of establishing Mephistopheles as a gentleman of fashion."[14] Webb notes several examples of this: "In his first speech to the Lord [Mephistopheles] says: 'thou . . . once more art kind enough / To interest thyself in our affairs' where the German simply says 'thou approachest' *(dich . . . nahst).* . . . Mephistopheles continues to use phrases which evoke the world of high society: 'Thou tookedst not my visits *in ill part*'; 'Though I should *scandalize* this company'; 'I take care *to keep on good terms with him*' (the italicized phrases are Shelley's additions)."[15] This aristocratic Mephistopheles, Webb goes on to say, may well "owe something to

Byron's version of Satan in *The Vision of Judgment,* which like Goethe's *Prologue* was modeled on the book of Job and which, like Shelley's translation, was destined for the *Liberal.*"[16]

The following passages from Shelley's rendering of *Faust* are, I think, particularly good examples of how he used Byron's urbane style to give Mephistopheles' speeches a free-flowing and conversational vitality:

> MEPHISTOPHELES Be guided now by me, and you shall buy
>   A pound of pleasure with a dram of trouble.
>   I hear them tune their instruments—one must
>   Get used to this damned scraping. Come, I'll lead you
>   Among them; and what there you do and see
>   As a fresh compact 'twixt us two shall be.
>   How say you now? this space is wide enough—
>   Look forth, you cannot see the end of it—
>   An hundred bonfires burn in rows, and they
>   Who throng around them seem innumerable;
>   Dancing and drinking, jabbering, making love,
>   And cooking . . . Now tell me, friend,
>   What is there better in the world than this?
>   . . . In truth, I generally go about
>   In strict incognito; and yet one likes
>   To wear one's orders upon gala days.
>   I have no ribbon at my knee; but here
>   At home, the cloven foot is honourable.
>   . . . Come now, we'll go about from fire to fire:
>   I'll be the pimp, and you shall be the lover.
>
> (scene 2.246–58; 261–70)

Mephistopheles' conversational style resembles that of the witty and disarmingly informal tempter of Byron's *The Deformed Transformed.* One also thinks of passages from *The Vision of Judgment* like the one in which the devil Asmodeus complains about having to carry Southey before St. Peter's celestial gate:

> Confound the Renegado! I have sprain'd
>   My left wing, he's so heavy; one would think
> Some of his works about his neck were chain'd.
>   But to the point: while hovering o'er the brink
> Of Skiddaw (where as usual it still rain'd),

I saw a taper, far below me, wink,
And stooping, caught this fellow at a libel—
No less on History than the Holy Bible. (681–88)

Of course, Shelley was bound by his role as translator (the mention of the cloven foot in his translation is no reflection on Byron), but the speech of his Mephistopheles has an aristocratic tone and a quick-paced flow which seem to reflect Byron's influence. In his translation Shelley also uses colloquial expressions such as "buy a pound of pleasure with a dram of trouble" and "one must get used to this damned scraping," expressions which compare with Asmodeus's "confound the Renegado!" Although Shelley was trying to be faithful to Goethe's text as he perceived it, Byron's verse was clearly on his mind, and his attempt to translate *Faust* for Byron's benefit appears to have resulted in an interesting cross-pollination of ideas and style, in Shelley's curiously Byronic Mephistopheles and the Mephistophelian Caesar of Byron's *The Deformed Transformed*. And one wonders if Shelley's association of Byron with Mephistopheles may have influenced Byron's image of himself as a witty and detached observer of life (see, for example, *Don Juan*, 13.54–56).

It is not surprising that *The Triumph of Life* was also shaped, in part, by Shelley's interest in *Faust*. The compulsive activity of Life's pageant may well owe something to Goethe's *Walpurgisnacht* scene, which, of course, Shelley translated. Webb suggests that Shelley uses his image of "the blind million [who] rush impetuously / To meet the evil ones" (237–38) from his translation of *Faust* to develop the frenzied scene in *The Triumph of Life*, which describes "The million with fierce song and maniac dance / Raging around" (110–11).[17] Robinson notes, moreover, that Faust's urge to pursue the sun at the end of day and achieve immortality is reversed in *The Triumph of Life*.[18] Shelley's inversion of these lines (26–28) suggests, Robinson argues, that the poet of Shelley's fragment is concerned with night rather than day, and that his fascination may well be with death rather than eternal life. Whether one agrees with this interpretation or not, it is clear that Shelley's interest in *Faust* and his translation of the *Walpurgisnacht* scene were important factors in the composition of *The Triumph of Life*.

Shelley's response to *Faust* was shaped, as his letters suggest, by a depressed and almost morbid state of mind. His tendency to view *Faust* as a somber, if thought-provoking work, is reflected in a letter to John Gisborne: "I have been reading over & over again Faust, & always with sensations which no other composition excites. It deepens the gloom and augments the rapidity of the ideas & would therefore seem to be an unfit study for any person who is a prey to the reproaches of memory, & the delusions of an imagination not to be restrained.—And yet the pleasure of sympathizing with emotions known only to few, although they derive their sole charm from despair & scorn of the narrow good we can attain in our present state, seems more than to cure the pain which belongs to them."[19] According to Jerrold Hogle, Shelley feels "caught as he reads [Goethe's] *Tragödie* between the despairing 'gloom' and the hopeful and striving 'rapidity' of thought that [he mentions in the letter quoted above]. As a . . . result, all the major figures and symbols in *The Triumph*—Rousseau, the speaker, the chariot, the 'etherial gloom' of Life itself, and even the most benign projectors of self-images seeking knowledge of themselves—are presented as similarly oscillating between both inclinations at key points."[20] But although Hogle is right to emphasize the influence of Shelley's emotional response to *Faust* on *The Triumph of Life,* I disagree with his assumption that the "rapidity of . . . ideas" that Shelley mentions in his letter are necessarily "hopeful and striving." In my view, *Faust* influenced Shelley most profoundly in the "gloom" it inspired in him, and in the "despair and scorn" of life Shelley saw in it, sentiments which are reflected in Rousseau's "deep scorn" (191) and the poet's "despair" (231) in *The Triumph of Life.*

As I have already mentioned, Shelley also associated *Faust* with Byron, for whom he translated it orally, and who, by 1822, had become a disturbing symbol of poetic success. In a June letter to Gisborne, Shelley revealed both his strong identification with the character of Faust and his wistful envy of Byron: "Jane brings her guitar, and if the past and present could be obliterated, the present would content me so well that I could say with Faust to the passing moment, 'Remain, thou, thou art so beautiful.' . . . I write little now. It is impossible to compose except under the strong excitement or assurance of finding sympathy with what you write. . . . Byron is in this respect fortunate. He touched a chord to which a million hearts responded."[21] During the last months of his life Shelley found himself hypersensitive to "the reproaches of memory and the delusions of an imagination not to be restrained," a state of mind exacerbated by his obsessive study of *Faust* and by the presence of Byron. As G. M. Matthews notes, the context of Shelley's quotation from *Faust* in the passage cited above is significant; it comes from the scene in which Faust makes his bargain with Mephistopheles: "Werd ich zum Augenblicke sagen: / Verweile doch! du bist so schön! / Dann magst du mich in Fesseln schlagen, / Dann will ich gern zugrunde gehn!" (1699–1703).[22] Was Shelley yearning for death? We will never know. This much, however, is clear: *The Triumph of Life* was written by a man who had come to question his own poetic gift, and who appears to have abandoned his once cherished notion of man's power to shape his own world. That this poem exists even in its fragmentary state is a tribute to Shelley's determination and strength as he battled against his self-doubts and the sense that his poetry might never find the "sympathy" of other discerning minds.

In *The Triumph of Life* Shelley seems to be indicating that none of the consolations that Julian offers Maddalo in *Julian and Maddalo* can truly help alleviate man's miserable lot. Nature, as a source of lasting joy, is rejected in the opening lines of the poem, and, although in *Julian and Maddalo* Julian asserts that every man has the power to find "love, beauty and truth" (174) in his own mind, the poet of *The Triumph of Life* is unable to resist the hellish vision of reality which seems to force itself upon his weary and passive brain. Julian's hypothesis that the chains which bind man's spirit may prove "Brittle . . . as straw" (182) is not confirmed by the vision of Life's pageant, in which some of the world's greatest men are chained helplessly to Life's car. And the idea that a beautiful feminine vision, like Maddalo's daughter, can uplift someone in despair has no currency in *The Triumph of Life,* in which the vision of the lovely "shape all light" (352) is followed by Rousseau's fall into the vicissitudes of hellish reality. Thus, as this chapter will suggest, the discussion in *Julian and Maddalo* ends, from Shelley's point of view, with the admission that man's Promethean aspirations may well be doomed to failure.

* * *

The Triumph of Life commences with a description of the Sun "rejoicing in his splendour" (3), an opening which is used by many critics as support for their belief that Shelley's optimism, somewhat battered but still intact, is present in his last work. In fact, G. M. Matthews believes that "Nothing in Shelley's other poems matches, for controlled exuberance, the celebration of generative life and law"[23] in the five different manuscript beginnings of *The Triumph of Life*. I disagree, however, with the idea that *The Triumph* opens with a simple paean to the sunrise which turns mysteriously into a pessimistic vision. The Sun himself is an ambiguous figure, both paternal and tyrannical, who, in one of Shelley's discarded drafts, presides over a miserable world in which "Every successive region slowly rose / Out of the death of daily life, and bore / Its portion in the ruin of repose."[24] Shelley describes this "father" (18) of nature in terms taken from Byron's *The Vision of Judgment* and used in reference to the archangel Michael, who "flew forth in glory and in good" (*The Vision of Judgment,* 233).[25] The Sun, pictured "hastening to his task / Of glory and of good" (1–2), seems, like the heavenly functionary of Byron's satire, almost too "good"—the hyperbole is self-deflating. More significantly, however, the Sun is perceived by the narrating poet as an unwelcome influence which obscures his own vision of "the stars that gem / The cone of night" (22–23). Even though the Sun of *The Triumph of Life* emanates rejoicingly through the "smiling air" (14), his effect on the poet's vision is negative as he blots out the poet's "stars" and thus makes way for the hellish pageant of Life that follows.

The ironically described sunrise at the opening of *The Triumph of Life* represents Shelley's rejection of Wordsworth's pantheistic vision, just as the depiction of Life's pageant later on in the poem portrays Shelley's fatalistic attitude toward quotidian existence.[26] Although the Sun is worshipped by all of nature, whose "altars" (5), "orison" (7), and "incense" (12) are symbolic of Wordsworth's "natural piety," the poet directs his gaze toward the fleeing night and away from the coming light of day (26–27). While the rest of the earth unites in its devotion to the Sun, the poet finds himself alienated from the natural world, whose

external workings have little to do with his troubled mental state. Even
the most breathtaking sunrise cannot change his essential condition,
in which he is trapped between "Heaven" (28) and the "Deep" (27),
or the "gulph of death" (*Adonais*, 35) which will inevitably claim him.
Toward the end of his life Shelley had come to believe that the notion
that life on earth is the only possible source of man's happiness was
"absurd" and even "demoniacal." In a letter to John Gisborne he wrote:
"Perhaps all discontent with the *less* . . . supposes the sense of a just
claim to the *greater*, & . . . we admirers of Faust are in the right road to
Paradise.—Such a supposition is not more absurd, and is certainly less
demoniacal than that of Wordsworth—where he says

> This earth
> Which is the world of all of us, & where
> *We find our happiness or not at all.*"[27]

This misreading of Wordsworth, who, in the passage quoted by
Shelley, is opposing "the world of all of us" to fanciful utopias rather
than to "Paradise," suggests that at this stage of his career Shelley was,
in a sense, "demonizing" the older poet. He was closing his Wordsworth
and opening his Goethe with a vengeance. Thus at the beginning of
The Triumph of Life Shelley, who had been accused of imitating Wordsworth in his earlier poetry,[28] describes how Wordsworth's pantheistic
Sun outshines his more esoteric starlight with more than a tinge of
bitterness in his ironic presentation of the tyrannical "father." In *The
Triumph* Shelley not only rejects Wordsworth's vision, he also partially
repudiates some of his earlier, more Wordsworthian visions: "we admirers of Faust," not Wordsworth, he writes, "are in the right road to
Paradise."

The beginning of *The Triumph of Life* can be compared to a passage
from Byron's *Manfred* describing Manfred's state of alienation from
nature, a passage which owes a debt, in turn, to Goethe's *Faust*. In
this section of Byron's dramatic poem Manfred is, like the poet of *The
Triumph*, on a mountain, watching the dawn but refusing to see any
consolation in its beauty:

> MAN.   My mother Earth!
> And thou fresh breaking Day, and you, ye Mountains,
> Why are ye beautiful? I cannot love ye.

And thou, the bright eye of the universe,
That openest over all, and unto all
Art a delight—thou shin'st not on my heart. (1.2.7–12)

Likewise, the Sun does not shine on the poet's heart in Shelley's fragment. Instead of being uplifted by nature's beauty, the poet turns away from the pantheistic vision it presents, a vision whose "Sweet talk in music" (39) drowns out the poet's own thoughts, which must, therefore, "remain untold" (21). Like Manfred, the poet is primarily interested in his own mental state—to him the influence of nature is oppressive rather than inspirational.

The poet is physically inert and his mind, overpowered first by the light of the Sun and then by the "beams that quench the Sun" (102), becomes a medium for visions rather than a creator of them. This reflects the lack of artistic motivation Shelley refers to in a March 1822 letter to Leigh Hunt: "What motives have I to write.—I *had* motives— and I thank the god of my heart they were totally different from those other apes of humanity who make mouths in the glass of time—but what are *those* motives now?"[29] Likewise, the narrator's evident paralysis represents his creative inertia and, appropriately, the passive voice describes what happens to his mind: a Vision "was rolled" (40) on his weary brain. As the poem unfolds the poet's passivity continues. Rousseau refers to him as a "spectator" (305) who observes life's pageant but does not take part in it. To use Maddalo's phrase, the narrator is a "passive thing" (*Julian and Maddalo,* 161) and, in general, the great men presented in *The Triumph of Life* seem equally helpless, especially with respect to the deformed figure of Life. Similarly, Rousseau seems powerless to control the visions that come to him, whether they take the form of a shifting "shape all light" (353), or of a harshly lit triumph. Only the "sacred few" (128) remain untouched by Life's obscuring light, but no poet is specifically named as being part of this saved remnant (although one might suppose that Keats, who died young, might make one of their number). Instead, the image of the poet presented in *The Triumph of Life* is of a tortured, paralyzed being struggling against influences which obliterate his thoughts. This view contrasts sharply with Julian's idea that man can create his own inner mental paradise, regardless of his situation in life. Although Shelley presents the human imagination as a powerful agency elsewhere in his writings, in *The Triumph of Life* he portrays the poet as a helpless perceiver of visions which force themselves upon his consciousness, not as one of "the unacknowledged legislators of the World."

But not everyone in the poem is victimized by Life—in the midst of the section describing the poet's "waking dream" is the passage about "the sacred few" mentioned above, which some critics use to support their contention that this part of the poem contains a positive element. According to Donald Reiman, for example, the sacred few "Offer the hope of human salvation" and "Everywhere in *The Triumph* the dark side of human experience is balanced by positive alternatives."[30] With respect to the description of those who "could not tame / Their spirits to the Conqueror" (128–29), however, it is important to recognize that these lines are heavily influenced by Byron's *Prophecy of Dante,* which presents a generally pessimistic view of man's lot.[31] In the *Prophecy* Dante says: "few shall soar upon that eagle's wing, / And look in the sun's face with eagle's gaze" (3.70–71). Moreover, as the sacred few fly "back like eagles to their native noon" (131), the "few" of Dante's vision "long to flee / Back to their native mansion" (3.169–70). The great men who escape Life's corrupting influence in the *Prophecy* do so by dying before they can be afflicted with "infection, and despair" (3.173), just as in *The Triumph* the sacred few flee earth "as soon / As they had touched the world with living flame" (129–30). In both poems "vulture passions" (*Prophecy,* 3.174) rend apart many would-be Prometheans. And, even if a great man should resist all temptations and succeed in becoming passionless, the world responds by making him a martyr, which is the fate of Socrates and Jesus Christ (134), the only two heroes specifically alluded to by Shelley's narrator. As Dante explains, every Prometheus ends up "chain'd to his lone rock by the sea-shore" (4.19). Little optimism can be found in the assertion that great men escape corruption only through premature death or through superhuman self-control and eventual self-sacrifice. Moreover, the multitudes of exceptional people who fall prey to Life's temptations dwarf the few beings who escape "to their native noon." Even Byron's Dante cannot confidently include himself in the company of those who "could resist themselves" (3.181), and Shelley's Rousseau laments the fact that he has been "overcome" (240) by his own heart. The idea of the sacred few in *Prophecy* and *The Triumph* is presented more as an impossible ideal than an attainable reality, and it serves to emphasize rather than put limits on Life's terrible power.

While the poet turns away from the Sun's splendor, he cannot escape the "cold glare" (77) which follows, a harsh radiance which makes his eyes "sick" (298). This new vision is much more powerful and therefore more threatening than the Wordsworthian glimpse of nature that begins the poem. Life's harsh light effectively defoliates the scene presented to the helpless poet, rendering him a starkly hellish view of people tortured along "a public way" (43), swept along by Life's chariot "with impotence of will" (170). The "path" is a place "where flowers never grew" and where the multitudes do not hear "fountains" or feel the "breeze" which inspires pastoral poetry (65–72). Even the powerful Sun of the poem's opening is "obscured with [   ] light" (78) which, "intenser than the noon" (77), outshines the Sun just as the Sun's brightness erases the poet's starry skies. Thus the real "triumph" in *The Triumph of Life* is not attained by Wordsworthian nature. It is, rather, a despairing vision of Life, with its failed Prometheuses and its scornful insights into man's folly, that triumphs in this unfinished masterpiece.

*   *   *

The occupant of the chariot passing before the poet's eyes is identified by a corrupted Rousseau, who also describes the many historical and literary figures in Life's pageant. The poet's guide through this pageant is both self-critical and critical of mankind. A deformed parody of natural imagery resembling an "old root" whose "thin discoloured hair" (182–86) looks like bleached grass, this "strange distortion" (183) on the hillside represents a worldview which is antithetical to the vision which opens the poem. He directs the poet's attention to the maenadic dance of mankind and the solemn procession of failed Prometheans, much as Maddalo introduces Julian to the inmates of the Venetian madhouse and a Maniac whose poetic imagination has been darkened by suffering. As Rousseau tells the poet, the scene before them can be described as an expression of "deep scorn" (191), or of a worldview which holds mankind in contempt. Part of Rousseau's "scorn" is directed toward the creature he has become, a parody of the historical Rousseau, "distorted" like the other "busy phantoms" by Life's miscreative ray (531–34). Like the Maniac, who feels compelled to wear a "mask of fals[e]hood" (308), Rousseau has been forced to assume a "disguise" (204) which he "disdains to wear" (205). He criticizes himself, the world in general, and the great men chained to the triumphal chair, accentuating the negative aspects of an already pessimistic perspective on human existence. Under the influence of his deformed guide, the poet is overcome with despair and disgust (231–32). And Rousseau's description of the earlier stages of Life's pageant (434–543) which the poet hears later on in the poem is, if anything, more steeped in contempt for mankind than the first vision which rolls across the poet's brain. Although Rousseau seems a much more emotional and sympathetically drawn figure than the coldly intellectual Lucifer of Byron's *Cain,* he, like Lucifer, presents a view of life which emotionally devastates the sensitive being whom he instructs. In both *The Triumph* and *Cain* the futility of seeking knowledge is juxtaposed with the tragic reality of man's hellish condition, which demands some kind of remedy. The poet's "despair" (231) as he asks "why God made irreconcilable / Good & the means of good" (230–32) echoes Cain's sentiments, as Rousseau's determination to satiate the poet's "thirst of knowledge" (194) with obscure visions parallels, in many ways, Lucifer's attempt to educate and confuse Cain. Of course, we must allow for the possibility that, had Shelley lived to complete the poem, Rousseau would have offered the narrator some form of consolation. But in the fragment Shelley left, the poet, like Cain, can only recoil in disgust from the vision of life his guide reveals to him, a vision fraught, like Byron's mystery play, with both irony and tragedy.

Rousseau's entrance into the poem is prompted by the poet's questions about the shape of Life (177–78), questions which elicit some very pessimistic responses. The kind of knowledge Rousseau presents to the poet leads to sorrow rather than contentment. His promise to tell the poet about the grim pageant contains a warning: "If thirst of knowledge doth not . . . abate, / Follow it even to the night, but I / Am weary" (194–96). Moreover, Rousseau's own fall into the world of experience, as he reveals in his vision of the shape all light, takes place after he questions the shape about his past and present, as well as the reasons behind his past and present (398). After this short interrogation, the shape offers Rousseau her cup and Rousseau perceives a deforming vision. As Byron's *Manfred* says, "Sorrow is knowledge" (1.1.10) and "The Tree of Knowledge is not that of Life" (1.1.12). While nature cannot offer any consolation to the poet, knowledge actually serves to drive him to despair. The vision of the shape of Life categorically refuses to offer any kind of consolation to him, and the information that Rousseau provides is far from comforting.

The poet's and Rousseau's descriptions of Life's triumph take up more than two-thirds of Shelley's fragment and dominate the poem he left us in a way that the scenes involving the paternal Sun and the shape all light do not. Life and its vicissitudes present a problem which, in the context of *The Triumph of Life*, appears insurmountable. This does not mean, however, that Shelley believes that this pessimistic view of mankind's condition presents a complete picture of human existence. Ironically, the "cold glare" which reveals deformities also blinds. Rousseau has holes for eyes (187–88) and, in his function as a guide to the daydreaming poet, he can be regarded as a blind man leading the victim of a strange trance into a surrealistic world. Moreover, Life's charioteer, although he possesses four faces and, presumably, eight eyes, has all of his eyes "banded" (100). Even though these "banded eyes could pierce the sphere / Of all that is, has been, or will be done" (103–4), the chariot itself is badly guided (105). Similarly, the "light's severe excess" (424) leads to everything being "distorted" (531). While Shelley recognizes the potentially destructive power of Life, which obliterates Wordsworthian pantheism, he uses irony to expose its reductive nature. And the fact that at the close of the fragment the poet still asks "what is Life?" (544) indicates that he cannot unreservedly accept a despairing outlook on human existence.

As part of his response to the poet's questions, Rousseau describes an earlier incarnation of himself who differs radically from the decayed creature the poet meets. In fact, Rousseau, as Shelley depicts him in *The Triumph* and as Byron portrays him in *Childe Harold's Pilgrimage*, canto 3, manifests two contrasting personalities.[32] Shelley and Byron depict the historical Rousseau, whose "life was one long war with self-sought foes" (*Childe Harold*, 3, stanza 80), the great thinker who inspired the French Revolution (*The Triumph*, 206–7). But they are also fascinated with the Rousseau who wrote of love in *Julie; ou, La Nouvelle Héloïse* (see *Childe Harold*, 3, stanza 79), a work which, Shelley believed, was created by "a mind so powerfully bright as to cast a shade of false-hood on the records that are called reality."[33] As the Rousseau of *The Triumph of Life* becomes enamored of a mysterious shape all light, the Rousseau of Byron's *Childe Harold,* canto 3, loves "ideal beauty, which became / In him existence, and o'erflowing teems / Along his burning page, distempered though it seems" (3.740–42).

In their relatively sympathetic responses to Rousseau, Shelley and Byron differed from most of their countrymen who, as Edward Duffy writes, employed "an insular optics that, seeing Rousseau plain as a *philosophe,* either elided the man of feeling or brutalized him into a psychopath whose every word and deed epitomized just that kind of self-indulgence to be expected when the universalizing reason . . . presumed to set the affective life free from the bonds of place and circumstance."[34] Shelley and Byron never succeed, however, in resolving the political Rousseau and his more idyllic, sentimental persona into an integrated personality, and thus *The Triumph* and *Childe Harold,* 3, present a puzzling and contradictory version of Rousseau. But in Shelley's last major poem the "powerfully bright" vision of the author of *Julie* is erased (see *The Triumph,* 405–6), and Rousseau metamorphoses into the eyeless, deformed creature who greets the poet, a flawed political writer whose "words were seeds of misery" (280) and who helps to create "a world of agony" (295). Rousseau, the would-be Prometheus, becomes Rousseau, the prophet of suffering.

Shelley's own fall from optimism to pessimism is perhaps most forcibly expressed in the way *The Triumph,* at least in its fragmentary form, contrasts with *Prometheus Unbound,* the most coherent and comprehensive presentation of his idealism. As Life's pageant unfolds, the poet witnesses a "wild dance" (138) which has its counterpart in the Dionysian revelry of the last act of *Prometheus Unbound.*[35] In the earlier poem the moon itself moves "Maniac-like" (4.470) and a chorus of Spirits and Hours dance "Ceaselessly and [are] rapid and fierce and free" (4.163). But whereas this maniacal activity is an expression of joyful freedom, the demonic parody of act 4 of *Prometheus Unbound* in *The Triumph of Life* depicts dancers who are miserable, obscene, and bound to Life's car. There are also parallels between the description of Life's chariot and the portrayal of the Moon Spirit's chariot in *Prometheus Unbound.* But while "the Mother of Months is borne" (4.207) alive in the chariot in *Prometheus Unbound*, the image in *The Triumph* is one of death: the young Moon bears "the ghost of her dead Mother" (84).[36] And, unlike the vision in Shelley's lyrical drama which presages a rebirth for man in a new and better world, the parodic version in *The Triumph* is the harbinger of Life's destructive storm.

The element of parody continues in the description of the shape of Life. Like Demogorgon, Life is a "mighty Darkness" (*Prometheus Unbound*, 2.4.2) who uses a "ghastly charioteer" (2.4.144) to convey him about. Moreover, the description of the spirits guiding the cars of the Immortal Hours in *Prometheus Unbound* also has a parallel in *The Triumph*: as the charioteers summoned by Demogorgon look both "behind" (2.4.133) and "before" (2.4.137), the four faces of Life's charioteer can look at "all that is, has been or will be done" (104). But while the charioteers commanded by Demogorgon are keen-sighted, the eyes of Life's conductor are banded, and the chariot itself is poorly guided. Both the sinister "Shape" of *The Triumph*, likened to "dark ether" (85), and the darkness representing the shapeless Demogorgon are mysterious but extremely powerful figures with the potential to dominate anyone who lacks self-control, whether a willful god like Jupiter or the earthly "Anarchs" (*The Triumph*, 285) dealing in blood and gold. The shape of Life serves, however, to chain men, whereas Demogorgon's function is to free the universe from bondage. Thus Life acts as a kind of demonic Demogorgon, and his pageant of suffering is an ironic parody of the joyous celebration presented in *Prometheus Unbound*.

But perhaps the most powerful reversal of the optimistic movement in *Prometheus Unbound* takes place in the last part of *The Triumph of Life*, in which strength and beauty fall off the forms that Rousseau observes. After the world is redeemed in *Prometheus Unbound* "ugly human shapes and visages" (3.4.65) come to look like "mild and lovely forms / After some foul disguise had fallen" (3.4.69–70), while in *The Triumph* the positive characteristics fall off and ugliness is revealed: "From every firmest limb and fairest face / The strength and freshness fell like dust, and left / The action and the shape without the grace" (520–22). According to the Spirit of the Earth in *Prometheus Unbound*, beauty and goodness are intrinsic qualities in men. Rousseau's vision contradicts this idea, however, since it depicts "strength and freshness" as masks (536) which slough off to reveal man's true debility. In *The Triumph of Life* man's inherent weakness leads to his eventual corruption and seemingly precludes the kind of universal regeneration described in act 4 of *Prometheus Unbound.* Moreover, since the "sacred few" who, like Prometheus, have remained unconquered by Life, flee the fallen world by returning to their "native noon" or by being martyred, no great men remain who are capable of leading mankind out of its state of progressive decay.

Thus Shelley revises his earlier poetry through the deft use of irony in his last major poem. This pervasive use of irony in *The Triumph of Life* may well stem from Byron, who was perhaps the most accomplished ironist of his day.[37] According to Ross Woodman, even before the composition of *The Triumph* Shelley had "dimly perceived the possibility, essentially Byronic in nature, of viewing his earlier visionary hopes in ironic terms" and created in his unfinished "Charles the First" a character, Archy the court jester, who mocks Shelley's Promethean meliorism as "New devil's politics" (line 365).[38] *The Triumph of Life* embodies a much darker vision of the world than even Shelley's tragedy *The Cenci* because it repudiates the Shelleyan idealism of *Prometheus Unbound* and because it is not limited to a specific historical situation: *The Triumph* looks at mankind throughout recorded history and finds it fallen and virtually beyond redemption. Of course, Shelley may have ended the poem, had he lived, on a positive note, but as it stands *The Triumph of Life,* like the compositions of Shelley's Maniac, seems "charactered in vain / On [an] unfeeling leaf which burns the brain / And eats into it . . . blotting all things fair / And wise and good which time had written there" (*Julian and Maddalo,* 478–81).

The "waking dream" that is *The Triumph of Life* has many difficulties for the poet who tries to understand it, who, lost in the vision that takes over his brain, has only the slightest connection to any form of concrete reality. The shape of Life is never clearly described—the poet uses similes and metaphors to approximate what he perceives, as the chariot advances "Like the young Moon" (79) which, in turn, is compared to an infant bearing "her dead Mother" (84), while Life itself is "as one whom years deform" (88), a "shape" defined only by its misshapen outline. Beyond this lack of clarity, the absence of a motivating force behind the visions the poet and Rousseau observe adds to the confusing nature of the poem. In *The Cenci,* for example, there is a reasonable explanation for Beatrice's corruption and the change of her worldview: her brutalizing conflict with a tyrannical father ends in her transformation into a being who sees the world as "tedious, false and cold" (5.4.80). But in *The Triumph of Life* there is no conflict. Abruptly, an "icy cold" (78) vision making the poet's eyes "sick" (298) invades his consciousness, a vision which does not appear to be psychologically motivated and is not the instrument of a tyrant such as Cenci or Jupiter. This hellish view of life is dominated not by an anthropomorphic being but by Life itself, an abstraction borne by a charioteer who has all four of his faces banded. The progress of the car, like the movement of the pageant, is random, and sightless chance governs the dream world of *The Triumph of Life.*

The vision of human existence as a phenomenon like the scattering of autumn leaves or the drifting of "bubbles on an eddying flood" (458) is not an attractive one to the poet, who attempts to posit some kind of absolute above the mutable world. He speaks of the "sacred few" who fly away to their "native noon," a realm somehow removed from Life's reality, and of the "true Sun" (292), the absolute which priestcraft attempts to eclipse. But as the skeptical Rousseau reminds the poet, "Figures ever new / Rise on the bubble, paint them how you may" (248–49)—the poet's ideals, the "native noon" and the "true Sun," are his own creations, images of light which may be as illusory as the shape all light whom Rousseau encounters in his ephemeral Eden. In a canceled draft, Rousseau speaks of "truth & its inventors" (26),[39] implying that truth does not exist in an absolute sense but is invented by man. Similarly, Byron expresses epistemological incertitude in several sections of his *Don Juan,* including the following stanza:

"Que sçais-je?" was the motto of Montaigne,
　　As also of the first Academicians:
That all is dubious which Man may attain,
　　Was one of their most favourite positions.
There's no such thing as certainty, that's plain
　　As any of Mortality's Conditions:
So little do we know what we're about in
This world, I doubt if doubt itself be doubting. (9.129–36)

In *The Triumph,* however, the vicissitudes of Life are less doubtful than are dreams of paradise. To Rousseau, Heaven is something he imagines (333), whereas Hell is grounded in reality, in "the harsh world in which [he wakes] to weep" (334). He and the poet can dream of an absolute, a Heaven in which the sufferings inflicted by the conqueror Life do not exist, but such imaginings are simply new figures on the world's "false & fragile glass" (247), as arbitrary as the beliefs satirized in Life's vision.

Finding no evidence of a benevolent god, the poet despairingly blames man's lot on an evil or capricious deity who, he says, "made irreconcilable / Good and the means of good" (230–31). But the idea of a wrongheaded god has no more validity in the world of Life's triumph than the idea of a "true Sun" has. In *The Triumph of Life* the shape of Life, not God, is the random and motiveless force that fetters mankind. Accordingly, the mind-reading Rousseau demands that the poet pay attention to Life's pageant rather than concern himself with an irrelevant deity, telling him to behold the "spoilers spoiled" (235) who, more than God, are to blame for man's wretched condition. In the fragment Shelley left us the protagonist seems powerless to transform his and Rousseau's pessimistic vision. Lacking even an evil god to blame for the tragic human condition, the reclining poet observes and asks questions but remains inactive, for there is nothing he can do, no one, except an ambiguous shape in his dream, that he can defy. Shelley's Promethean myth of man's power to change the world and perfect himself has no currency in *The Triumph of Life,* in which Necessity is equated with Life instead of Demogorgon, and enchains man rather than releasing him. At least Prometheus is able to personify his problems in the tyrant Jupiter and, in pitying Jupiter, become free—the poet of *The Triumph of Life* cannot even invent a deity to rebel against, and remains the helpless prey of visions which occur without any form of causation and which lead him to confusion and despair.

This fatalistic attitude toward the phenomena of the mind is consistent with the pessimistic view Byron expresses in *Childe Harold's Pilgrimage,* canto 4, a poem which in 1818 Shelley had attacked for embodying "the most wicked & mischievous insanity that was ever given forth."[40] According to Byron, every sufferer of Life's miseries is vulnerable to memories

which shall wound,
Striking the electric chain wherewith we are darkly bound;
   And how and why we know not, nor can trace
   Home to its cloud this lightning of the mind,
   But feel the shock renew'd. (4.206–10)

And in *Childe Harold,* canto 4, and *The Triumph* not even beautiful visions can prevail over despair. Like Shelley's shape all light, Byron's nymph Egeria is a mysterious and "beautiful" (4.1035) entity associated with a cave and a fountain, and as Rousseau's encounter with the shape all light ends in Life's despairing vision, Byron's meditation on Egeria gives way to expressions of nihilism:

Of its own beauty is the mind diseased,
And fevers into false creation
. . .
Where are the charms and virtues which we dare
Conceive in boyhood and pursue as men,
The unreach'd Paradise of our despair[?] (4.1090–98)

While Byron insists on the power of humankind's "faculty divine" (4.1139), and Shelley invokes "the sacred few," visions like the shape all light and Egeria are presented as too intangible and illusory to provide any protection from despair.

Moreover, the *Walpurgisnacht*-like spectacle of the maddened lovers in *The Triumph of Life* forcibly recalls Byron's description in *Childe Harold,* 4, of self-destructive love. In *The Triumph* young lovers, caught in

     rapid whirlwinds[,] . . . glow
Like moths by light attracted and repelled,
   Oft to new bright destruction come and go,
. . . the fiery band which held
   Their natures, snaps . . . ere the shock cease to tingle
One falls and then another in the path
   Senseless. (144–60)

Similarly, Byron presents love in *Childe Harold,* 4, as a form of insanity:

Who loves, raves—'tis youth's frenzy—but the cure
Is bitterer still; as charm by charm unwinds
Which robed our idols, and we see too sure

Nor worth nor beauty dwells from out the mind's
Ideal shape of such; yet still it binds
The fatal spell, and still it draws us on,
Reaping the whirlwind from the oft-sown winds;
The stubborn heart, its alchemy begun,
Seems ever near the prize,—wealthiest when most undone.
   (1099–1107)

In *Childe Harold,* 4, and *The Triumph* passionate love is presented as a whirlwind which destroys its deluded victims—rather than allowing its devotees to transcend life, love makes them all the more vulnerable to life's vicissitudes. As Byron writes in *Childe Harold,* "Circumstance, that unspiritual god / And miscreator, makes and helps along / Our coming evils with a crutch-like rod" (4.1122–24). Byron's rod-wielding "Circumstance," like Shelley's deformed shape of Life, has the power to overwhelm a helpless humanity.

The triumph of Life described by the poet and Rousseau is not, then, the triumph of Life in all of its variety, including its sublime as well as its horrible aspects—it is, rather, the triumph of a certain poetic perspective on Life, characterized by irony and fatalism. But every triumph implies a defeat, and the chief victims in the poem are the poet and Rousseau, whose own visions have been silenced by the "savage music, stunning music" (453) of Life's "new Vision" (434). As it stands, a fragment frozen by Shelley's death, *The Triumph of Life* suggests that Shelley, as well as his protagonist, has felt the effects of Life's omnipotent ray. Writing to Leigh Hunt on 10 April 1822, about three months before his death, Shelley laments: "Alas, how I am fallen from the boasted purity in which you knew me once exulting!"[41] Maddalo's pronouncement on Julian's meliorism seems to sum up Shelley's unfinished masterwork: "we aspire / How vainly to be strong!" (177–78).

EIGHT

Byron Puffs the Snake

The Island (1823), Byron's treatment of the mutiny on the *Bounty* story, has been generally ignored or underrated. For example, Andrew Rutherford dismisses *The Island* as a "rag-bag of old Byronic themes" which has little intrinsic merit or originality.[1] Studies by P. D. Fleck and Robert Hume argue, however, that *The Island* does differ from Byron's other works, both in its authorial comments on the Byronic hero and in its mixture of heroic, tragic, romantic, and even comic perspectives.[2] And, as Jerome McGann notes, "*The Island* is unique among Byron's works in the way it lays out an unequivocal program for the possession of the earthly paradise."[3] While *The Island* certainly does not rival *Don Juan,* it does represent a new direction in Byron's poetry, a direction which he did not live to develop. It is also his most Shelleyan poem, which—far from being a "rag-bag of old Byronic themes"—goes beyond these themes to treat many of the ideas and aspirations of his drowned friend. As Charles Robinson notes, *The Island* is essentially "an elegy on Shelley."[4]

Although it superficially resembles Byron's oriental tales, *The Island* has some important differences from these earlier works. Describing his new poem to Leigh Hunt, Byron wrote that he had made a special effort to avoid "running foul of my own 'Corsair' and style"—he, like Shelley, had come to see the limitations of the Byronic hero.[5] In *The Island* not only does Byron criticize a Byronic hero (Fletcher Christian), he also describes how a potential Corsair (Torquil) turns into a Shelleyan hero and achieves the kind of paradise the narrator of *Epi-*

psychidion desperately longs for. In *The Island* Byron rejects the darker perspective on life presented in his own oriental tales and asserts the possibility of a Shelleyan utopia, revealing an ability to question, even condemn, the pessimistic outlook on life with which he is most often associated.

But while many of the ideas embodied in *The Island* were probably inspired by Shelley, the poem may also have been influenced by another member of the Pisan circle. On 14 January 1822 a swashbuckling figure named Edward John Trelawny joined the circle and immediately inspired Byron with feelings of insecurity. The problem was that Trelawny seemed more of a Byronic hero than Byron himself: " 'I have met today the personification of my Corsair,' [Byron] told Teresa after Trelawny's first call upon him. 'He sleeps with the poem under his pillow, and all his past adventures and present manners aim at this personification.'—'I feel curious to see him,' said Teresa. 'You will not like him,' Byron firmly replied."[6] Byron and this new Corsair became instant competitors and, according to Trelawny, he proved the more adept swimmer, much to Byron's mortification.[7] But Trelawny, who was a gifted storyteller, also served to inspire Shelley to write what Mary Shelley later dubbed *An Unfinished Drama*. The setting of this *Unfinished Drama,* Mary writes in her notes to the fragment, is an island of the South Seas: "An Enchantress, living in one of the islands of the Indian Archipelago, saves the life of a Pirate, a man of savage but noble nature. She becomes enamoured of him; and he, inconstant to his mortal love, for a while returns her passion; but at length, recalling the memory of her whom he left, and who laments his loss, he escapes from the enchanted island and returns to his lady. His mode of life makes him again to go to sea, and the Enchantress seizes the opportunity to bring him, by a spirit-brewed tempest, back to her island."[8] While the plot of the *Unfinished Drama* differs greatly from Byron's *The Island,* there is a significant similarity between the two works in their presentation of love on an isolated tropical island. Like Torquil, the hero of *The Island,* the pirate of Shelley's fragment is "a simple innocent boy" (85) who must be rescued by his beloved. Since the *Unfinished Drama* was "undertaken for the amusement of the individuals who composed [the Shelleys'] intimate society,"[9] it is likely that Byron at least heard of this project, and certainly possible that it, along with the poets' friendship with the corsair-like Trelawny, inspired him to write a South Sea adventure of his own.

One of the most important differences between *The Island* and Byron's earlier tales is that *The Island*, like Shelley's *Unfinished Drama*, is far removed from Europe and unpolluted by the "sordor of civilisation" (2.69). By placing the poem in the "infant world" (4.420) of Toobonai, Byron allows his protagonist, Torquil, to escape the crushing weight of history and the world of experience. Moreover, Torquil has no forebears to leave him legacies of guilt and violence—his only parent is the sea off the Hebrides. This "tempest-born" (2.168) being, once Christian disappears from the scene, has no connection with the world outside of his island paradise and does not have enough knowledge of sad reality to keep him from achieving a state of innocence. While the intense glare of a pessimistic vision obliterates the "silver music" (355) of the "shape all light" in Shelley's *The Triumph of Life*, Christian's despairing view of life in *The Island* cannot withstand the "untaught melodies" (2.103) of Toobonai, or the optimism of Neuha, whose "hopes ne'er drew / Aught from Experience, that chill touchstone, whose / Sad proof reduces all things from their hues" (2.146–48). Nature and innocence, not the scornful, despairing outlook of Christian, triumph in Byron's last major work, in which Torquil finds his antitype and regains paradise. Although Shelley at the end of his career appeared ready to give up his visionary dreams, Byron had enough respect for his friend's idealism to be willing to explore it in a work whose setting is so exotic that it is unburdened with the problems of Western civilization—the priestcraft and superstition which frustrated Shelley's "passion for reforming the world."

But while he allowed himself to be influenced by Shelley in his last poem, Byron also revised Shelley's vision, putting it in a particular historical context and arguing for the realism of some of his descriptions. The sourcebook for *The Island* is William Bligh's actual narrative of the mutiny on the *Bounty*, and Torquil is modeled on a real person, a man named George Stewart who, like Torquil, married a Tahitian girl.[10] Moreover, Byron wrote many notes supporting the realism of the scenes he describes. Even the cave in the "central realm of earth" (4.119) where Neuha and Torquil find refuge is, Byron writes, "no fiction," and has its original in the Tonga Islands."[11] Byron's stance in *The*

Island is not entirely vatic and, in his presentation of Ben Bunting and his panegyric on tobacco, Byron seems to be trying to create a contrast to his portrait of the idyllic love of Torquil and Neuha, to assert that even a poem with visionary elements cannot ignore the existence of mundane reality.[12] Although *The Island* is a romance and not simply a narrative of fact, Byron, unlike Shelley, employs nonfictional elements in his work in an attempt to give credibility to a worldview which might otherwise seem hopelessly unrealistic. As Byron explained in a letter to John Murray, no work should be a complete fabrication: "I hate things *all fiction* . . . there should always be some foundation of fact for the most airy fabric—and pure invention is but the talent of a liar."[13]

Byron's revisionary attitude toward Shelley's myth in *The Island* can best be described, I think, by Harold Bloom's term *Tessera*, which has to do with a poet's effort to "complete" the work of another poet "by so reading the parent-poem as to retain its terms but to mean them in another sense, as though the precursor had failed to go far enough."[14] Byron's poem is actually more optimistic than the works by Shelley which seem to have influenced it because it presents paradise on earth as something that can be achieved without undue suffering. As opposed to Shelley's Prometheus, who experiences aeons of pain before he can liberate himself, and Laon, who is finally put to death after living a life marked by mental and physical torture, Torquil finds Eden through his love for Neuha and, rather than being captured or slain by the forces of law and tyranny, escapes from the fallen world with his beloved. In Toobonai Torquil merges both with his antitype and nature itself, and, despite the fact that he has implicated himself in the guilty, mutinous deeds of his comrades, he is able to achieve a state of relative innocence and happiness. Unlike Prometheus, he does not go through a self-conscious internal struggle—Torquil is prone to "strive much more than wonder at [his] fate" (3.30)—but he nevertheless succeeds in finding refuge with Neuha in a well-provisioned cave that has many similarities to Prometheus's "Cave all overgrown." Not only does Byron present Shelley's visionary hopes in a real historical setting, he also depicts a hero, Torquil, who combines in "one absorbing soul" (2.305) with his beloved, who successfully rebels against the established order (Captain Bligh and England), and attains, without much struggle, a paradise isolated from the fallen world. In adopting elements of Shelley's myth Byron seeks to go beyond them, to "complete" his dead friend's vision and to put it in the context of his own kind of tale—to make Shelley's vision, to a certain extent, his own.

While *The Island* builds on Shelley's work as the basis of its vision of paradise regained, it also constitutes a palinode with respect to a number of Byron's own poems. For example, *Don Juan,* according to Byron, refuses to "exalt the *sentiment* of the passions," serving instead to strip off and mock this "illusion";[15] but much of *The Island* is taken up with a celebration of the passion of love which, far from being an illusion, is the force which saves Torquil from Christian's bloody fate. *The Island* also contrasts with Byron's *Sardanapalus:* Torquil's heart, like Sardanapalus's, is "tamed to [a] voluptuous state, / At once Elysian and effeminate" (*The Island,* 2.312–13), but, unlike Sardanapalus, Torquil escapes the destructive vortex of the violent outer world and lives to experience, indefinitely, the "Elysian and effeminate" existence that Sardanapalus cannot maintain. Whereas in *Sardanapalus* the political situation in Assyria helps cause the protagonist's fall, in *The Island* Torquil not only survives but succeeds in living in total harmony with nature and his antitype, while Christian, the Byronic hero, dies a violent and meaningless death. Sardanapalus is destroyed by his culture; Torquil is subsumed and re-created by the culture of the islanders.

In *The Island,* then, the Byronic hero perishes and Torquil is left to realize his potential and "form a nation's glory" (2.205) rather than its grief. In fact, Torquil and Christian can be considered as separate sides of a single personality, and Christian's death can be seen as the purging of antisocial and self-destructive elements which keep the Torquil part of the personality from fulfilling itself. If Byron's Cain had been able to eliminate that part of his nature that hungers for greatness and is prone to violence, perhaps he too could have achieved paradise with his antitype (Adah). For the Shelleyan hero to survive, the Byronic facets of his being must be eliminated. Accordingly, Shelley, in his preface to *Prometheus Unbound,* rejects Milton's Satan as the possible model for his hero, and Byron, in his late romance, has Christian self-destruct so as to leave the "infant world" of Toobonai free of the "hell" (1.164) that this satanic figure has within himself.

But in order to make it possible for Torquil to attain paradise, Byron
must do more than simply eradicate Christian. He must also free his
protagonist from traditional morality, the "duty" and "conscience"
(1.60–63) embodied in the person of Captain Bligh. The mutineers, in
their unjustified rebellion against Bligh and their country, are tainted
by corruption, and their paradise is "guilt-won" (3.39). Thus Torquil
brings a past to the island, an original sin that disqualifies him, it would
seem, for residence in Eden. But Torquil's memory is at least temporarily washed clean. Neuha, "Rapt in the fond forgetfulness of life"
(2.332), sings to him her Lethean song, and he enters a world in which
only the present matters, in which clock time and the mundane England
of Captain Bligh no longer exist. As Byron says, the lovers "never
paused o'er time . . . / What deem'd they of the future or the past? / The
present, like a tyrant, held them fast" (2.348–53). There is, moreover,
no "adulterous whisper" (2.338) to make Torquil and Neuha ashamed
of their passion. And, by obliterating Torquil's memory of his duty and
unlawful rebellion, Neuha's "untaught melodies" succeed in bringing
her lover into touch with his "Childhood's sympathy" (2.278) with
nature. While Bernard Blackstone's assertion that *The Island* embodies
Byron's "urge to regress to an infantile state of irresponsibility"[16] may
be an exaggeration, it does seem that the first condition of attaining
paradise in the poem is the ability to ignore adult obligations. This
does not mean that Torquil becomes an infant mentally, but that with
Neuha's help he can imaginatively re-create the joys of childhood and
transcend the world of experience. Likewise, Byron, in his description
of lovers' happiness, is moved to remember the "infant rapture" (2.290)
associated with the Loch-na-gar and the Highland linns (2.291–93) of
his own boyhood. There is something incompatible between the re-
sponsibilities of Bligh's workaday world and this imaginative recreation
of one's youth, and thus Torquil must turn from the *Bounty* and the
clock time of England and totally immerse himself in Neuha's song in
order to regain what Wordsworth calls the "visionary gleam."

But while Torquil manages to escape guilt and the avenging forces
of justice, the rest of the mutineers are either killed or dragged off
in chains to England. According to Robert Hume, the punishment of
Christian and his henchmen supports the idea that Toobonai is not a

true paradise: "*The Island* is primarily a story of crime and retribution, and the 'utopia' it presents, far from being an ideal, actually constitutes a temptation for the crime."[17] In my view, however, the fate of these other mutineers reflects more on their inability to become part of the natural world than on any negative qualities in Toobonai itself. Byron uses the rock image to demonstrate the essential difference between Christian, who is aloof and self-absorbed, and Torquil, who is more in tune with the habitat and people of the island. After the fight with the forces of the law, Christian becomes a rock-like being, "Still as a statue" (3.91), as he stands "Fast by the rock" (3.93), stifling his own breast until "his form seemed turned to flint" (3.96). He is "Like an extinct volcano" (3.140), a sterile, smouldering being incapable of the positive act of creation. That Christian is apart from the natural order is demonstrated by the fact that he commits suicide by smashing himself on a rock, in "rage 'gainst the earth which he forsook" (4.340). But while a rock forms Christian's grave, the "black rock" (4.10) into which Neuha leads Torquil saves his life. Torquil enters a "central realm of earth" (4.119), becoming part of the natural world instead of setting himself, like Christian, against it. And, once inside the rock, he finds it full of provisions, vegetable symbols of fertility (4.169–72) which stand in stark contrast to the barrenness of the rock imagery associated with Christian. *The Island* does present a kind of "utopia," but it is only available to those who do not, like Christian, become calcified in their isolation from the natural world. Torquil is able to find sustenance even in a seemingly sterile rock and survival in a dive into the ocean which, as far as Torquil's pursuers are concerned, could only result in death. Instead of being a story of "crime and retribution," *The Island* is a tale of paradise regained by a mutineer who adapts himself to his environment and who is ennobled by the love he feels for his antitype.

Thus, while the other rebels suffer for their temerity in taking over the *Bounty,* Torquil escapes vengeance and, in fact, becomes a happier person for his stay in Toobonai. As Byron makes clear, Torquil has the potential to become either a "patriot hero or despotic chief" (2.204), and the fact that Christian identifies himself with his younger friend indicates that, if not for the positive influences of Neuha and Toobonai, Torquil may well have become another self-destructive Byronic hero.

Torquil's abandonment of his duty has a positive result and is a course
of action which, Byron suggests, could be recommended to some of the
world's leaders:

> Had Caesar known but Cleopatra's kiss,
> Rome had been free, the world had not been his.
> And what have Caesar's deeds and Caesar's fame
> Done for the earth? We feel them in our shame.
> The gory sanction of his Glory stains
> The rust which tyrants cherish on our chains. (2.318–23)

Torquil's "voluptuous state" leads him away from the destruction he
could cause in the violent world of empire-building, in which men like
Bligh, motivated by ambition and dreams of glory, create misery and
live loveless existences. And Torquil escapes the fate of the other mutineers, not because he is any less guilty of mutiny than his fellow rebels
but because he is able to erase that guilt through his baptism, or symbolic death and rebirth, at sea. As a native of an island of the Hebrides,
moreover, Torquil can adapt himself to Toobonai, whereas the other
mutineers, despite their will to live in this paradise, are still too much a
part of civilization to transcend the fatal conflicts of the outside world.

The Island is less an indictment of the mutineers' irresponsibility than
it is a critique of the kind of hero they seek to become. These "new-born
heroes" (1.103) cannot emulate the islanders whom they befriend—
descendants of "The naked knights of savage chivalry" (2.217)—but
are also too uncivilized to respect discipline, to act as Bligh bids them
to. Their bravery, Byron tells us, can be compared to the courage of the
Greeks at Thermopylae (4.260), but they do not fight for a good cause
and, Byron says, " 'tis the cause makes all" (4.261). Like the Byronic
heroes of the oriental tales, the mutineers go by their own code rather
than by standard morality, and they have no principles to defend. Byron
rejects this kind of individual heroism, dismissing Christian as a "poor
victim of self-will" (4.287). According to the vision presented in The
Island, man, to live well and honorably, must subordinate himself to a
cause, even if it is a jingoistic one. The Romantic rebel is cursed by his
inability to achieve Rousseau's state of nature and at the same time by
his failure to suppress his individuality in becoming an integral part
of the social world. His only hope, then, is to erase his egoistic self

and avoid the painful dilemmas that mar his existence in sad reality. While Christian can only fight and be crushed, Torquil achieves a state of blissful forgetfulness and, unlike the tragic Rousseau of *The Triumph of Life,* manages to maintain it. He is a new kind of hero who lives in harmony with nature, and he stands in stark contrast to the Byronic hero who lives in eternal enmity with both nature and himself.

* * *

The island of Toobonai itself, as the title of the poem suggests, is the central image of Byron's last major work. It stands as a multifaceted symbol which is interpreted in different ways by the rebels, Christian, the islanders themselves, and Neuha and Torquil. According to the mutineers, Toobonai represents paradise. At the beginning of *The Island* Byron alludes to Milton's description of Adam and Eve leaving Eden (*Paradise Lost,* 12.646) in reference to the *Bounty*'s departure from Toobonai. "The waters with their world were all before" (1.5), he writes, noting that the paradisiacal South Sea islands are "Behind" (1.6), growing increasingly distant from the ocean-weary rebels. The mutineers, inspired by the island they have left, have developed a kind of collective myth, which makes Toobonai its paradise, and "the uncertain wave" (1.32) of the dangerous sea its hell. Weary of being "driven / Before the mast by every wind of heaven" (1.112–13), they long for the womblike peace and security of "the cave / Of some soft savage" (1.31–32). In essence, their myth is extremely simple, even childlike, and does not make sufficient allowances for the power of the outside world to exact retribution on those who break its laws. They cherish the unrealistic hope that somehow "their distant caves / Might . . . be missed amidst the world of waves" (3.35–36), again contrasting the dangerous ocean and the caves which offer them an illusory security. Unfortunately for the mutineers, their half-baked myth is shattered by the forces of law and order, and, after they are defeated in battle, they find themselves silenced as well: "Each sought his fellow's eyes, as if to call / On him for language which his lips denied, / As though their voices with their cause had died" (3.82–85). Their imaginations fail to take into account the outside world and collapse as soon as reality asserts itself in the form of a "wicked-looking craft" (2.513).

Christian, on the other hand, never has any illusions of attaining paradise. Like Milton's Satan, he carries hell within him, shouting: "I am in hell! in hell!" (1.164). Moreover, Christian also resembles Satan in his determination to be free at all costs. As he tells Torquil: "For me, my lot is what I sought; to be, / In life or death, the fearless and the free" (3.163–64). Byron reinforces this idea of Christian's satanic nature by picturing his once graceful locks of hair as rising "like startled vipers" (4.90) and using the simile "like a serpent" (3.336) to describe Christian preparing to commit suicide. If Torquil is hopeful, Christian is the embodiment of despair, and even the sight of Torquil and Neuha together in "Nature's ecstasy" (3.200) fails to uplift his spirits. He can only feel a "gloomy joy / Mixed with those bitter thoughts the soul arrays / In hopeless visions of . . . better days" (3.204–6). Unlike Torquil, whose mind is totally focused on the present, the past distorts Christian's outlook and makes it impossible for him to see anything positive in the world around him. His myth focuses on himself, and the island attracts him simply because, burdened by no laws, he is allowed to express himself freely. In Toobonai there is no one to contradict Christian's negative, destructive vision, to make him remain a part of the social order he despises. He dies fighting for his freedom, even though this freedom is essentially a sterile thing, which creates nothing and cannot allay Christian's desperate unhappiness. Like the Lucifer of Byron's *Cain,* he revolts to assert his own selfhood, not to pursue any altruistic goals. In the end he describes himself as mad (3.146) and his myth of absolute freedom—of his right to be God in his solipsistic little universe—becomes little more than an expression of his paranoid and violent nature. Christian, with both Maddalo's negative view of the world and Maddalo's leadership qualities, leads himself and his men to destruction. In presenting the Byronic hero as a homicidal madman, Byron repudiates the protagonists of many of his earlier poems, along with the view of the world they profess.

In contrast, the myth that the islanders present seems like the expression of perfect mental health, grounded in reality but offering the possibility of happiness. The "ditty of Tradition's days" (2.79) sung by the natives of Toobonai expresses nature's harmony in a simple way, uncomplicated by modern sophistication. "Rung from the rock, or mingled with the wave" (2.88), the islanders' song is both spontaneous and naturalistic. Instead of monuments or "Hieroglyphics . . . /

For sages' labours, or the student's dream" (2.93–94), the Toobonai natives create a harmony which embodies "The first, the freshest bud of Feeling's soil" (2.96). Since nothing is written down, everything envisioned by the islanders is "first," and the influences that stifle the vision of Shelley's Rousseau are nonexistent. After describing the song of Toobonai, Byron asks: "what can our accomplished art / Of verse do more than reach the awakened heart?" (2.101–2). This sentiment recalls Shelley's belief that "the power of awakening in others sensations like those which animate [a poet's] own bosom" is an "essential attribute of Poetry" (see the preface to *The Revolt of Islam*).[18] The immediacy of the islanders' vision of life makes them tend, however, toward realism rather than the creation of myths—even the appearance of a woman from the deep, which makes some of the natives think that a "Goddess" (4.212) has manifested herself, is ultimately explained as a natural phenomenon. And although the mutineers have a romantic view of the island, the islanders recognize that Toobonai is no paradise. They have been attacked in the past by warriors from Fiji (2.35) and, while they enjoy the present, they do so with the knowledge that death awaits them: "to-morrow we may die" (2.46). The islanders present a bifocal view of the world which includes both hope and realism, and this double vision is expressed at the end of their song: "We too will see Licoo; but—oh! my heart!— / What do I say?—to-morrow we depart!" (2.63–64).[19] Their perspective on life is healthier and more balanced than the mutineers' fearful search for refuge and Christian's asocial search for absolute freedom, but it falls short of the dream shared by Torquil and Neuha of an earthly paradise.

With Neuha's help Torquil ultimately frees himself from the influence of Christian and the other mutineers, and comes to accept a perspective on the world which incorporates both the islanders' child-like sensitivity to nature and many of Shelley's ideals. Although Torquil, unlike Shelley, adopts a simple, nonintellectual perspective on life, Toobonai becomes for him an island of love which has much in common with the "Elysian isle" (539) of Shelley's *Epipsychidion*. Robinson asserts, moreover, that there are similarities between Shelley, as Byron saw him, and Torquil, who has blue eyes, fair hair, and is "Eager to hope, but not less firm to bear, / Acquainted with all feelings save despair" (2.163–78).[20] The description of the love between Torquil and

Neuha reminds one of Shelley's vision of love in his essay "On Love" and in *Epipsychidion,* especially since they unite with each other "in one absorbing soul" (2.305) and an "all-absorbing flame" (2.378). And Torquil's metamorphosis into a Shelleyan hero, during which he must "Strip off [his] fond and false identity" (2.392), parallels the transformation of the happy inhabitants of Prometheus's redeemed world in *Prometheus Unbound,* who cast off the "foul disguise" (3.4.70) of their corrupt former selves.

Before he can establish his Shelleyan outlook on life, however, Torquil must overcome Christian's influence. Even when Neuha and Torquil are alone, Christian looms in the background. The sun sets over them violently, in a way that prefigures Christian's death, descending "fiery, full, and fierce, as if he left / The World for ever, earth of light bereft, / [and] Plunged with red forehead down along the wave, / As dives a hero headlong to his grave" (2.362–65). In describing Christian's negative influence on Torquil, Byron, whether consciously or unconsciously, depicts a relationship which has some resemblances to his own association with Shelley during the last months of Shelley's life. Although Torquil is ultimately successful in attaining paradise with Neuha, he cannot free himself from Christian's influence, or the influence of sad reality, until after he has experienced and transcended the dark Byronic vision of life. Until then, Torquil's love for Neuha has some negative characteristics: it is a "desolating joy" (2.112) and they delight in their love as "martyrs revel in their funeral pyre" (2.116). Like Shelley, Torquil finds his own perspective at least temporarily obscured by a Byronic influence, the "hopeless visions" (3.206) Christian has of human existence.

The imperfect Eden of the lovers' first idyll is essentially static, and Byron, with his sense of the dynamic and changing nature of life, follows his description of their happiness with an abrupt fall into the everyday world of a gruff, unsentimental sailor. The fact that Torquil responds so readily to Ben Bunting's call to arms and is, moreover, willing to part from his antitype, indicates that he still has ties to sad reality. After he leaves Neuha, Torquil's descent into hell is almost immediate: abruptly, the clear blue sky of the lovers' tryst (2.414) gives way to the "polluted Heaven" (3.4) made infernal by the "sulphury vapours" (3.3) of battle. Torquil finds himself in Christian's destructive world and becomes scarred psychologically by his collision with sad reality: "his worst wound was within" (3.99). In order to escape from his pursuers and recover from his contact with violence and death, Torquil retreats to a cave with a submarine entrance, an enclosure which, like Cythna's ocean cavern, leads to the mental recuperation of those who seek refuge in it.

Although the idea of the sea cave is ostensibly taken from William Mariner's *Account of the Natives of the Tonga Islands,* its function in the poem has some similarities to the role of the "cave / Above the waters" (7.2929–30) in *The Revolt of Islam.*[21] Like Torquil, Cythna, after receiving serious psychic wounds in the violent outer world, enters her cave by diving to an underwater aperture. The enclosures in both poems are similar to religious sanctuaries: Cythna recuperates from her rape by Othman in a "hupaithric temple" (7.2935), while Torquil seeks refuge from his pursuers in "a Chapel of the Seas" (4.160). Despite the fact that a tyrant imprisons Cythna in her cave, whereas Torquil hides in his, these sea caverns resemble each other as works of nature, works of art, and as places in which a person suffering from life's vicissitudes can recover. Torquil's "Gothic canopy" is "upreared by Nature's architect" (4.146–47); Cythna's "strange dungeon" (7.2953) is created by Earth (7.2946). Moreover, the cave in *The Island* is full of sculptures, "Fantastic faces" (4.156) formed "with a little tinge of phantasy" (4.155), while the sea cave of *The Revolt of Islam* contains "shapes like statues" (7.2945). But most significantly, each enclosure seems to heal the wounds of a world-weary protagonist. Cythna becomes a poet who strengthens her mental vision by experiencing the "war of earthly minds" (7.3134) that she imagines in the waves of the cave's fountain. Torquil, on the other hand, has Neuha to help him recover from his bout with sad reality: while Christian and his cohorts are hunted down, Torquil and Neuha make a "harmony" (4.229) in their island cave. In both cases the cave is a central image, embodying nature and mental rebirth, and Cythna and Torquil emerge from their enclosures with a renewed faith in their ideals and the possibility of paradise on earth.

In Neuha's cave Torquil regains the innocence he lost when he joined Christian and the mutineers in their war against society. More than this, he comes to accept nature's ceaseless flux, the creation, destruction, and recreation of worlds shaped by earthquake "When the Poles crashed, and water was the world" (4.150), or obliterated by "some earth-absorbing fire" (4.151). Unlike Byron's Cain, who despairs over Lucifer's vision of a universe undergoing successive apocalypses and rebirths, Torquil does not concern himself with the impermanence of material reality. On the contrary, he contents himself with the kind of existence that Cain, with his aspirations, thinks insufficient, an existence in which personal happiness, not man's condition as a whole, is preeminent. With Neuha's help, Torquil, rejecting European culture and the Western sky-god who obsesses Cain, substitutes for them the traditions of Toobonai and a tellurian goddess who conducts him into a "central realm of earth" (4.119), a cave full of fertility symbols (4.169–74). He thus frees himself from the Biblical myth of guilt and retribution haunting the other mutineers in "their guilt-won Paradise" (3.39) and becomes part of the verdant, unself-conscious world of nature.

In his cave Torquil encounters the Christian tradition of the Old World as a darkness which is overcome by a shaft of light: "As in some old cathedral's glimmering aisle / The dusty monuments from light recoil, / Thus sadly in their refuge submarine / The vault drew half her shadow from the scene" (4.133–36). The allusion to Genesis at the beginning of *The Island*, in which the retreating night is described "Dividing darkness from the dawning main" (1.8), parallels the cave's metamorphosis from a dark cathedral full of "dusty monuments" to a tiny paradise illuminated by Neuha's pine torch. If they are to regain paradise, Torquil and Neuha must re-create their world. Thus, after setting her lover up in the safety of a natural refuge, Neuha places their adventures within the framework of the island's poetic tradition, telling him the "olden tale of Love" (4.192) that is the inspiration for her actions. In becoming part of Toobonai's continuing myth, Torquil is freed from the Old World and its traditions, and from the influences of the despotic Captain Bligh and the nihilistic Christian. By presenting Torquil with a new tradition Neuha gives him more than the confused murmur that greets Rousseau at the beginning of his dream in *The Triumph of Life*, but less than the overpowering visions which can obliterate a newly formed imagination.

Although little is presented in *The Island* describing Torquil's utopia in his "yet infant world" (4.420) after the ship from England has left, his position as an Adam in a South Seas Eden contrasts sharply with

Christian's fate as a satanic being destroyed by his conflict with the representatives in the Old World. While Christian finds himself in an imaginative cul-de-sac as a would-be epic hero in an age in which gunpowder has made epic heroism obsolete (3.47–50), Torquil becomes a new kind of solipsistic hero, passive rather than active, who tries to avoid strife rather than seek it. Neuha and Torquil create their own poetic vision, a tale which replaces the "olden tale of Love" which precedes it—even their cave is renamed "Neuha's Cave" (4.414) as the islanders acknowledge the primacy of their "new tradition." And their happiness is more secure than the contentment of ignorance because they have survived the world of experience. The Eden of Torquil and Neuha is "perilously earned" (4.418) by Neuha's foresight in preparing the cave and Torquil's trust in diving after her into the depths. As Prometheus is redeemed through his love for Asia, Torquil's devotion for Neuha ultimately saves him from Christian's hell on earth.

* * *

Neuha's beneficial influence over Torquil is so strong that the reader may be tempted to dismiss Christian and the violence associated with him as simply a momentary tempest which briefly interrupts the idyll. One must remember, however, that the subtitle of the poem is "Christian and his Comrades," and that although Christian remains largely in the background of the poem, he performs an important function. In fact, even his tendency to recede from Torquil's consciousness is significant, since Torquil must repress his awareness of Christian in order to identify himself totally with Neuha. The real conflict in *The Island* is between Christian and Neuha, who influence the impressionable Torquil in drastically different ways, much as Lucifer and Adah influence Cain. Because he is essentially passive, Torquil sees Christian and Neuha as models rather than rivals. It is not in his nature to contend with others and, in this, he is an exemplary Shelleyan hero. Unlike the bound Prometheus, he would never set himself in fruitless opposition to a god or swear vengeance, and the violence of the mutineers' last stand sickens him. Torquil's personality is not developed enough to be fully independent: he first falls under Christian's control and participates in the mutiny and then becomes totally dominated by Neuha and the worldview that she represents.

After Christian dies, however, Torquil is left without a leader and without a potential rival and thus has nothing, once the "wicked-looking craft" departs, to revolt or contend against. Whereas Don Juan's paradisiacal tryst with Haidée is brutally interrupted by her piratical father and the world of experience, Byron saves the equally passive Torquil from a similar fate in *The Island* by having the Corsair-like Christian killed and making the representatives of the outside world sail away on their warship. In the "yet infant world" of Toobonai the Shelleyan hero finds it possible to avoid the negative influence of his European past and of a Byronic contemporary, two factors which haunted Shelley in his own search for a poetic utopia. After Christian's death the harmony that Torquil and Neuha create together is one of "Peace and Pleasure" (4.418), free from the effects of Christian's disruptive presence.

But Torquil is not the only one who must deal with the somber figure of the self-destructive Christian—Byron must also come to terms with this character from his violent oriental tales, a character that threatens the peace of Byron's most pastoral poem. At times, Byron's denunciations of Christian and his fellow mutineers seem almost shrill, as if Byron, in his attempts to exorcise his own Byronic hero, felt compelled to go to extremes. When Christian's locks rise melodramatically, "like startled vipers," Byron enters the realm of parody, and Byron's description of Christian's death, which the mutineer punctuates by shooting a pursuer with a coat button, is gratuitously and senselessly violent. Christian appears to represent a part of Byron's work, perhaps of Byron's own personality, that Byron, in his last major poem, is at pains to reject and then to kill. And in putting Christian to death Byron also repudiates Maddalo's pessimistic vision. If Maddalo's view of life cannot be refuted or obliterated by a more persuasive vision of the world, it *can* be consigned, as Christian is, to a violent death.

Thus while Byron appears to have overshadowed Shelley's later career, Shelley haunted Byron's imagination after his drowning, and inspired Byron to write his most Shelleyan poem. Far from an affirmation of "the necessity of self-discipline,"[22] *The Island* is an assertion of the possibility of a Shelleyan hero achieving happiness and escaping the outside world through an apparent death at sea, which is really a rebirth into a new and better existence. Torquil's disappearance into the ocean and resurrection is, perhaps, Byron's sentimental revision of

Shelley's own, more disfiguring fate, which prompted Trelawny to use a quotation from *The Tempest* for the drowned poet's epitaph: "Nothing of him that doth fade, / But doth suffer a sea change / Into something rich and strange."[23] Byron, who was horrified by the state of Shelley's mangled body, plotted a much better "sea change" for his Shelleyan hero, who not only survives drowning but lives to flourish in an island paradise similar to that envisioned by the speaker of *Epipsychidion*.

Even though it remains an isolated case in Byron's poetry, *The Island* stands as an important memorial to Shelley. In the last part of his life Byron sensed that there is, as Julian says, "something nobler than to live and die" (*Julian and Maddalo*, 187), and that a man like Torquil, too young to be spoiled by cynicism, could achieve this "something nobler." In the end the strong influence the two poets had over each other made them reverse their philosophical positions until, incongruously, Byron began to sound like Julian and Shelley like Maddalo. Byron, the so-called pessimist, created an idealistic idyll in his last major work, whereas Shelley, the "beautiful and ineffectual angel," concluded his career with a corrosive vision of bitter reality.

* * *

Both Shelley and Byron died relatively young men, and one is left to wonder how their relationship would have changed had they known each other longer. The tension in Pisa looms large only, perhaps, because it immediately preceded Shelley's drowning. In a sense the conversation begun in Venice is a fragment broken off, like Shelley's *The Triumph of Life*, by death. We can never know whether its ending would have been positive or negative.

What we are left with, then, is a relationship between two important poets which seems, on the whole, to have helped both of them develop and refine their poetic visions, their philosophical beliefs, and their aesthetic tastes. The philosophical discussions of Shelley and Byron were not actuated by the desire of either poet to clear an imaginative space for himself or to escape the influence of another strong poet. Rather, they sought, in their constant arguments, their unwavering attention to each other's beliefs, to better understand themselves, their poetry, and the world in which they lived. Shelley and Byron did not need to misread each other, as Shelley, in Harold Bloom's opinion, felt compelled to misread Wordsworth; in fact, they understood each other with a clarity, almost an objectivity, which is rare in poetic relationships.

The conversation of Shelley and Byron evolved until the poets came almost to resemble each other. As they considered Byronic and Shelleyan heroes in their works they both came to see the limitations of their perspectives, and Shelley, in *The Triumph of Life*, seems to be repudiating his Julian persona much as Byron, in *The Island*, exorcises the Byronic hero. Neither Shelley nor Byron let their conversation become a repetitive argument in which they merely contradicted each other— their interaction helped them grow and change as poets, and it should, perhaps, come as no surprise that their later works seem so remarkably different from many of their earlier productions.

Writing of Byron and Shelley, Algernon Charles Swinburne notes their commitment to the passionate exploration of nature: "[Shelley and Byron] were not content to play with [nature's] skirts and paddle in her shadows. Their passion is perfect, a fierce and blind desire which exalts and impels their verse into the high places of emotion and expression. They feed upon nature with a holy hunger, follow her with a divine lust as of gods chasing the daughters of men."[24] This passion and determination to attain in their works "the high places of emotion and expression" is common to both poets. They are, in a sense, overreachers, and when their poems fail it is most often because they try to do too much rather than too little. The poets' efforts to go beyond the poetry of their era, to use verse as it had never been used before, led them to create their greatest works: in *The Triumph of Life* and *Don Juan* we have poems which defy convention and point ahead to the modern age.

In different ways Byron and Shelley were both Promethean figures, and if Byron's Prometheus was a bitterly defiant prisoner and Shelley's was a triumphant rebel-turned-pacifist, each poet had the Promethean aspiration to change his world, to create poetry that was new and went against the accepted notions of the day. Their relationship has a special importance because the issues they stood for were seminal and reverberated throughout the literature that followed. And it has that rare quality among poetic associations of being consistently beneficial, like Goethe's friendship with Schiller, or Robert Frost's short relationship with Edward Thomas.[25] Poets often compete against each other to the detriment of their work, but they also can inspire one another to test their limitations, to dare to go beyond that which they had done before. It is, as Shelley writes, impossible "to exclude from [a poet's] contemplation the beautiful which exists in the writings of a great contemporary," and that contemplation, in the case of Shelley and Byron, helped to inspire each of them in their Promethean quests.

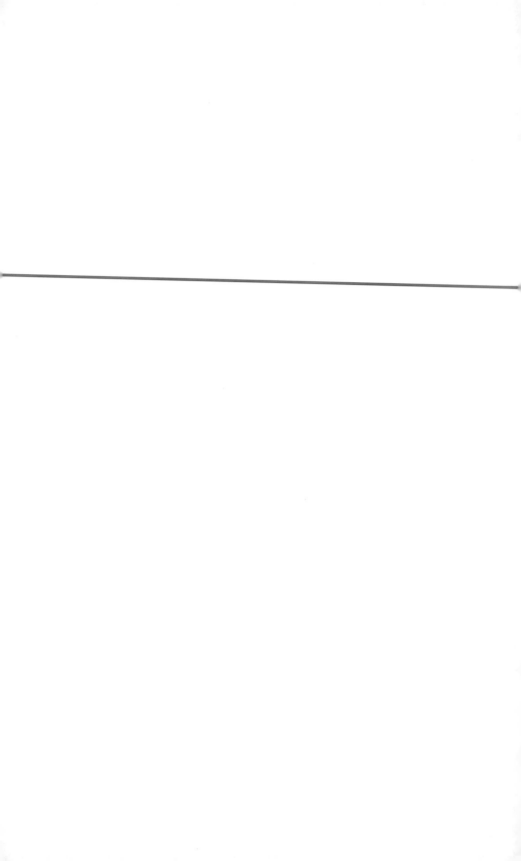

Byron and Shelley in
Mary Shelley's *The Last Man*

Although forbidden "to bring dear S[helley]'s name before the public again during Sir T[imothy Shelley]'s life,"[1] Mary Shelley did manage to present a fictional version of her husband in *The Last Man*. She used, of course, some poetic license in this portrait of Shelley—writing to John Bowring, she indicated that the novel's Shelleyan character, Adrian, is not identical to the original: "I have endeavoured, but how inadequately to give some idea of [Shelley] in my last published book—the sketch has pleased some of those who best loved him—I might have made more of it but there are feelings which one recoils from unveiling to the public eye."[2] To Teresa Guiccioli she wrote: "Have you read my Last Man—You will find in Lord Raymond and Count Adrian faint portraits but *I hope* not displeasing to you of B[yron] and S[helley]."[3] Although *The Last Man* is a work of fiction rather than a description of the Shelley-Byron relationship, in the Adrian-Raymond sections of the novel Mary Shelley presents an important, if somewhat subjective, appraisal of the two poets she knew so well.

Mary Shelley, like Shelley himself in *Julian and Maddalo*, saw Byron and Shelley as men who, despite their differences, were united in their compassion for suffering humanity. *The Last Man* contains some penetrating examples of Adrian-Shelley and Raymond-Byron in conversation: "we remained to discuss the affairs of nations, and the philosophy of life. The very difference of our dispositions gave zest to these conversations. Adrian had the superiority in learning and eloquence; but

Raymond possessed a quick penetration, and a practical knowledge of
life, which usually displayed itself in opposition to Adrian, and thus kept
up the ball of discussion."[4] This recalls, of course, *Julian and Maddalo,*
in which the idealisms of Julian-Shelley are met by Maddalo-Byron's
terse response: "You talk Utopia." Earlier in the novel, however, when
Adrian and Raymond first meet, their relationship is not as convivial,
and Mary Shelley describes an opposition which approaches antagonism: "At this time Lord Raymond returned from Greece. No two
persons could be more opposite than Adrian and he. With all the in-
congruities of his character, Raymond was emphatically a man of the
world. . . . Adrian felt that he made a part of a great whole. . . . His soul
was sympathy, and dedicated to the worship of beauty and excellence.
Adrian and Raymond now came into contact, and a spirit of aversion
rose between them. Adrian despised the narrow views of the politician,
and Raymond held in supreme contempt the benevolent visions of the
philanthropist" (31).

Thus in *The Last Man* Mary Shelley radically alters the history of
the Shelley-Byron relationship; whereas Shelley and Byron began on
friendly terms and experienced tensions during the later period of the
association, Adrian and Raymond at first despise each other and then
become friends. There is a sense in *The Last Man* that if Shelley's death
had not put a premature end to his friendship with Byron, the poets'
relations would have improved, and Shelley might even have joined
Byron in the struggle in Greece. Mary Shelley makes Adrian Raymond's biggest supporter: when Raymond proposes going to Greece in
the novel, the sickly and weak Adrian immediately agrees to join him,
and, earlier in the novel, Adrian enthusiastically supports Raymond's
election as Lord Protector of England.

In essence, the arguments of Adrian and Raymond are seen as stimulating rather than antagonistic, as when the characters discuss plans
for civic improvement: "Raymond talked of his new buildings; of his
plan for an establishment for the better education of the poor; as usual
Adrian and he entered into argument, and time slipped away unper-
ceived" (99). The "as usual" reflects Mary Shelley's own experience
of the poets' many dialogues—even after Shelley's death, the voice of
Byron led her to expect an answering remark from her husband: "when
Albè [Byron] ceases to speak I expect to hear *that other* voice, & when I

hear another instead, it jars strangely with every association. . . . when Albe speaks & Shelley does not answer, it is as thunder without rain."[5] Although Adrian and Raymond, like their models, often disagree, not all of their conversations turn into arguments—when Raymond decides to leave his estranged wife and his post as Lord Protector of England to join the Greek revolution, Adrian dismisses Verney's objections and agrees to join Raymond. Adrian becomes, in fact, Raymond's most generous and consistent supporter, and their relationship is ultimately positive.

This does not mean, of course, that Mary Shelley neglects to point out the characters' failings as well as their virtues. In the first part of the novel Adrian is consistently seen as weak, sickly, and reclusive, without any discernible goals or useful occupations. He is never able to find that antitype or ideal woman always sought by Shelley—Adrian's passion for Evadne comes to nothing when she becomes infatuated with Raymond. In fact, Evadne's rejection of Adrian leads to Adrian's mental breakdown and virtual retirement—only when the world is being ravaged by the plague is Adrian able to take on an important role. Before then, Adrian derides those who would attempt to drag him, "a poor visionary from the clouds" (68), into the public arena. In post-revolutionary Europe, Mary Shelley seems to be suggesting, Shelley lacked the political acumen to forward his social agenda—it would have taken a major catastrophe to enable him to demonstrate his heroic qualities. Thus she has the visionary Adrian note that the plague, by rendering politics irrelevant, has finally allowed him to become his country's benefactor: "I cannot intrigue, or work a tortuous path through the labyrinth of men's vices and passions; but I can bring patience, and sympathy, and such aid as art affords, to the bed of disease" (179).

Moreover, the Byronic Raymond, although far more active and effective than Adrian in the first section of the novel, proves self-destructive. Although able to rise to the position of Lord Protector, he is unable to control his passions—as Raymond himself says, his inability to rule himself makes him an unfit ruler of men: "I undertook a task to which I am unequal. I cannot rule myself. My passions are my masters; my smallest impulse my tyrant" (109). In this analysis of Byron, Mary Shelley seems to agree with Shelley's description of Maddalo-Byron in his preface to *Julian and Maddalo:* "His passions and his powers are incomparably greater than those of other men; and, instead of the latter having been employed in curbing the former, they have mutually lent each other strength. His ambition preys upon itself." Raymond, a self-described "victim of ambition" (141), fails (like Byron) as a husband, and then is crushed and mutilated by a falling ruin when he decides to invade the plague-infested Constantinople by himself. Although this portrait of Byron is full of praise—he is "a transcendent power, whose intents, words, and actions [are] worthy to be recorded in letters of gold" (150)—there is a pessimistic sense in the novel that this charismatic and talented figure is too changeable, perverse, and self-destructive to be able to do much for his fellow man.

It is significant that Adrian is only able to become a leader after Raymond's death—it is almost as if Mary Shelley suspected that Byron's presence inhibited her husband's productivity, and that Shelley would have been able to accomplish a great deal had Byron disappeared from the scene. Although much of Adrian's life is marked by mental and physical breakdowns, after Raymond's death he becomes an able and vigorous ruler of England: "[Lionel Verney] was struck by the improvement that appeared in the health of Adrian. He was no longer bent to the ground, like an over-nursed flower of spring. . . . His eyes were bright, his countenance composed, an air of concentrated energy was diffused over his whole person, much unlike its former languor" (181). It would seem, then, that Raymond benefits far more from the relationship than does Adrian, who flourishes only in Raymond's absence. This is not, however, because only Adrian is supportive—before Raymond decides on his own candidacy for the post of Lord Protector, he tries to nominate Adrian for the position. But Adrian, who, like Shelley, is self-deprecating and perhaps overmodest, never accepts Raymond's support. One suspects that Mary Shelley believed that her husband could have used his connection to Byron more effectively—perhaps with John Murray, the publisher Mary Shelley herself approached after Byron's death—but that Shelley refused to do so. It seems clear, however, that in *The Last Man* Raymond gets far more from his relationship with Adrian than Adrian gets in return, and this may well reflect Mary Shelley's opinion of the Shelley-Byron association. Like Edward

Trelawny, Mary Shelley must have been at times sorely tempted to ask Byron to "puff the Snake."[6]

The Adrian-Raymond portion of *The Last Man* stands, then, as an intriguing memorial to the Shelley-Byron relationship. Perhaps because she wrote it with the poets' premature deaths in mind, Mary Shelley presents Promethean aspirations in *The Last Man* as heroic but ultimately doomed. The kinship of *The Last Man* with Byron's gloomy "Darkness" has often been noted, but Byron's poem is presented as a dream vision, and *The Last Man,* according to the "Author's Introduction," is a document based on Sibylline leaves—Sibylline leaves which contain "truths" (4). It is significant, moreover, that Mary Shelley puts one of the most despairing utterances of the novel in the mouth of her Shelley-like Adrian (with imagery derived from *The Triumph of Life*): "I have done my best; with grasping hands and impotent strength, I have hung on the wheel of the chariot of plague; but she drags me along with it, while, like Juggernaut, she proceeds crushing out the being of all who strew the high road of life. Would that it were over—would that her procession achieved, we had all entered the tomb together!" (289). But although *The Last Man* is a novel of almost unrelieved pessimism, Mary Shelley presents the Adrian-Raymond association as an essentially positive and supportive relationship. Thus, when Raymond-Byron decides to exile himself from England, it is Adrian-Shelley, his "companion, the outcast's friend" (110), who instantly agrees to accompany him on his final quest.

Cash Rules: Money and the Byron-Shelley Relationship

Ready cash is a nonliterary factor that may well have affected the Shelley-Byron association. Shelley essentially despised wealth, complaining while in Edinburgh of being "chained to the filth & *commerce*"[1] of that city, but Byron, especially in his later years, had a great appreciation for cash. In *Don Juan* he humorously dedicates a passage to misers and the object of their worship:

> Love or lust makes man sick, and wine much sicker;
>   Ambition rends, and gaming gains a loss;
> But making money, slowly first, then quicker,
>   And adding still a little through each cross
> (Which *will* come over things) beats love or liquor,
>   The gamester's counter, or the statesman's *dross.*
> Oh Gold! I still prefer thee unto paper,
> Which makes bank credit like a bark of vapour. (12.25–32)

Although, as Doris Langley Moore has demonstrated, Trelawny was grossly exaggerating when he wrote that Byron was a member of "that great sect that worships golden images,"[2] Byron's attitude toward financial matters was in sharp contrast to Shelley's relative carelessness with money, and this difference seems to have been an important factor during the last months of their association.

Of course, both poets had gone through periods of financial embarrassment during their careers, but while Byron worked to build capital and avoid money problems, Shelley went from eluding warrants of arrest for debt in England to incurring increasingly ruinous post obit loans in Italy. As Doris Moore notes, "When it was borne in upon [Byron] at last that he had been the victim of innumerable great and small impositions, he over-reacted in his typical manner, and determined to make known his love of money and his resolution never to be cheated again."[3] In Ravenna Byron appointed an Italian, Lega, to act as his secretary and do his bookkeeping, and Lega's overzealousness on his master's behalf may well have added to Byron's reputation for avarice. Moreover, Byron often presented himself to his friends as a miser—in a 27 January 1819 letter to Douglas Kinnaird he wrote: "I have imbibed such a love for money that I keep some Sequins in a drawer to count, & cry over them once a week."[4] By 23 February 1822 he was writing to Kinnaird that "Cash is Virtue,"[5] and in 1823, after Shelley's death, he reaffirmed his greed: "I loves lucre."[6] But, as Doris Moore observes, "if we set Byron's reputation for avarice against his actual expenditure, we find that the letters in which he boasted of loving lucre have little relation to what he did with it when he began to have it in comparative abundance."[7] In fact, Lega's list of Byron's charitable contributions for March 1822 reveals that Byron was consistently generous to the poor and handicapped, and also gave money to nuns and monks.[8]

Unfortunately, while Byron was gathering his growing wealth and entrusting it to the painstaking and scrupulous Lega, Shelley, in 1822, estimated that he owed between £20,000 and £25,000, mostly in loans taken out against his expected inheritance.[9] According to Doris Moore,

> Shelley . . . from early youth had lived and assisted his friends mainly by reckless borrowing on terms even more ruinous than those Byron had consented to at eighteen. . . . [H]e had made disastrous use of his expectations from the entailed estate of his father, and until the latter should die, his own consisted of nothing but debts, the major part of which were the consequence of his approaches to two authors much older than himself, both of whom he had informed, before meeting them, that he was the son of a man of property. William Godwin and Leigh Hunt had known exactly how to welcome that kind of admirer.[10]

Moreover, unlike Byron, Shelley handled his own financial affairs—he had no Lega to manage expenses and discourage borrowing. It is perhaps not surprising, then, that during the time they lived in close proximity in Pisa financial matters would cause tension between the poets, especially since Shelley was put in the delicate position of having to negotiate with Byron for loans to finance Leigh Hunt and *The Liberal.* Shelley, who had relatively few funds, was prepared to be generous, whereas Byron, who was quite wealthy, seemed begrudging in his expenditures.

Byron's apparent stinginess became especially offensive to Shelley's circle of friends when he declined to honor a bet he had made with Shelley regarding the poets' legacies. In his journal entry for 25 December 1821, Edward Ellerker Williams wrote that "It was on this day that Lord B. and S[helley] proposed to give a thousand pounds to the other who first came to their estate."[11] But although Lady Noel (Lady Byron's mother) died on 28 January 1822,[12] and Byron came into an estate of £10,000 a year, he never paid Shelley the £1,000 he had wagered. Characteristically, Shelley never complained about not getting the money, but given his financial predicament, Byron's non-payment must have rankled. Of course, Byron made frequent loans to Shelley: in fact, Byron lent his friend £50 just before Shelley's death by drowning.[13] But one wonders whether or not the difficult last months of the poets' association may have been more adversely affected by Shelley's financial woes and his belief in Byron's stinginess than by their poetic rivalry.

It may, moreover, be significant that several pages of the manuscript of *The Triumph of Life* (probably composed in May and June 1822) are marked with what seem to be financial calculations, as if even in the middle of poetic composition money considerations were a distracting influence on Shelley. Although the poet condemns "Anarchs" who "spread the plague of blood and gold abroad" (285–87), one page of the manuscript is half-covered with numbers (including "250 crowns"), and two other pages have calculations jotted down in the margins.[14] While Byron could write in relative freedom from financial worries, the Shelleys must always have felt the pressure of being constantly in debt and short of cash.

Thus the poets' attitudes toward money affected both their lives and their careers, although not always in the way one would expect. While Byron had the reputation for being the more penurious of the two,

Shelley was able to persuade him to abandon the best-selling poetry of his early career and write works which were condemned by the same upper-class reading public who had made Byron famous. And Byron broke with John Murray, who published his works in expensive octavo and quarto volumes, and began selling cheaper editions of his poems to a less genteel audience. On the other hand, Shelley's financial feckless-ness at times inspired him to write (unsuccessfully) for money, as he essentially did when he wrote *The Cenci,* to be produced on the London stage. But while Byron was able to attain the kind of financial secu-rity that allowed him the freedom to write what he liked, financial ruin haunted Shelley from the moment he eloped with Harriet Westbrook. Moreover, the poets' different experiences with money are sometimes reflected in their works. Whereas "Cash rules the grove" (12.14) in *Don Juan,* money in Shelley's poetry is often condemned as bloody and corrupt: in Shelley's "The Mask of Anarchy" England is presented as a "lost country bought and sold / With a price of blood and gold" (293–94), and in *The Cenci* the psychopathic Count Cenci finds that gold can buy the pope himself, and allow him to commit unspeakable crimes. Although Shelley would have liked to have been able to tran-scend something as sordid as money, it nevertheless had an important effect on his and Byron's lives and careers, afflicting nearly every facet of Shelley's life while at the same time enabling Byron to write in de-fiance of prevailing literary tastes and, after Shelley's death, present a £4,000 loan to the government of Greece.

Notes

1. Shelley, Byron, and Their Conversations

1. Stephen C. Behrendt, in *Shelley and His Audiences,* 173, mentions the canceled lines of Shelley's "Sonnet to Byron," in which Shelley seems to wish that he, with his "witchcraft scarce," could compete with "the gilded throne" of Byron's popularity.

2. Charles E. Robinson, *Shelley and Byron: The Snake and Eagle Wreathed in Fight,* 8.

3. Ibid., 68.

4. Behrendt, 170. See also Warren S. Stevenson, *Poetic Friends: A Study of Literary Relations during the English Romantic Period.*

5. Robinson, *Shelley and Byron,* 59.

6. Ibid., 200.

7. Ibid., 214.

8. Ibid., 220–21.

9. Ibid., 81.

10. For an excerpt of Byron's and Shelley's discussion of *Hamlet,* see Walter Edwin Peck, *Shelley: His Life and Work,* 2:421–32; and on the authenticity of this discussion, see Earl R. Wasserman, "Shelley's Last Poetics: A Reconsideration," 505–8 and nn.

11. To Leigh Hunt, 15 August 1819, PBSL, 2:108.

12. For the fashionable talk of Shelley's Mephistopheles see Timothy Webb, *The Violet and the Crucible: Shelley and Translation,* 186–87.

13. John Buxton, *Byron and Shelley: The History of a Friendship,* 268.

14. P. M. S. Dawson, "Byron, Shelley, and the 'New School,'" 89–108. For

a different view of the poets' responses to Keats, see J. Drummond Bone, "Byron, Shelley and Contemporary Poetry 1820–1822," 69–77. According to Bone, while both poets perceive a "disordered profusion" in Keats's verse, "Shelley accepts [it] as an index of hidden value. Byron sees it as a sign of an emptiness revealed by attempts to conceal it" (71).

15. To Lord Byron, 16 April 1821, PBSL, 2:284; and to John Murray, 30 July 1821, BLJ, 8:163.

16. Robinson, *Shelley and Byron*, 159.

17. Thomas Medwin, *Medwin's Conversations of Lord Byron*, 97; and to Percy Bysshe Shelley, 26 April 1821, BLJ, 8:103.

18. To Mary Shelley, 7 August 1821, PBSL, 2:317.

19. G. M. Matthews, "On Shelley's 'The Triumph of Life,' " 104.

20. Charles E. Robinson, "Shelley to Byron in 1814: A New Letter," 104–10.

21. William Michael Rossetti, ed., *The Diary of Dr. John William Polidori, 1816*, 121.

22. To Maria Gisborne, 22 November 1822, in Betty T. Bennett, ed., *The Letters of Mary Wollstonecraft Shelley*, 1:290–91.

23. Mary Wollstonecraft Shelley, *Frankenstein, or The Modern Prometheus*, 227.

24. See Geoffrey Matthews and Kelvin Everest, eds., *The Poems of Shelley*, 1:519.

25. Edward John Trelawny, *Records of Shelley, Byron, and the Author*, 122.

26. Donald H. Reiman and Kenneth Neill Cameron, eds., *Shelley and His Circle: 1773–1822*, 5:198.

27. Newman Ivey White, *Shelley*, 2:714 n. 46.

28. See Judith Chernaik and Timothy Burnett, "The Byron and Shelley Notebooks in the Scrope Davies Find," 36–49.

29. Matthews and Everest, eds., *The Poems of Shelley*, 1:521.

30. To Thomas Love Peacock, 12 July 1816, PBSL, 1:486.

31. Reiman and Cameron, eds., *Shelley and His Circle*, 5:198.

32. Richard Holmes, *Shelley: The Pursuit*, 687.

33. To Leigh Hunt, 26 August 1821, PBSL, 2:343.

34. Quoted and discussed by Reiman in Reiman and Cameron, eds., *Shelley and His Circle*, 5:246.

35. Trelawny, 80.

36. Nathaniel Brown, *Sexuality and Feminism in Shelley*, 41.

37. To Thomas Love Peacock, [17 or 18] December 1818, PBSL, 2:58.

38. Brown, 2.

39. To Thomas Love Peacock, 8 October 1818, PBSL, 2:44.

40. To John Gisborne, 22 October 1821, PBSL, 2:363.

41. Brown, 80.

42. PBSL, 2:58.

43. Louis Crompton, *Byron and Greek Love: Homophobia in 19th-Century England*, 244.

44. Doris Langley Moore, *Lord Byron: Accounts Rendered*, 439.

45. Crompton, 8.

46. Ibid., 288.

47. Brown, 21.

48. To Thomas Love Peacock, 8 October 1818, PBSL, 2:42.

49. To Mary Shelley, 7 August 1821, PBSL, 2:323.

50. See PBSL, 2:318n, for Richard Belgrave Hoppner's letter detailing the allegations against Shelley.

51. To Mary Shelley, 16 August 1821, PBSL, 2:339.

52. Ibid., 10 August 1821, PBSL, 2:323.

53. Ibid., 15 August 1821, PBSL, 2:336.

54. To Thomas Love Peacock, [10?] August 1821, PBSL, 2:331.

55. To Mary Shelley, 15 August 1821, PBSL, 2:339.

56. Ernest J. Lovell, ed., *His Very Self and Voice: Collected Conversations of Lord Byron*, 273.

57. Peck, 2:432.

58. Holmes, 689.

59. Medwin, *Medwin's Conversations of Lord Byron*, 268n.

60. Ibid., 155n.

61. Trelawny, 73.

62. To Leigh Hunt, 10 April 1822, PBSL, 2:405.

63. To Horace Smith, 21 May 1822, PBSL, 2:423.

64. To Horace Smith, 25 January [1822], PBSL, 2:379.

65. To Claire Clairmont, [February 1822?], PBSL, 2:392.

66. Trelawny, 100.

67. Ibid., 121–22.

68. See letter to John Murray, 19 January [1830], in Bennett, ed., *The Letters of Mary Wollstonecraft Shelley*, 2:102.

69. Robinson, *Shelley and Byron*, 230.

70. To Horace Smith, 29 June 1822, PBSL, 2:443.

71. See Harold Bloom, *The Anxiety of Influence*.

72. The Blake texts cited here are taken from David V. Erdman, ed., *The Complete Poetry and Prose of William Blake*, 129, 180.

73. Jerome J. McGann, *The Romantic Ideology: A Critical Investigation*, 124.

74. Robinson, *Shelley and Byron*, 241–44.

75. Ibid., 244.

76. Robinson, "Shelley to Byron in 1814: A New Letter," 105, 108.
77. To Charles Ollier, 6 September 1819, PBSL, 2:118.
78. See PBSL, 2:470.
79. This translation of Julia Kristeva's remarks is taken from Parisier Plottle and Hanna Charney, eds., *Intertextuality: New Perspectives in Criticism,* 2:xiv.
80. See letter to Leigh Hunt, 29 May 1819, PBSL, 2:96.
81. Thomas Moore, *Letters and Journals of Lord Byron,* 316.
82. In fact, Moore warned Byron against Shelley's influence—see Shelley's letter to Horace Smith, 11 April 1822, 2:412. For an account of the Byron-Moore relationship, see Thérèse Tessier, "Byron and Thomas Moore: A Great Literary Friendship," 46–58.
83. See Trelawny, *Records of Shelley, Byron, and the Author.*

2. In Switzerland: Wordsworth and Science

1. See Lovell, ed., *His Very Self and Voice,* 182–83, 185.
2. See Robert Brinkley, "Documenting Revision: Shelley's Lake Geneva Diary and the Dialogue with Byron in *History of a Six Weeks' Tour,*" 66–82.
3. To Thomas Love Peacock, 15 May 1816, PBSL, 1:475.
4. Medwin, *Medwin's Conversations of Lord Byron,* 194.
5. See, for example, Byron's 19 January 1821 letter to John Murray, in which he calls Wordsworth "Turdsworth the great Metaquizzical poet" (BLJ, 8:66).
6. Lovell, ed., *His Very Self and Voice,* 129.
7. Medwin, *Medwin's Conversations of Lord Byron,* 194.
8. To Leigh Hunt, 30 October 1815, BLJ, 4:324.
9. G. Kim Blank, *Wordsworth's Influence on Shelley: A Study of Poetic Authority,* 44.
10. See the 14 September 1814 entry in Mary Shelley's journal: "[Shelley] brings home Wordsworths Excursion of which we read a part—much disapointed—He is a slave" *(sic).* I am quoting from Paula R. Feldman and Diana Scott-Kilvert, eds., *The Journals of Mary Shelley: 1814–1844,* 1:25.
11. Matthews and Everest, eds., *The Poems of Shelley,* 1:514–15.
12. To Thomas Love Peacock, 25 July 1818, PBSL, 2:26.
13. Medwin, *Medwin's Conversations of Lord Byron,* 194.
14. Jonathan Wordsworth also detects the influence of William Wordsworth's "The Forsaken Indian Woman" (of *Lyrical Ballads*) on Byron's *The Prisoner of Chillon* (1816). See Jonathan Wordsworth, " 'Tis to Create': A Fragment of Biography," 45.
15. See Michael G. Cooke, "Byron and Wordsworth: The Complementarity

of a Rock and the Sea," 32–38, for an analysis of "The Dream" as "Byron's counterpart to 'Tintern Abbey' " (32).

16. McGann notes this echo in McGann and Weller, eds., *Lord Byron: The Complete Poetical Works*, 4:456.

17. To Augusta Leigh, 13 January 1817, BLJ, 5:159.

18. See Robinson, *Shelley and Byron*, 35–37.

19. Matthews and Everest, eds., *The Poems of Shelley*, 1:535.

20. To Thomas Love Peacock, 17 July 1816, PBSL, 1:490.

21. Mary Wollstonecraft Shelley, *Frankenstein, or the Modern Prometheus*, 227.

22. Percy Bysshe Shelley, *Zastrozzi and St. Irvyne*, 180. Also see Holmes, 40.

23. Holmes, 38, 80.

24. To Elizabeth Hitchener, 23 November 1811, PBSL, 1:142.

25. See Kenneth Neill Cameron, *The Young Shelley: Genesis of a Radical*, 248.

26. Matthews and Everest, eds., *The Poems of Shelley*, 1:374.

27. See Cameron, *The Young Shelley*, 262.

28. John Clubbe, "The Tempest-Toss'd Summer of 1816: Mary Shelley's *Frankenstein*," 27–28.

29. See Robinson, *Shelley and Byron*, 254–55, for a summary of the evidence supporting Shelley's influence on "Darkness." Cyrus Redding claimed that " 'Darkness' originated in a conversation with Shelley, as [he and Byron] were standing together, . . . looking upon the Lake of Geneva. Shelley said, 'What a change it would be if the sun were to be extinguished at this moment; how the race of man would perish, until perhaps only one remained—suppose one of us! How terrible would be his fate!' " (Cyrus Redding, *Literary Reminiscences and Memoirs of Thomas Campbell*, 1:301.)

30. To Thomas Love Peacock, 23 July 1816, PBSL, 1:499.

31. See Feldman and Scott-Kilvert, eds., *The Journals of Mary Shelley*, 1:121.

32. PBSL, 1:499.

33. See Feldman and Scott-Kilvert, eds., *The Journals of Mary Shelley*, 1:116–17 and n.

34. See Matthews and Everest, eds., *The Poems of Shelley*, 1:536–37.

35. Martin J. S. Rudwick, *The Meaning of Fossils: Episodes in the History of Palaeontology*, 109.

36. Clubbe, 30.

37. Carl Grabo, *A Newton Among Poets: Shelley's Use of Science in* Prometheus Unbound, 177.

38. Ibid., 180.

39. Kenneth Neill Cameron, *Shelley: The Golden Years*, 553.

40. McGann and Weller, eds., *Lord Byron: The Complete Poetical Works*, 6:229. See also Byron's letter to Thomas Moore, 19 September 1821, BLJ, 8:216: "I

have gone upon the notion of Cuvier, that the world has been destroyed three or four times, and was inhabited by mammoths, behemoths, and what not; but *not* by man till the Mosaic period, as, indeed, it proved by the strata of bones found;— . . . I have, therefore, supposed Cain to be shown, in the *rational* Preadamites, beings endowed with a higher intelligence than man, but totally unlike him in form, and with much greater strength of mind and person."

41. Medwin, *Medwin's Conversations of Lord Byron,* 157.

42. Ibid., 188. Like many of his contemporaries, Byron confused comets with meteors, and attributed great destructive power to them: in *Manfred* he describes how Manfred's "star" is "A pathless comet" and "The menace of the universe" (1.1.110–19).

43. See McGann and Weller, eds., *Lord Byron: The Complete Poetical Works,* 4:459n, 465n.

44. See Holmes, 328; and Lovell, ed., *His Very Self and Voice,* 185–86.

45. Holmes, 328.

46. See Percy Bysshe Shelley, *Zastrozzi and St. Irvyne,* 123, 159; and Robinson, *Shelley and Byron,* 241–42.

47. Matthews and Everest, eds., *The Poems of Shelley,* 1:519.

48. Wordsworth, 46.

49. See Holmes, 686.

3. The Conversational Style of Byron and Shelley

1. To Leigh Hunt, 15 August 1819, PBSL, 1:108.

2. See preface to William Wordsworth, *Literary Ballads,* in W. J. B. Owen, ed., *Wordsworth's Literary Criticism,* 74.

3. Earl R. Wasserman, *Shelley: A Critical Reading,* 57.

4. Harold Bloom, "The Unpastured Sea: An Introduction to Shelley," 380.

5. The lines "if you can't swim / Beware of Providence" seem particularly prescient in light of the fact that Shelley died of drowning.

6. Donald Davie, *Purity of Diction in English Verse,* 144.

7. See Peck, 2:421–32.

8. Ibid., 425. Neville Rogers, in *Shelley at Work: A Critical Inquiry,* 16–17, 156–57, refers to another *Julian and Maddalo*–style conversation in which Shelley, under the name of Lionel (a name he uses for his personae in *Rosalind and Helen* and *The Boat on the Serchio,* and which Mary Shelley uses for her own persona in *The Last Man*), discusses the works of Keats with an unnamed character who may well be modeled on Byron. Certainly, Byron was capable of

discussing Keats's poetry in the language used by Lionel's friend, who refers to a book of Keats's verse as "a new knot of abortions" (Rogers, 257).

9. Kelvin Everest, "Shelley's Doubles: An Approach to 'Julian and Maddalo,'" 80.

10. William Keach, *Shelley's Style*, 22.

11. Journal, 16 November 1813, BLJ, 3:207; and to Samuel Rogers, 27 February 1814[?], BLJ, 4:74.

12. See Timothy Clark, *Embodying Revolution: The Figure of the Poet in Shelley*, 208.

13. McGann and Weller, eds., *Lord Byron: The Complete Poetical Works*, 4:450.

14. To Lord Byron, 9 July 1817, PBSL, 1:547.

15. Bernard A. Hirsch, "'A Want of That True Theory': *Julian and Maddalo* as Dramatic Monologue," 14.

16. See Carlos Baker, *Shelley's Major Poetry: The Fabric of a Vision*, 128–35.

17. To Lord Byron, 24 September 1817, PBSL, 1:556–57.

18. Donald H. Reiman and Sharon B. Powers, eds., *Shelley's Poetry and Prose*, 475.

19. See Webb, 186–87. Byron himself saw a Mephistophelian element in his tendency to observe humanity in a detached, ironic way. In canto 13 of *Don Juan* (written after Shelley's death) he writes: "For my part, I am but a mere spectator, / And gaze where'er the palace or the hovel is, / Much in the mode of Goethe's Mephistopheles" (13.54–56).

20. Medwin, *Medwin's Conversations of Lord Byron*, 119.

21. Detached Thoughts, no. 55, BLJ, 9:31.

22. To Thomas Love Peacock, 8 October 1818, PBSL, 2:42.

23. PBSL, 2:42.

24. Richard Cronin, *Shelley's Poetic Thoughts*, 57–58.

25. To Douglas Kinnaird, 31 August 1820, BLJ, 7:167.

26. Cronin, 57–58.

27. Robinson describes the relationship between the first two cantos of *Don Juan* and Shelley's *The Witch of Atlas* in *Shelley and Byron*, 268 n. 10.

28. Brian Nellist, "Shelley's Narratives and 'The Witch of Atlas,'" 178.

29. Jerome J. McGann, "A Reply to George Ridenour," 576.

4. *The Cenci* and Sad Reality

1. Robinson, *Shelley and Byron*, 144.

2. To John Murray, 4 January 1821, BLJ, 8:57.

3. To Percy Bysshe Shelley, 26 April 1821, BLJ, 8:103.

4. To Thomas Love Peacock, 20 July 1819, PBSL, 2:102.

5. Reiman and Cameron, eds., *Shelley and His Circle*, 7:46.

6. To Mary Shelley, 7 August 1821, PBSL, 2:317.

7. Robinson, *Shelley and Byron*, 159.

8. Ibid., 156.

9. Many critics have, in fact, condoned Beatrice's revenge. See, for example, Stuart Curran's judgment in his influential study of the tragedy, *Shelley's "Cenci": Scorpions Ringed with Fire*, 140: "only by killing her father in line with the principles of divine justice can Beatrice hope for absolution from the evil into which her father has plunged her."

10. Medwin, *Medwin's Conversations of Lord Byron*, 119.

11. To Leigh Hunt, 26 August 1821, PBSL, 2:345.

12. Bennett, ed., *The Letters of Mary Wollstonecraft Shelley*, 2:163.

13. Medwin, *Medwin's Conversations of Lord Byron*, 97.

14. Ibid., 119–20.

15. To John Taaffe, Jr., to Percy Bysshe Shelley, and to the Earl of Guilford, all dated 12 December 1821, BLJ, 9:78–79.

16. See Reiman and Powers, eds., *Shelley's Poetry and Prose*, 237.

17. Medwin, *Medwin's Conversations of Lord Byron*, 156.

18. See to Thomas Love Peacock, 22 July 1816, PBSL, 1:499.

19. For a discussion of the influence of the *Relation* on *The Cenci*, see Curran, *Shelley's "Cenci,"* 40–46.

20. E. F. Bleiler, ed., *Three Gothic Novels*, 260.

21. James B. Twitchell, *The Living Dead: A Study of the Vampire in Romantic Literature*, 80.

22. Terry Otten, "Christabel, Beatrice, and the Encounter with Evil," 20.

23. *On the Devil, and Devils* was probably written in mid-November 1819. See Stuart Curran and Joseph Anthony Wittreich, Jr., "The Dating of Shelley's 'On the Devil, and Devils,'" 83–94.

24. Roger Ingpen and Walter E. Peck, eds., *The Complete Works of Percy Bysshe Shelley*, 7:101.

25. For a more wide-ranging discussion of the vampire myth as it is used in *Manfred* and *The Cenci*, see Twitchell, 74–92.

26. To Lord Byron, 9 July 1817, PBSL, 1:547.

27. Andrew Nicholson, ed., *Lord Byron: The Complete Miscellaneous Prose*, 100–101. Although Byron blamed Robert Southey for the gossip, it is more likely that Henry Brougham was the real culprit—see Nicholson, 374–75 n. 62.

28. To Maria Gisborne, 16 November 1819, PBSL, 2:154.

29. Ingpen and Peck, eds., *The Complete Works of Percy Bysshe Shelley*, 7:95.

30. To Elizabeth Hitchener, 20 June 1811, PBSL, 1:109.

31. See Michael Worton, "Speech and Silence in *The Cenci*," 105–24; and Anne McWhir, "The Light and the Knife: Ab/Using Language in *The Cenci*," 145–61, for discussions of Beatrice's refusal to put Cenci's rape of her into words.

32. Ingpen and Peck, eds., *The Complete Works of Percy Bysshe Shelley*, 2:375.

33. Reiman and Cameron, eds., *Shelley and His Circle*, 7:28.

34. To Thomas Love Peacock, 17 or 18 December 1818, PBSL, 2:58.

35. Ingpen and Peck, eds., *The Complete Works of Percy Bysshe Shelley*, 2:159.

36. Jerrold E. Hogle, *Shelley's Process: Radical Transference and the Development of His Major Works*, 162. Hogle also discusses Shelley's redefinition of Catholic myth in *Adonais* (see 317–19).

37. To Augusta Leigh, 27 May 1817, BLJ, 5:228, italics Byron's.

38. Lovell, ed., *His Very Self and Voice*, 210.

39. To Lord Byron, 16 [for 17] April 1821, PBSL, 2:283.

40. To Horace Smith, 11 April 1822, PBSL, 2:412.

41. Reiman and Cameron, eds., *Shelley and His Circle*, 7:xli.

42. Ibid., 7:xlii.

43. To Mary Shelley, Friday [10 August] 1821, PBSL, 2:322.

44. Robinson, *Shelley and Byron*, 126.

45. Ibid.

46. Ibid., 134.

47. For a lengthy comparison of *Prometheus Unbound* and *The Cenci*, see Stuart Curran, *Shelley's Annus Mirabilis: The Maturing of an Epic Vision*, 120–33.

48. To Charles Ollier, 6 September 1819, PBSL, 2:117.

49. To Thomas Love Peacock, 15 February 1820 [for 1821], PBSL, 2:262.

50. Ravenna Journal, 18 February 1821, BLJ, 8:47.

5. Byron's *Sardanapalus:* The Shelleyan Hero Transformed

1. McGann and Weller, eds., *Lord Byron: The Complete Poetical Works*, 6:604.

2. Ibid., 6:604, 625.

3. Ravenna Journal, 28 January 1821, BLJ, 8:36.

4. Martyn Corbett, *Byron and Tragedy*, 114.

5. To John Murray, 3 November 1821, BLJ, 9:54.

6. To Leigh Hunt, 26 August 1821, PBSL, 2:345.

7. Lovell, ed., *His Very Self and Voice*, 277.

8. To Richard Belgrave Hoppner, 10 September 1820, BLJ, 7:174.

9. Bennett, ed., *The Letters of Mary Wollstonecraft Shelley,* 1:232.

10. Detached Thoughts, no. 53, BLJ, 9:30.

11. Richard Lansdown, *Byron's Historical Dramas,* 150.

12. Ibid., 168.

13. Bernard Blackstone, *Byron: A Survey,* 234.

14. Jerome J. McGann, *Fiery Dust: Byron's Poetic Development,* 228–30.

15. Marilyn Butler, "John Bull's Other Kingdom: Byron's Intellectual Comedy," 283.

16. Samuel C. Chew, Jr., *The Dramas of Lord Byron: A Critical Study,* 112.

17. Jerome Christensen, *Lord Byron's Strength: Romantic Writing and Commercial Society,* 298–99.

18. Lady Blessington, *Conversations of Lord Byron,* 53. Also see letter to Thomas Moore, 4 March 1822, BLJ, 9:119.

19. For an informative discussion of *The Revolt of Islam* and Laon's and Cythna's progress toward their deaths, see Richard Haswell, "Shelley's *The Revolt of Islam:* 'The Connexion of Its Parts,'" 81–102.

20. Malcolm Kelsall, *Byron's Politics,* 117–18.

21. Charles J. Clancy, "Death and Love in Byron's *Sardanapalus,*" 58.

22. See, for example, Malcolm Kelsall, "The Slave-Woman in the Harem," 326.

23. Gordon Spence, "Moral and Sexual Ambivalence in *Sardanapalus,*" 69.

24. Sardanapalus's hedonism is not, of course, very Shelleyan.

25. Ravenna Journal, 31 January 1821 (midnight), BLJ, 8:41.

26. Lansdown, 149.

27. Detached Thoughts, no. 84, BLJ, 9:41.

28. Sardanapalus's "effeminacy" has been treated in a number of articles, including Susan Wolfson's "'A Problem Few Dare Imitate': *Sardanapalus* and 'Effeminate Character,'" 867–902.

29. See Kelsall, *Byron's Politics,* 3.

6. The Diabolical Discourse of Shelley and Byron

1. To John Gisborne, 12 January 1822, PBSL, 2:376.

2. Ibid., 26 January 1822, PBSL, 2:388.

3. For evidence about when Byron received *Queen Mab,* see Robinson, *Shelley and Byron,* 244.

4. Thomas Medwin, *The Life of Percy Bysshe Shelley,* 334.

5. To John Murray, 3 November 1821, BLJ, 9:53.

6. See Reiman and Powers, eds., *Shelley's Poetry and Prose*, 14n; and Shelley's 16 June 1821 letter to John Gisborne, PBSL, 2:300–301.

7. To John Murray, 12 October 1817, BLJ, 5:268.

8. Wolf Z. Hirst, "Byron's Lapse into Orthodoxy: An Unorthodox Reading of *Cain*," 153.

9. James Rieger, *The Mutiny Within: The Heresies of Percy Bysshe Shelley*, 198.

10. A short discussion of the biblical and Miltonic references to Cain as artist can be found in Peter L. Thorslev, Jr., *The Byronic Hero*, 94.

11. To James Hogg, 24 March [1814], BLJ, 4:84.

12. Shelley mentions Tubal-Cain in "Letter to Maria Gisborne": "forms of unimaginable wood, / To puzzle Tubal Cain and all his brood" (50–51).

13. For a provocative discussion of Cain's process of self-definition, see Leonard Michaels, "Byron's Cain," 74.

14. To Leigh Hunt, 27 September 1819, PBSL, 2:122.

15. Ravenna Journal, 31 January 1821 (midnight), BLJ, 8:41.

16. To John Murray, 3 November 1821, BLJ, 9:54.

17. To Richard Belgrave Hoppner, 10 September 1820, BLJ, 7:174 and n.

18. Alan Richardson, *A Mental Theater: Poetic Drama and Consciousness in the Romantic Age*, 4.

19. Ibid., 14.

20. Ibid., 115.

21. McGann and Weller, eds., *Lord Byron: The Complete Poetical Works*, 6:252.

22. Trelawny, 103.

23. Ibid., 310 n. 17.

24. See C. Darrel Sheraw, "Coleridge, Shelley, Byron and the Devil," 6–9.

25. Ingpen and Peck, eds., *The Complete Works of Percy Bysshe Shelley*, 7:104.

26. Ibid., 7:89.

27. To John Gisborne, 10 April 1822, PBSL, 2:407.

28. Ingpen and Peck, eds., *The Complete Works of Percy Bysshe Shelley*, 7:97.

29. Ibid., 7:94.

30. Richardson, 61.

31. To Horace Smith, 11 April 1822, PBSL, 2:412.

32. To John Murray, 3 November 1821, BLJ, 9:53.

33. Ingpen and Peck, eds., *The Complete Works of Percy Bysshe Shelley*, 3:15.

34. See Robinson, *Shelley and Byron*, 213.

35. Webb, 186.

7. Byron, Goethe, and *The Triumph of Life*

1. G. M. Matthews, "On Shelley's 'The Triumph of Life,'" 105.

2. I essentially agree with Karen A. Weisman's statement that *The Triumph of Life* "is preoccupied by poetry's relationship to quotidian existence" (see Weisman, "Shelley's Triumph of Life over Fiction," 337).

3. Harold Bloom, *Poetry and Repression: Revisionism from Blake to Stevens,* 104.

4. See Baker, 258; and Robinson, *Shelley and Byron,* 228–30.

5. To John Gisborne, 22 October 1821, PBSL, 2:364. The translation is taken from Walter Kaufmann, trans., *Goethe's Faust,* 113.

6. Holmes, 693

7. Medwin, *Medwin's Conversations of Lord Byron,* 155. Holmes notes that the "burning" of *The Deformed Transformed* was "a stage device," since Byron had another copy in his desk (see Holmes, 689).

8. Trelawny, 103.

9. Medwin, *Medwin's Conversations of Lord Byron,* 261.

10. For approximate dates for *The Deformed Transformed* and Shelley's reading of it, see Charles E. Robinson, "The Devil as Doppelgänger in *The Deformed Transformed:* The Sources and Meaning of Byron's Unfinished Drama," 182–202.

11. Holmes, 693; and Medwin, *The Life of Percy Bysshe Shelley,* 331.

12. Quotations from Shelley's "Scenes from the 'Faust' of Goethe" are taken from Ingpen and Peck, eds., *The Complete Works of Percy Bysshe Shelley,* 4:322–40.

13. To John Gisborne, 10 April 1822, PBSL, 2:407.

14. Webb, 186.

15. Ibid.

16. Ibid.

17. Ibid., 185–86.

18. Robinson, *Shelley and Byron,* 222–23. Edward Duffy, in *Rousseau in England: The Context for Shelley's Critique of the Enlightenment,* 127, also discusses the significance of Shelley's "revision" of Goethe's lines.

19. To John Gisborne, 10 April 1822, PBSL, 2:406.

20. See Hogle, 334.

21. To John Gisborne, 18 June 1822, PBSL, 2:436.

22. G. M. Matthews, "On Shelley's 'The Triumph of Life,'" 132n.

23. Ibid., 121.

24. "Discarded Opening-'C,'" Donald H. Reiman, ed., *Shelley's "The Triumph of Life": A Critical Study,* 236.

25. Reiman notes this echo in ibid., 22n.

26. The vision of Life in Shelley's last major work has much in common with the perspective of Raymond, the "Byron" of Mary Shelley's *The Last Man*. Mary has this Byronic figure lament his inability to dream: "Happy are the dreamers . . . so that they be not awakened! Would I could dream! but 'broad and garish day' [cf. *The Cenci*, 2.2.177] is the element in which I live; the dazzling glare of reality inverts the scene for me." Likewise, the failure of the narrator of *The Triumph* to avert his gaze from "the dazzling glare of reality" leads to his hellish vision of Life's pageant. See Mary Wollstonecraft Shelley, *The Last Man*, 34.

27. To John Gisborne, 10 April 1822, PBSL, 2:406–7. See *The Prelude* (1805), 10.709–27. These lines were first published in *The Friend* for 26 October 1809 and reprinted in the collected edition of 1815.

28. This accusation was made in a *Quarterly Review* article, which Shelley mistakenly attributed to Southey. See letter to Charles Ollier, 15 October 1819, PBSL, 2:127.

29. To Leigh Hunt, 2 March 1822, PBSL, 2:394.

30. Reiman, ed., *Shelley's "The Triumph of Life,"* 35, 84.

31. Robinson, *Shelley and Byron*, 228–30, uses these allusions to Byron's *The Prophecy of Dante* to argue that Shelley meant "to announce in *The Triumph of Life* that Byron was the main cause of his purgatorial torments" and therefore "used Byron's own words to damn himself to the vexations of such a purgatory."

32. See Clark, 231, for a discussion of how *Childe Harold*, canto 3, influenced Shelley's pessimistic portrayal of Rousseau in *The Triumph of Life*. Also see Duffy, 71–75, 86–151, for a discussion of how Byron and Shelley responded to Rousseau.

33. To Thomas Love Peacock, 12 July [1816], PBSL, 1:485.

34. Duffy, 57.

35. Ross Woodman discusses this parallel in *The Apocalyptic Vision in the Poetry of Shelley*, 194.

36. See Reiman, ed., *Shelley's "The Triumph of Life,"* 29n.

37. Edward Botstetter writes that Shelley's last poems "reveal an increasing effort to express in informal, economic language a detached and even ironic contemplation of men and things as they are—and in this possibly they reflect the influence of Byron." See Edward E. Botstetter, *The Romantic Ventriloquists: Wordsworth, Coleridge, Keats, Shelley, Byron*, 238–39.

38. Woodman, 184. The quotation from "Charles the First" is taken from Ingpen and Peck, eds., *The Complete Works of Percy Bysshe Shelley*, 4:157.

39. Reiman, ed., *Shelley's "The Triumph of Life,"* 241. See also Donald H. Reiman, ed., *The Bodleian Shelley Manuscripts: Peter Bell the Third and The Triumph*

of Life, 186–87, for a facsimile of the manuscript page from which this quotation was taken. Shelley first wrote "truth & its creators" and then crossed out "creators" and wrote "inventors" underneath.

40. To Thomas Love Peacock, 17 or 18 December 1818, PBSL, 2:58.

41. To Leigh Hunt, 10 April 1822, PBSL, 2:405.

8. Byron Puffs the Snake

1. Andrew Rutherford, *Byron: A Critical Study*, 202.

2. Robert D. Hume, "*The Island* and the Evolution of Byron's 'Tales,'" 174–75, 181.

3. McGann, *Fiery Dust*, 198.

4. Robinson, *Shelley and Byron*, 237.

5. To Leigh Hunt, 25 January 1823, BLJ, 10:90.

6. Iris Origo, *The Last Attachment*, 298.

7. Of course, Trelawny's extreme jealousy of Byron makes him an unreliable source. See Trelawny, 96.

8. Ingpen and Peck, eds., *The Complete Works of Percy Bysshe Shelley*, 4:137.

9. Ibid.

10. Ernest Hartley Coleridge, ed., *The Works of Lord Byron. Poetry*, 5:605n. James McKusick argues that Byron also found information on George Stewart from an appendix to the minutes of the court-martial written by Edward Christian, the brother of Fletcher Christian (see James C. McKusick, "The Politics of Language in Byron's *The Island*," 846–47).

11. Coleridge, ed., *The Works of Lord Byron. Poetry*, 5:629n.

12. McKusick notes Ben Bunting's "subversive linguistic role": "Just as in *Don Juan*, where the narrator's jocular asides frequently expose the youthful hero's unconscious hypocrisy, so . . . the intrusive presence of Ben Bunting, as an agent of heteroglossia, represents the return of the linguistic repressed in the guise of crude vernacular epithets" (McKusick, 851).

13. To John Murray, 2 April 1817, BLJ, 5:203.

14. Bloom, *The Anxiety of Influence*, 14.

15. To John Murray, 6 July 1821, BLJ, 8:148.

16. Bernard Blackstone, *The Lost Travellers: A Romantic Theme with Variations*, 212.

17. Hume, 172.

18. See Coleridge, ed., *The Works of Lord Byron. Poetry*, 5:603 n. 2; and Thomas Hutchinson, ed., *Shelley: Poetical Works*, 35.

19. I am indebted to P. D. Fleck for this idea. See P. D. Fleck, "Romance in Byron's *The Island,*" 173.

20. Robinson, *Shelley and Byron,* 238.

21. Robinson makes this point in ibid., 239. Also see Blackstone, *The Lost Travellers,* 264.

22. Hume, 178.

23. PBSL, 2:445–46 n. 4.

24. Clyde K. Hyder, ed., *Swinburne as Critic,* 41.

25. For a narrative description of the Frost-Thomas relationship, see John Lehmann, *Three Literary Friendships,* 133–65.

Appendix A

1. To Leigh Hunt, 22 August [1824], in Bennett, ed., *The Letters of Mary Wollstonecraft Shelley,* 1:444.

2. To John Bowring, 25 February [1826], in ibid., 1:512.

3. To Teresa Guiccioli, 20 August 1827, in ibid., 1:566.

4. Mary Wollstonecraft Shelley, *The Last Man,* 65.

5. Feldman and Scott-Kilvert, eds., *The Journals of Mary Shelley: 1814–1844,* 2:439.

6. See Trelawny, 80–81.

Appendix B

1. To Elizabeth Hitchener, [16] October 1811, PBSL, 1:151.

2. Trelawny, 217.

3. Doris Langley Moore, *Lord Byron: Accounts Rendered,* 241.

4. To Douglas Kinnaird, 27 January 1819, BLJ, 6:98.

5. Ibid., 23 February 1822, BLJ, 9:113.

6. Ibid., 18 January 1823, BLJ, 10:87.

7. Doris Langley Moore, *Lord Byron: Accounts Rendered,* 243.

8. Ibid., 264–65.

9. See PBSL, 2:408.

10. Doris Langley Moore, *Lord Byron: Accounts Rendered,* 350.

11. Quoted from PBSL, 2:390n.

12. Leslie A. Marchand, *Byron: A Portrait,* 366.

13. Doris Langley Moore, *Lord Byron: Accounts Rendered,* 336.

14. See Reiman, ed., *The Bodleian Shelley Manuscripts,* 209, 213, 227.

Bibliography

Baker, Carlos. *Shelley's Major Poetry: The Fabric of a Vision.* Princeton, N.J.: Princeton University Press, 1948.

Behrendt, Stephen C. *Shelley and His Audiences.* Lincoln: University of Nebraska Press, 1989.

Bennett, Betty T., editor. *The Letters of Mary Wollstonecraft Shelley.* 3 volumes. Baltimore: Johns Hopkins University Press, 1980–88.

Blackstone, Bernard. *Byron: A Survey.* London: Longman, 1975.

———. *The Lost Travellers: A Romantic Theme with Variations.* London: Longman, 1962.

Blank, G. Kim. *Wordsworth's Influence on Shelley: A Study of Poetic Authority.* New York: St. Martin's, 1988.

Bleiler, E. F., editor. *Three Gothic Novels.* New York: Dover, 1966.

Blessington, Lady. *Conversations of Lord Byron.* Edited by Ernest J. Lovell, Jr. Princeton, N.J.: Princeton University Press, 1969.

Bloom, Harold. *The Anxiety of Influence.* New York: Oxford University Press, 1973.

———. *Poetry and Repression: Revisionism from Blake to Stevens.* New Haven, Conn.: Yale University Press, 1976.

———. "The Unpastured Sea: An Introduction to Shelley." In *Romanticism and Consciousness: Essays in Criticism.* Edited by Harold Bloom. New York: Norton, 1970. 374–401.

Bone, J. Drummond. "Byron, Shelley and Contemporary Poetry, 1820–1822." In *Paradise of Exiles: Shelley and Byron in Pisa.* Edited by Mario Curreli and Anthony L. Johnson. Salzburg: Universität Salzburg, 1988. 69–77.

Botstetter, Edward E. *The Romantic Ventriloquists: Wordsworth, Coleridge, Keats, Shelley, Byron.* Seattle: University of Washington Press, 1963.

Brinkley, Robert. "Documenting Revision: Shelley's Lake Geneva Diary and the Dialogue with Byron in *History of a Six Weeks' Tour.*" *Keats-Shelley Journal* 39 (1990): 66–82.

Brown, Nathaniel. *Sexuality and Feminism in Shelley.* Cambridge, Mass.: Harvard University Press, 1979.

Butler, Marilyn. "John Bull's Other Kingdom: Byron's Intellectual Comedy." *Studies in Romanticism* 31 (Fall 1992): 281–94.

Buxton, John. *Byron and Shelley: The History of a Friendship.* New York: Harcourt, Brace and World, 1968.

Byron's Letters and Journals. Edited by Leslie A. Marchand. 12 volumes. Cambridge, Mass.: Harvard University Press, 1973–82.

Cameron, Kenneth Neill. *Shelley: The Golden Years.* Cambridge, Mass.: Harvard University Press, 1974.

———. *The Young Shelley: Genesis of a Radical.* New York: Macmillan, 1950.

Chernaik, Judith, and Timothy Burnett. "The Byron and Shelley Notebooks in the Scrope Davies Find." *Review of English Studies* n. s. 29 (February 1978): 36–49.

Chew, Samuel C., Jr. *The Dramas of Lord Byron: A Critical Study.* 1915. New York: Russell and Russell, 1964.

Christensen, Jerome. *Lord Byron's Strength: Romantic Writing and Commercial Society.* Baltimore: Johns Hopkins University Press, 1993.

Clancy, Charles J. "Death and Love in Byron's *Sardanapalus.*" *Byron Journal* 10 (1982): 56–70.

Clark, Timothy. *Embodying Revolution: The Figure of the Poet in Shelley.* Oxford: Clarendon, 1989.

Clubbe, John. "The Tempest-Toss'd Summer of 1816: Mary Shelley's *Frankenstein.*" *Byron Journal* 19 (1991): 26–40.

Coleridge, Ernest Hartley, editor. *The Works of Lord Byron: Poetry.* 7 volumes. London: John Murray, 1898–1904.

Complete Poetry and Prose of William Blake, The. See David V. Erdman, editor.

Complete Works of Percy Bysshe Shelley, The. See Roger Ingpen and Walter E. Peck, editors.

Cooke, Michael G. "Byron and Wordsworth: The Complementarity of a Rock and the Sea." In *Lord Byron and His Contemporaries: Essays from the Sixth International Byron Seminar.* Edited by Charles E. Robinson. Newark: University of Delaware Press, 1982. 19–42.

Corbett, Martyn. *Byron and Tragedy.* New York: St. Martin's, 1988.

Crompton, Louis. *Byron and Greek Love: Homophobia in 19th-Century England.* Berkeley: University of California Press, 1985.

Cronin, Richard. *Shelley's Poetic Thoughts*. New York: St. Martin's, 1981.

Curran, Stuart. *Shelley's Annus Mirabilis: The Maturing of an Epic Vision*. San Marino, Calif.: Huntington Library, 1975.

————. *Shelley's "Cenci": Scorpions Ringed with Fire*. Princeton, N.J.: Princeton University Press, 1970.

Curran, Stuart, and Joseph Anthony Wittreich, Jr. "The Dating of Shelley's 'On the Devil, and Devils.'" *Keats-Shelley Journal* 21–22 (1972–73): 83–94.

Davie, Donald. *Purity of Diction in English Verse*. New York: Schocken, 1967.

Dawson, P. M. S. "Byron, Shelley, and the 'New School.'" In *Shelley Revalued: Essays from the Gregynog Conference*. Edited by Kelvin Everest. Totowa, N.J.: Barnes and Noble, 1983. 89–108.

Duffy, Edward. *Rousseau in England: The Context for Shelley's Critique of the Enlightenment*. Berkeley: University of California Press, 1979.

Erdman, David V., editor. *The Complete Poetry and Prose of William Blake*. Revised edition. New York: Doubleday, 1988.

Everest, Kelvin. "Shelley's Doubles: An Approach to 'Julian and Maddalo.'" In *Shelley Revalued: Essays from the Gregynog Conference*. Edited by Kelvin Everest. Totowa, N.J.: Barnes and Noble, 1983. 63–88.

Feldman, Paula R., and Diana Scott-Kilvert, editors. *The Journals of Mary Shelley: 1814–1844*. 2 volumes. Oxford: Clarendon, 1987.

Fleck, P. D. "Romance in Byron's *The Island*." In *Byron: A Symposium*. Edited by John D. Jump. London: Macmillan, 1975. 163–83.

Grabo, Carl. *A Newton Among Poets: Shelley's Use of Science in Prometheus Unbound*. Chapel Hill: University of North Carolina Press, 1930.

Haswell, Richard. "Shelley's *The Revolt of Islam*: 'The Connexion of Its Parts.'" *Keats-Shelley Journal* 25 (1976): 81–102.

Hirsch, Bernard A. "'A Want of That True Theory': *Julian and Maddalo* as Dramatic Monologue." *Studies in Romanticism* 17 (Winter 1978): 13–34.

Hirst, Wolf Z. "Byron's Lapse into Orthodoxy: An Unorthodox Reading of *Cain*." *Keats-Shelley Journal* 39 (1980): 151–72.

Hogle, Jerrold E. *Shelley's Process: Radical Transference and the Development of His Major Works*. New York: Oxford University Press, 1988.

Holmes, Richard. *Shelley: The Pursuit*. New York: Dutton, 1975.

Hume, Robert D. "*The Island* and the Evolution of Byron's 'Tales.'" In *Romantic and Victorian: Studies in Memory of William H. Marshall*. Edited by W. Paul Elledge and Richard L. Hoffman. Rutherford, N.J.: Fairleigh Dickinson University Press, 1971. 158–80.

Hutchinson, Thomas, editor. *Shelley: Poetical Works*. 1904. Corrected by G. M. Matthews. Oxford: Oxford University Press, 1971.

Hyder, Clyde K., editor. *Swinburne as Critic*. Boston: Routledge and Kegan Paul, 1972.

Ingpen, Roger, and Walter E. Peck, editors. *The Complete Works of Percy Bysshe Shelley*. 10 volumes. London: Ernest Benn, 1926–30.

Journals of Mary Shelley: 1814–1844. See Paula R. Feldman and Diana Scott-Kilvert, editors.

Kaufmann, Walter, translator. *Goethe's* Faust. Garden City, N.Y.: Doubleday, 1961.

Keach, William. *Shelley's Style*. New York: Methuen, 1984.

Kelsall, Malcolm. *Byron's Politics*. Totowa, N.J.: Barnes and Noble, 1987.

———. "The Slave-Woman in the Harem." *Studies in Romanticism* 31 (Fall 1992): 315–31.

Lansdown, Richard. *Byron's Historical Dramas*. Oxford: Clarendon, 1992.

Lehmann, John. *Three Literary Friendships*. New York: Holt, Rinehart and Winston, 1983.

Letters of Mary Wollstonecraft Shelley, The. See Betty T. Bennett, editor.

Letters of Percy Bysshe Shelley, The. Edited by Frederick L. Jones. 2 volumes. Oxford: Clarendon, 1964.

Lord Byron: The Complete Miscellaneous Prose. See Andrew Nicholson, editor.

Lord Byron: The Complete Poetical Works. Edited by Jerome J. McGann and Barry Weller. 6 volumes. Oxford: Oxford University Press, 1980–91.

Lovell, Ernest J., editor. *His Very Self and Voice: Collected Conversations of Lord Byron*. New York: Macmillan, 1954.

McGann, Jerome J. *Fiery Dust: Byron's Poetic Development*. Chicago: University of Chicago Press, 1968.

———. "A Reply to George Ridenour." *Studies in Romanticism* 16 (1977): 571–83.

———. *The Romantic Ideology: A Critical Investigation*. Chicago: University of Chicago Press, 1983.

McGann, Jerome J., and Barry Weller, editors. See *Lord Byron: The Complete Poetical Works*.

McKusick, James C. "The Politics of Language in Byron's *The Island*." *ELH* 59 (1992): 839–56.

McWhir, Anne. "The Light and the Knife: Ab/Using Language in *The Cenci*." *Keats-Shelley Journal* 38 (1989): 145–61.

Marchand, Leslie A. *Byron: A Portrait*. Chicago: University of Chicago Press, 1970.

Marchand, Leslie A., editor. See *Byron's Letters and Journals*.

Matthews, G. M. "On Shelley's 'The Triumph of Life.'" *Studia Neophilologica* 34 (1962): 104–34.

Matthews, Geoffrey, and Kelvin Everest, editors. *The Poems of Shelley.* Volume 1. London: Longman, 1989.

Medwin, Thomas. *The Life of Percy Bysshe Shelley.* Edited by H. Buxton Forman. London: Oxford University Press, 1913.

———. *Medwin's Conversations of Lord Byron.* Edited by Ernest J. Lovell. Princeton, N.J.: Princeton University Press, 1966.

Michaels, Leonard. "Byron's Cain." *PMLA* 84 (1969): 71–78.

Moore, Doris Langley. *Lord Byron: Accounts Rendered.* London: John Murray, 1974.

Moore, Thomas. *Letters and Journals of Lord Byron.* London: John Murray, 1920.

Nellist, Brian. "Shelley's Narratives and 'The Witch of Atlas.'" In *Essays on Shelley.* Edited by Miriam Allott. Totowa, N.J.: Barnes and Noble, 1982. 160–90.

Nicholson, Andrew, editor. *Lord Byron: The Complete Miscellaneous Prose.* Oxford: Clarendon, 1991.

Origo, Iris. *The Last Attachment.* New York: Charles Scribner's Sons, 1949.

Otten, Terry. "Christabel, Beatrice, and the Encounter with Evil." *Bucknell Review* 17 (1969): 19–31.

Owen, W. J. B., editor. *Wordsworth's Literary Criticism.* London: Routledge and Kegan Paul, 1974.

Peck, Walter Edwin. *Shelley: His Life and Work.* 2 volumes. Boston: Houghton Mifflin, 1921.

Plottle, Parisier, and Hanna Charney, editors. *Intertextuality: New Perspectives in Criticism.* New York: New York Literary Forum, 1978.

Poems of Shelley, The. See Geoffrey Matthews and Kelvin Everest, editors.

Redding, Cyrus. *Literary Reminiscences and Memoirs of Thomas Campbell.* Volume 1. London: Charles J. Skeet, 1860.

Reiman, Donald H., editor. *The Bodleian Shelley Manuscripts: Peter Bell the Third and The Triumph of Life.* New York: Garland, 1986.

———. *Shelley's "The Triumph of Life": A Critical Study, Based on a Text Newly Edited from the Bodleian Manuscript.* 1965. New York: Octagon, 1979.

Reiman, Donald H., and Kenneth Neill Cameron, editors. *Shelley and His Circle: 1772–1822.* 8 volumes. Cambridge, Mass.: Harvard University Press, 1961–86.

Reiman, Donald H., and Sharon B. Powers, editors. *Shelley's Poetry and Prose.* New York: Norton, 1977.

Richardson, Alan. *A Mental Theater: Poetic Drama and Consciousness in the Romantic Age.* University Park: Pennsylvania State University Press, 1988.

Rieger, James. *The Mutiny Within: The Heresies of Percy Bysshe Shelley.* New York: George Braziller, 1967.

Robinson, Charles E. "The Devil as Doppelgänger in *The Deformed Trans-formed:* The Sources and Meaning of Byron's Unfinished Drama." *Bulletin of the New York Public Library* 74 (1970): 177–202.

———. *Shelley and Byron: The Snake and Eagle Wreathed in Fight.* Baltimore: Johns Hopkins University Press, 1976.

———. "Shelley to Byron in 1814: A New Letter." *Keats-Shelley Journal* 35 (1986): 104–10.

Rogers, Neville. *Shelley at Work: A Critical Inquiry.* Oxford: Clarendon, 1956.

Rossetti, William Michael, editor. *The Diary of Dr. John William Polidori, 1816.* London: Elkin Mathews, 1911.

Rudwick, Martin J. S. *The Meaning of Fossils: Episodes in the History of Palaeon-tology.* London: MacDonald, 1972.

Rutherford, Andrew. *Byron: A Critical Study.* Stanford, Calif.: Stanford Univer sity Press, 1962.

Shelley, Mary Wollstonecraft. *Frankenstein, or The Modern Prometheus.* Edited by James Rieger. Chicago: University of Chicago Press, 1974.

———. *The Last Man.* Edited by Hugh J. Luke, Jr. Lincoln: University of Nebraska Press, 1965.

Shelley, Percy Bysshe. *Zastrozzi and St. Irvyne.* Edited by Stephen C. Behrendt. Oxford: Oxford University Press, 1986.

Shelley: Poetical Works. See Thomas Hutchinson, editor.

Shelley's Poetry and Prose. See Donald H. Reiman and Sharon B. Powers, editors.

Sheraw, C. Darrel. "Coleridge, Shelley, Byron and the Devil." *Keats-Shelley Journal* 33 (1972): 6–9.

Spence, Gordon. "Moral and Sexual Ambivalence in *Sardanapalus.*" *Byron Jour-nal* 12 (1984): 59–69.

Stevenson, Warren S. *Poetic Friends: A Study of Literary Relations during the English Romantic Period.* New York: Peter Lang, 1989.

Tessier, Thérèse. "Byron and Thomas Moore: A Great Literary Friendship." *Byron Journal* 20 (1992): 46–58.

Thorslev, Peter L., Jr. *The Byronic Hero.* Minneapolis: University of Minnesota Press, 1962.

Trelawny, Edward John. *Records of Shelley, Byron, and the Author.* Edited by David Wright. Harmondsworth, England: Penguin, 1973.

Twitchell, James B. *The Living Dead: A Study of the Vampire in Romantic Literature.* Durham, N.C.: Duke University Press, 1981.

Wasserman, Earl R. *Shelley: A Critical Reading.* Baltimore: Johns Hopkins Uni-versity Press, 1971.

———. "Shelley's Last Poetics: A Reconsideration." In *From Sensibility to Romanticism: Essays Presented to Frederick A. Pottle.* Edited by Frederick W.

Hilles and Harold Bloom. New York: Oxford University Press, 1965. 487–
511.

Webb, Timothy. *The Violet and the Crucible: Shelley and Translation*. Oxford:
Oxford University Press, 1976.

Weisman, Karen A. "Shelley's Triumph of Life over Fiction." *Philological Quarterly* 71, no. 3 (Summer 1992): 337–60.

White, Newman Ivey. *Shelley*. 2 volumes. New York: Alfred A. Knopf, 1940.

Wolfson, Susan. " 'A Problem Few Dare Imitate': *Sardanapalus* and 'Effeminate
Character.' " *ELH* 58 (1991): 867–902.

Woodman, Ross. *The Apocalyptic Vision in the Poetry of Shelley*. Toronto: University of Toronto Press, 1964.

Wordsworth, Jonathan. " 'Tis to Create': A Fragment of Biography." *Wordsworth Circle* 20 (Winter 1989): 43–50.

Works of Lord Byron: Poetry, The. See Ernest Hartley Coleridge, editor.

Worton, Michael. "Speech and Silence in *The Cenci*." In *Essays on Shelley*. Edited
by Miriam Allott. Totowa, N.J.: Barnes and Noble, 1982. 105–24.

Index

Account of the Natives of the Tonga Island
   (Mariner), 143
Aeschylus, 94; *Prometheus Bound*, 60, 94
Antitype, 74, 76, 81, 84, 97, 133–35, 137,
   142, 153

Baker, Carlos, 48, 110
Behrendt, Stephen C., 2, 161n.1
Blackstone, Bernard, 79, 136
Blake, William, 18. Works: *Milton*, 18;
   Jerusalem, 18
Blank, Kim, 23
Blessington, Lady, 80
Bligh, William, 133
Bloom, Harold, 41, 109, 134, 147
Bone, J. Drummond, 162n.14
Botstetter, Edward, 173n.37
Bowring, John, 151
Brougham, Henry, 168n.27
Brown, Nathaniel, 10
Buffon, Georges, 28–31, 61
Butler, Marilyn, 79
Buxton, John, 4
Byron, Ada, 26
Byron, Allegra, 6, 12, 72
Byron, George Gordon, Lord: as aristo-
   crat, 3, 9; and Catastrophism, 33–36;

on *The Cenci*, 5, 56–57, 59; on the devil,
   101–7; friendship of, with Shelley, 1,
   4, 6–18; and homosexuality, 11; on
   incest, 9, 87; on Italian Catholicism,
   72; and Italian politics, 9, 59–60, 75,
   79; on Keats, 4–5; on poets, 83; as
   post-Waterloo liberal, 3, 90; reading
   of Shelley's works, 19–20, 78; on sexuality, 10; on Shelley's idealistic works,
   78; on Shelley's irreligion, 9; studied
   Armenian, 51–52; on Wordsworth,
   22–26. Works: *Beppo*, 40, 42, 54–55,
   73; *Cain*, 2–3, 9–10, 14, 21, 30, 32–34,
   66–67, 77–78, 84, 92–108, 122, 135,
   140, 144–45, 166n.40; *Childe Harold's
   Pilgrimage* (canto 1), 19, 80; *Childe
   Harold's Pilgrimage* (canto 2), 19; *Childe
   Harold's Pilgrimage* (canto 3), 8–9, 24–
   26, 45–46, 55, 67–68, 123–24, 173n.32;
   Childe Harold's Pilgrimage (canto 4), 10,
   128–30; *The Corsair*, 85, 131; "Darkness," 30, 33, 36, 60–61, 63, 95, 155,
   165n.29; *The Deformed Transformed*, 3–
   4, 14, 92, 101, 107, 111–14; "The Devil's
   Drive," 101; *Don Juan*, 5, 7, 10, 12–15,
   20, 23, 27, 35, 42, 45, 52–55, 84, 88,
   114, 127, 131, 135, 146, 148, 157, 160,

Byron, George Gordon, Lord (*continued*)
167nn. 19, 27; "The Dream," 24–25,
165n.15; *English Bards and Scotch Reviewers*, 19; "[Epistle to Augusta]," 24;
"Fragment of a Novel," 63; *The Giaour*,
47, 63–64, 85; *Heaven and Earth*, 33–34,
36, 95; *The Island*, 5, 10, 20, 34, 131–48;
"I Would I Were a Careless Child," 36;
"Lachin y Gair," 36; *Lament of Tasso*,
47–49; *Lara*, 19, 37, 66; *Manfred*, 2–3,
8–9, 48, 61–70, 73–75, 94, 98, 111, 118–
19, 123, 166n.42; *Marino Faliero*, 5, 53,
56–59, 75, 88; *Mazeppa*, 12, 14, *Poems
Original and Translated*, 19; *The Prisoner
of Chillon*, 9, 46–48, 164n.14; "Prometheus," 20, 50, 60, 63, 76, 83, 89,
94–95, 145, 148; *The Prophecy of Dante*,
75, 82–83, 94, 110, 120–21, 173n.31;
Sardanapalus, 4–5, 77–91, 111, 135;
"Some Observations upon an Article
in *Blackwood's Edinburgh Magazine*," 66;
"Sonnet on Chillon," 8; *The Two Foscari*, 59, 77; *The Vision of Judgment*, 42,
55, 101, 103, 105–6, 112–14, 117; *Werner*,
111
Byron, Lady (Annabella Milbanke), 7,
23, 26, 159
Byronic hero, 65–66, 82, 85, 88, 131–32,
135, 137–38, 140, 146, 148

Cameron, Kenneth Neill, 29, 32
Catastrophism, 31–36
Chaworth, Mary, 25
Chew, Samuel, 79
Christensen, Jerome, 79–80
Clairmont, Claire, 6–13, 15, 22, 30, 62, 66
Clancy, Charles J., 82
Clark, Timothy, 46
Clubbe, John, 29, 31
Coleridge, Samuel Taylor, 1, 26–27, 101,
109; relationship of, with Words-
worth, 1. Works: *Biographia Literaria*,
80; *Christabel*, 26, 61–63; "The Devil's

Thoughts," 101, 107; "Hymn: Before
Sun-rise, in the Vale of Chamouny,"
26; "Kubla Khan," 55; "To William
Wordsworth," 1
Conversation, of Shelley and Byron, 3–4,
17, 40, 47, 52, 61, 103, 108, 110, 151–53
Conversational style, 4, 39–43, 49, 55,
79–80, 112–13
Cooke, Michael C., 164n.15
Corbett, Martyn, 77
Crompton, Louis, 11
Cronin, Richard, 52–53
Curran, Stuart, 168n.9, 169n.47
Cuvier, Georges, 31, 33–36, 166n.46

Dante Alighieri, 47, 99, 109–10. Works:
Inferno, 47, 109; *Paradiso*, 109
Darwin, Erasmus, 22, 27
Davie, Donald, 42
Dramatic principles, 5, 56–59, 75
Duffy, Edward, 124, 172n.18

Everest, Kelvin, 8, 26, 44

Familiar style. *See* Conversational style
Fantasmagoriana, 36, 61–62
Fleck, P. D., 131, 175n.19
Fletcher, William (Byron's valet), 72
Frost, Robert, 148

Genesis, 96, 98, 102, 144
George IV, 35
Gibbon, Edward, 22
Gisborne, John, 10, 92, 112, 115, 118
Gisborne, Maria, 66
Godwin, William, 7, 158
Goethe, Johann Wolfgang von: friend-
ship of, with Schiller, 148; *Faust*, 4, 16,
21, 50, 62–63, 92, 101, 107, 110–18
Grabo, Carl, 32
Grimm, Friedrich, 99
Guiccioli, Teresa, 11, 13, 73, 132, 151

Haswell, Richard, 170n.19
Herodotus, 80
Hirsch, Bernard, 47
Hirst, Wolf, 95
Hitchener, Elizabeth, 28, 69
Hobhouse, John, 9
Hogg, James, 98
Hogg, Thomas Jefferson, 9, 28
Hogle, Jerrold, 72, 115
Holmes, Richard, 14, 36, 110, 112, 172n.7
Hoppner, Richard, 12, 78
Hume, Robert, 131, 136–37
Hunt, Leigh, 9, 13, 15–16, 23, 40, 58, 78, 119, 130–31, 158–59

Keach, William, 44
Keats, John, 4–5, 119, 166–67n.8; *Hyperion*, 4
Kelsall, Malcolm, 81
Kinnaird, Douglas, 53, 158
Kristeva, Julia, 20

Lansdown, Richard, 79, 83
Laplace, Pierre Simon de, 29
League of Incest, 66
Lega (Byron's Italian servant), 158
Lehmann, John, 175n.25
Leigh, Augusta, 26, 72
Lewis, Matthew "Monk," 26, 36–37, 62–63, 114; *Ambrosio, or The Monk*, 62
The Liberal (magazine), 13, 113, 159
Linguistic skepticism, 44–45, 49–51
Lowther family, 24

McGann, Jerome, 19, 36, 47, 55, 79, 131
McKusick, James C., 174nn. 10, 12
Mariner, William: *Account of the Natives of the Tonga Island*, 143
Matthews, G. M., 5, 8, 26, 109, 116–17
Maturin, Charles: *Bertram*, 57
Medwin, Thomas, 13–14, 22–23, 34, 50, 58–60, 78, 92, 111–12
Michaels, Leonard, 171n.13

Milbanke, Annabella. *See* Byron, Lady
Milton, John, 40, 102, 105; *Paradise Lost*, 98, 135, 139–40
Mirabeau, Comte de, 45
Money: and the Shelley-Byron relationship, 157–60
Montesquieu, 31
Moore, Doris Langley, 11, 157–58
Moore, Thomas, 9, 21; warned Byron against Shelley's influence, 164n.82
Murray, John, 59, 77, 94, 99, 134, 154, 160

Napoléon, 36, 67
Nellist, Brian, 53
Noel, Lady, 159

Ollier, Charles, 19, 75
O'Neill, Eliza, 57
Otten, Terry, 62

Parkinson, James, 31, 33
Peacock, Thomas Love, 8–9, 22, 24, 26, 30, 60, 70–71
Peck, Walter Edwin, 161n.10
Peterloo massacre, 75
Petrarch, Francesco, *Trionfi*, 17, 109
Phantasmagoriana. See Fantasmagoriana
Plato: *Symposium*, 11
Polidori, Dr. John William, 7, 22, 36, 61–62; *The Vampyre*, 7
Prometheus Bound (Aeschylus), 60, 94

Reiman, Donald, 8–9, 57, 73, 120
Relation of the Death of the Family of the Cenci, 61, 71–73
Richardson, Alan, 100, 106
Rieger, James, 97
Robinson, Charles E., 2–3, 5–6, 17–19, 56, 58, 73, 78, 110, 114, 131, 141, 165n.29, 172n.10, 173n.31
Rousseau, Jean-Jacques, 8, 22, 26, 46, 70, 110, 138; Shelley and Byron on,

Rousseau, Jean-Jacques (*continued*)
123–24; *Julie; ou, La Nouvelle Héloïse,*
123–24
Rudwick, Martin, 31
Rutherford, Andrew, 131

Saussure, Horace, 31
Schiller, Johann Christoph Friedrich, 148
Shakespeare, William, 5, 57. Works:
Hamlet, 4, 14, 43; *King Lear,* 16; *Macbeth,* 106; *The Tempest,* 147
Shelley, Clara, 12
Shelley, Mary (Godwin), 6–9, 12–13, 16,
22, 27, 30, 36–37, 57–59, 62, 66, 72,
132, 151–55. Works: *Frankenstein,* 7,
27, 29–30, 36; *The Last Man,* 151–55,
166n.8, 173n.26
Shelley, Percy Bysshe: on Byron's Christianity, 71–72, 106; on *Cain,* 92; on
Childe Harold's Pilgrimage (canto 4),
128; deference to Byron's rank, 9, 14;
on the devil, 101–7; on *Don Juan,* 7, 52;
friendship of, with Byron, 1, 4, 6–18;
on Goethe's *Faust,* 16, 110–12, 114–16,
118; on homosexuality, 11; on incest,
9, 66, 87; on Italian Catholicism, 71–
72; on Italian politics, 9, 59–60, 75;
on Keats, 4–5; on *The Lament of Tasso,*
48; linguistic skepticism of, 44–45,
49; on *Manfred,* 48; on *Marino Faliero,*
5, 57–59; as post-Waterloo liberal, 3,
90; reading of Byron's works, 19–20;
as rich landed gentry, 3; on science,
27–33; on sexuality, 10; on Wordsworth, 22–26. Works: *Adonais,* 55, 118,
169n.36; *Alastor,* 19, 25–26; *The Boat on
the Serchio,* 166n.8; *The Cenci,* 5, 20, 32,
56–77, 83, 86–91; 100–101, 127, 160,
168n.9, 173n.26; "Charles the First,"
5, 15–16, 126; *A Defence of Poetry,* 44;
"The Devil's Walk: A Ballad," 101;
"Discourse on the Manners of the
Antient Greeks Relative to the Sub-

ject of Love," 11; *Epipsychidion,* 13, 70,
80, 84–85, 131–32, 141–42, 147; "Feelings of a Republican on the Fall of
Bonaparte," 19; *Hellas,* 5, 19, 78, 101,
107; *History of a Six Weeks' Tour,* 47;
"Hymn to Intellectual Beauty," 8, 24;
Julian and Maddalo, 2–4, 7, 9, 12, 18, 21,
39–52, 58, 74, 79–80, 90, 94, 101, 103,
108, 110, 116, 119, 121, 130, 140, 146–
47, 151–52, 166n.8; *Laon and Cythna,*
8–9, 66; "Letter to Maria Gisborne,"
27, 41, 53, 171n.12; "Lines Written
among the Euganean Hills," 12, 80;
The Mask of Anarchy, 5, 160; "Mont
Blanc," 8, 24, 26, 30–31, 33; "Ode to
the West Wind," 33, 75; "On Life,"
49; "On Love," 142; *On the Devil, and
Devils,* 63, 69, 92, 101–2, 104–6; *Peter
Bell the Third,* 52–53, 101; *Prince Athanase,* 48; *Prometheus Unbound,* 2–3, 12,
20–21, 32–33, 35–36, 44, 49, 61, 64,
73–78, 80, 82, 84–86, 90–92, 94–100,
104, 106, 124–26, 128, 134–35, 145, 148;
Queen Mab, 6, 19–20, 28, 31, 33, 77–
78, 92–94, 103–4; *The Revolt of Islam,*
5, 8, 18, 20, 46, 77–78, 80–82, 85, 134,
141, 143; *Rosalind and Helen,* 166n.8;
St. Irvyne; or, The Rosicrucian, 27, 36,
63; "A shovel of his ashes took," 7,
37; "Sonnet to Byron," 1, 15, 161n.1;
"To Laughter," 8; "To Wordsworth,"
23; translation of Goethe's *Faust,* 4, 92,
101, 107, 110–14, 161n.12; *The Triumph
of Life,* 17, 21, 70, 98, 109–30, 133, 139,
141, 144, 148, 155, 159, 173nn. 26, 31;
An Unfinished Drama, 132–33; "Upon
the Wandering Winds," 8; "Verses
Written on Receiving a Celandine in
a Letter from England," 23–24; *The
Witch of Atlas,* 52–55, 167n.27; "Written
on Hearing the News of the Death of
Napoleon," 68; *Zastrozzi,* 63
Shelley, Timothy, 151

Shelleyan hero, 79–80, 82, 85, 131, 135, 142, 145–46
Simonides, 24
Smith, Horace, 15–16, 106
Sotheby, William: *Ivan*, 57
Southey, Robert, 111, 168n.27, 173n.28; "The Devil's Thoughts," 101, 107
Spence, Gordon, 82
Stevenson, Warren, 160n.4
Stewart, George, 133
Swinburne, Algernon Charles, 148

Tasso, Torquato, 99
Tessier, Thérèse, 164n.82
Thomas, Edward, 148
Thorslev, Peter L., 171n.10
Trelawny, Edward John, 14, 16, 21, 101, 111, 132–33, 147, 154–55, 157, 174n.7
Twitchell, James, 61

Vampirism, 63–65, 86

Wasserman, Earl R., 40, 161n.10
Webb, Timothy, 112–14, 161n.12
Weisman, Karen A., 172n.2
Westbrook, Harriet, 160
White, Newman Ivey, 8
Williams, Edward, 38, 159
Williams, Jane, 115
Wolfson, Susan, 170n.28
Woodman, Ross, 126
Wordsworth, Jonathan, 37, 164n.14
Wordsworth, William, 1, 8, 22–27, 53, 109–10, 117–18, 121, 123, 136, 148, 164n.5; relationship of, with Coleridge, 1. Works: *The Excursion*, 23, 25, 164n.10; "The Forsaken Indian Woman," 164n.14; "I Travelled Among Unknown Men," 22; "Lines Written a Few Miles above Tintern Abbey," 25, 165n.15; *Lyrical Ballads*, 23, 40; "Ode 1815," 24; *Peter Bell*, 53; *The Prelude*, 55

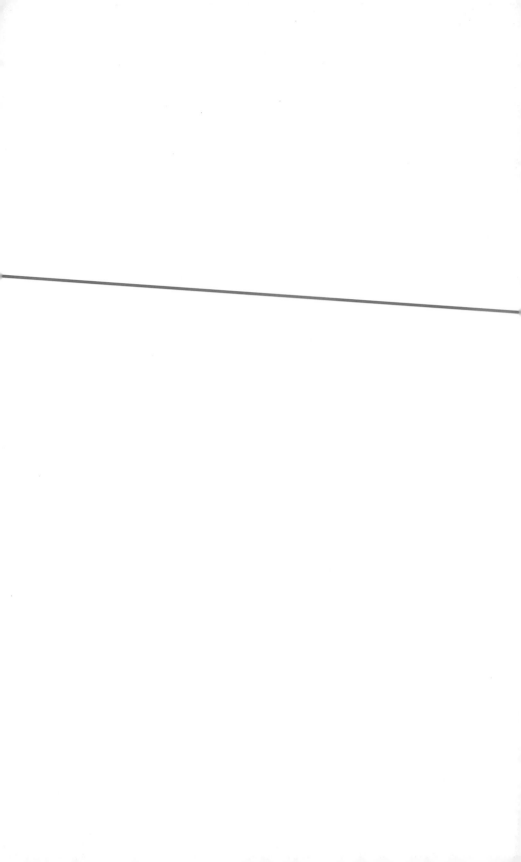